POSt roaD

Post Road publishes twice yearly and accepts unsolicited poetry, fiction, and nonfiction submissions. Complete submission guidelines are available at www.postroadmag.com.

Subscriptions: Individuals, $18/year; Institutions, $34/year; outside the U.S. please add $6/year for postage.

Post Road is a nonprofit 501(c)(3) corporation published in partnership with Literary Ventures Fund and the Lesley University MFA program. All donations are tax-deductible.

This issue of *Post Road* is made possible in part by generous support from the Cotton Charitable Trust.

Distributed by:

Ingram Periodicals, Inc., LaVergne, TN

Printed by:

BookMasters, Mansfield, OH

Post Road was founded in New York City in 1999 by Jaime Clarke and David Ryan with the following core editors: Rebecca Boyd, Susan Breen, Hillary Chute, Mark Conway, Pete Hausler, Kristina Lucenko (1999-2003), Anne McCarty and Michael Rosovsky.

Editors Emeritus include Sean Burke (1999-2001), Jaime Clarke (1999-2008), Mary Cotton, as Publisher and Managing Editor (2004-2008), Erin Falkevitz (2005-2006), Alden Jones (2002-2005), Fiona Maazel (2001-2002), Marcus McGraw (2003-2004), Catherine Parnell, as Managing Editor (2003), and Samantha Pitchel (2006-2008).

POSt roaD

Table of Contents

8   Contributor Notes

Fiction

14   Chris Stops the Boys   *Dawsen Wright Albertsen*
51   Whatever Happened to Harlan? A Report from the Field
      David Hollander
117 The Doctors   *Kirsten Menger-Anderson*
145 The Day They Were Shooting Dogs   *Samuel Reifler*
183 Body Language + Balloons and Clowns and Popcorn + Mash
      Kim Chinquee
201 Monster   *Rebekah Frumkin*
247 My First Real Home   *Diane Williams*
267 Transformations   *Alice Hoffman*

Nonfiction

49   Birthday   *Kim Goldberg*
61   Farewell   *Laura Didyk*
103 Little Orange Bottles   *Jeremy Rice*
155 Hold Your Horses the Elephants Are Coming   *Christopher Higgs*
197 Slow Freeze   *Laurah Norton Raines*
249 Rara Avis: How to Tell a True Bird Story   *Jackson Connor*

Criticism

83   Tiny Monuments: A Look at Snapshot Photography
      Hannah Lifson

Poetry

25   What We've Forgotten   *Lorraine Healy*
37   Suite for the Twentieth Century (for Carole Lombard) + Suite for
      the Twentieth Century (for Marilyn Monroe)   *Joseph Campana*
97   Cretaceous Moth Trapped in Amber (Lament in Two Voices) +
      Palinode for Being Thirty-four   *Katrina Vandenberg*

129 Dreaming of Rome + While Reading Pico della Mirandola's Oration on Human Dignity   *John Ruff*

165 My Older Brother, June Bug + Name I Will Never Forget
Jason Lee Brown

191 Die Fledermaus + Sisyphus in Paradise   *G. C. Waldrep*

215 Breathless, My Venom Spent, I Lay Down My Weapons + Horoscope   *Sarah Murphy*

259 What They Don't Tell You About Breast-Feeding + What I'm Not Telling You   *Liz Scheid*

Art

65 Portraits in Plasma   *Judith Page*

Theatre

169 Excerpt from *Gint* (an adaptation of Henrik Ibsen's *Peer Gynt*)
Will Eno

Etcetera

27 Conversation: Marion Ettlinger   *Adam Braver*

133 Journal: Black Rock City Journal   *Len Goldberg*

221 Journal: (Unexpurgated) Tour Journal   *Wesley Stace, John Wesley Harding, and George Fisher (of Henley)*

Recommendations

35 Mikhail Bulgakov   *Robert Olen Butler*

81 *Digressions on Some Poems by Frank O'Hara*, by Joe LeSueur
Allison Lynn

95 *Spin*, by Robert Charles Wilson   *Yael Goldstein*

101 William Faulkner's "The Bear"   *Allen Morris Jones*

113 The Promise of Failure, or Why You Should Drop Everything You're Doing and Read Richard Yates's *Revolutionary Road* Right Now!   *John McNally*

127 *A Sport and a Pastime*, by James Salter   *Noy Holland*

153 *Happy All the Time*: Loving Laurie Colwin   *Margo Rabb*

163 Kerouac's *On the Road* at Fifty   *Morris Dickstein*

179 *The Laws of Evening*, by Mary Yukari Waters   *Tod Goldberg*

187 *October Snow*, by Samuel Reifler   *Nelly Reifler*

195 *The Dog of the Marriage*, by Amy Hempel   *Perrin Ireland*

219 More Real Than Reality: The Frozen Art of Alistair MacLeod
Jon Clinch

265 *A Far Cry from Kensington*, by Muriel Spark   *David Leavitt*

fiction   chapbook

        comics

black   review

        poetry

                nonfiction

art

        warrior

Suscriptions: Submissions: Web:
One issue $10   BWR   webdelsol.com/bwr
One year $16   Box 862936   bwr@ua.edu
                    Tuscaloosa, AL 35486

BLACK WARRIOR REVIEW

Contributor Notes

Dawsen Wright Albertsen split his youth between St. Joseph, Missouri, and a farm north of Toledo, Iowa; graduated the University of Iowa; moved to Missouri, Louisiana, Illinois, California, and New York; worked nine years for two single-payer and one clinical research not-for-profit organizations; and now enjoys Brooklyn with cat, dog, and fiancé.

Jason Lee Brown teaches creative writing at Southern Illinois University–Carbondale, where he lives with his wife, Haruka. His work has appeared in *The Journal, Spoon River Poetry Review, Crab Orchard Review*, and *Ecotone*. He was recently nominated for Pushcart Prizes in fiction and poetry and has just finished editing the anthology *Best of the Midwest: Fresh Writing from Twelve States*.

Robert Olen Butler has published ten novels and four volumes of short fiction, one of which, *A Good Scent from a Strange Mountain*, won the 1993 Pulitzer Prize for Fiction. His most recent collection is *Severance*, from Chronicle Books, which contains sixty-two brief short stories told in the voices of newly severed heads. His new book is entitled *Intercourse* and also comprises brief short stories, 100 of them in fifty couples. He teaches creative writing at Florida State University and lives in Capps, Florida, population one, if you don't count his three bichon frises.

Joseph Campana is the author of *The Book of Faces*, with poems in or forthcoming in *Colorado Review, Hotel Amerika, New England Review, Michigan Quarterly Review, Poetry, TriQuarterly, Kenyon Review, FIELD*, and *Conjunctions*. He received a 2007 NEA Fellowship and teaches Renaissance literature and creative writing at Rice University.

Kim Chinquee's collection of flash fiction, *Oh Baby*, was published by Ravenna Press. Her recent stories appear in journals such as *Noon, Denver Quarterly, Conjunctions, New Orleans Review, Fiction, Mississippi Review, Notre Dame Review, Fiction International, Willow Springs, New York Tyrant, South Carolina Review, Arkansas Review*, and others. She received a 2007 Pushcart Prize.

Jon Clinch is the author of *Finn: A Novel*, published by Random House.

Jackson Connor lives with his wife and four kids in Ohio, where he studies and teaches writing. He earned an undergraduate degree from Penn State–Behrend and an MFA from the University of Utah.

Morris Dickstein teaches English at the Graduate Center of the City University of New York and is the author of *Gates of Eden, Leopards in the Temple*, and *A Mirror in the Roadway: Literature and the Real World*, published in paperback by Princeton University Press.

Laura Didyk, a Pushcart Prize nominee, received her MFA from the University of Alabama. Her work has appeared or is forthcoming in *Fence, Hayden's Ferry Review, Painted Bride Quarterly, New Orleans Review*, the *Sun, Alligator Juniper*, and others. She volunteers as a mentor for the PEN Prison Writing Program, works as an editor and writer at a nonprofit in Stockbridge, Massachusetts, and lives in Hudson, New York.

Will Eno is a Guggenheim fellow and a fellow of the Edward F. Albee Foundation. His play *Thom Pain (Based on Nothing)* was a finalist for the 2005 Pulitzer Prize. His play *Intermission* premiered at the Ensemble Studio Theatre's One-Act Marathon in June 2006. An excerpt of his play *Tragedy: A Tragedy* appeared in the June 2006 issue of *Harper's Magazine*. Will was at Princeton University in 2006, teaching playwriting and as a Hodder fellow. In the past year he was a fellow of the New York Public Library's Cullman Center for Scholars and Writers. His plays are published by Oberon Books, in London, and by Theatre Communications Group and Playscripts, both in the United States.

Rebekah Frumkin is a resident of Chicago, Illinois. Her stories have appeared in *Grimm Magazine*, the *Common Review*, and *Scrivener Creative Review*, among other places.

Kim Goldberg is a poet, author, and journalist on Vancouver Island. Her articles and essays on politics and current events have appeared in *Macleans, Canadian Geographic, Georgia Straight*, the *Progressive, Columbia Journalism Review, New Internationalist*, and numerous other magazines in North America and abroad for more than twenty years. She has recent poetry and prose in *PRISM International*, the *Dalhousie Review, Nimrod International Journal, CALYX, Tesseracts*, the *Arabesques Review*, and other literary magazines. Her latest book, *Ride Backwards on Dragon: A Poet's Journey through Liuhebafa*, was released last September from Leaf Press (www.leafpress.ca).

Len Goldberg is a CPA in Newton, Massachusetts, where he also resides with his wife. They will eagerly be returning to Burning Man in 2008.

Tod Goldberg is the author of the novels *Living Dead Girl*, a finalist for the Los Angeles Times Book Prize, and *Fake Liar Cheat*, and, most recently, the short story collection *Simplify*, winner of the Other Voices Short Story Collection Prize and a 2006 finalist for the SCIBA Book Award in fiction. He lives in La Quinta, California, with his wife, Wendy, and is currently a visiting assistant professor of creative writing in the MFA program at the University of California–Riverside.

Yael Goldstein is the author of the novel *Overture*, which will be released in paperback this August as *The Passion of Tasha Darsky*. She lives in Cambridge, Massachusetts.

Lorraine Healy is an Argentinean poet living on Whidbey Island, Washington. The winner of several national awards, including a Pushcart Prize nomination for 2004, she has been published extensively. She holds an MFA in poetry from New England College, in New Hampshire. She is the author of *The Farthest South* and *The Archipelago*.

Christopher Higgs lives in Clintonville, Ohio, with his true love and their ultra-pampered cat. He teaches at the Ohio State University. His recent work has been published or is forthcoming in *DIAGRAM, Salt Hill,* and *Beloit Fiction Journal*.

Alice Hoffman is the author of twenty-five works of fiction, including *Practical Magic, Turtle Moon, Here on Earth* and . She lives in Boston and New York City.

Noy Holland is the author of two collections of short fiction, *The Spectacle of the Body*, and *What Begins with Bird*. She teaches in the MFA program at the University of Massachusetts, Amherst.

David Hollander is the author of the novel *L.I.E.* and the creator of its protagonist, Harlan Kessler. Hollander's fiction and nonfiction have recently appeared in *McSweeney's, Unsaid,* the *New York Times Magazine,* and *Poets & Writers.*

Perrin Ireland is the author of the novels *Chatter* and *Ana Imagined,* and holds an MFA in writing and literature from Bennington College. She was previously a senior program officer for the National Endowment for the Arts and associate director for drama and arts for the Corporation for Public Broadcasting.

Allen Morris Jones has worked as a magazine editor, book editor, and critic. He's the author of a novel, *Last Year's River;* a book of scholarship, *A Quiet Place of Violence: Hunting and Ethics in the Missouri River Breaks;* and a tilted pile of published short stories, profiles, and personal essays. With William Kittredge he edited *The Best of Montana's Short Fiction.* He can be reached through his Web site, www.allenmorrisjones.com.

David Leavitt codirects the MFA program in creative writing at the University of Florida, where he edits the journal *Subtropics.* His most recent book is *The Indian Clerk.*

Hannah Lifson is a native New Yorker. For the past year she has spent her days off working for a snapshot collector. These days were the inspiration for her essay.

Allison Lynn is the author of the novel *Now You See It.* She lives in New York City.

John McNally is author of three works of fiction: *Troublemakers, The Book of Ralph,* and *America's Report Card.*

Kirsten Menger-Anderson is a San Francisco–based writer. Her first book of fiction, *Doctor Olaf van Schuler's Brain,* is forthcoming from Algonquin.

Sarah Murphy recently moved to Florida, where she is an assistant professor of English at Jacksonville University. She is currently involved in a production of *The Orpheus Project,* an interdisciplinary performance that explores the myth of Orpheus and Eurydice through music, dance, film, and poetry. Her work is forthcoming in *Pleiades* and *Court Green.*

Judith Page is a multimedia artist living in Brooklyn. In 2007 she created installations for the Aldrich Contemporary Art Museum, in Ridgefield, Connecticut, and Lesley Heller Gallery, in New York.

Margo Rabb's novel, *Cures for Heartbreak,* was published by Random House. Her short stories have been anthologized in *Best New American Voices* and *New Stories from the South;* have appeared in journals such as the *Atlantic Monthly, Zoetrope, One Story, New England Review,* and elsewhere; and have been broadcast on National Public Radio. Visit her online at www.margorabb.com.

Laurah Norton Raines teaches at Georgia State University, the same school that granted her MFA in creative writing. Laurah's work has appeared in a variety of journals, including *Fringe* and *Night Train.* She lives in Atlanta with her husband and two dogs.

Nelly Reifler is the author of the collection *See Through*. Her fiction has been published in such fine venues as *BOMB*, *McSweeney's*, *BlackBook*, and *jubilat*. A regular column on faith and religion (or the lack thereof) can be found at www.nextbook.org, and her lazily maintained Web site is www.nellyreifler.net.

Samuel Reifler is a lapsed Taoist who lives in Dutchess County, New York. He has written short fiction for numerous periodicals; his novella, *October Snow*, was published in 2004 by Pressed Wafer; his 1970 *I Ching: A New Interpretation for Modern Times* is in its tenth or eleventh printing (to his mild embarrassment).

Jeremy Rice is a senior creative writing major at the University of North Carolina–Asheville. He mostly writes fiction but has had both fiction and nonfiction pieces published in *Headwaters*, the literary magazine published through UNCA. He lives in Asheville with his girlfriend, Maggie, and is currently shopping around for low-residency MFA writing programs.

John Ruff teaches English at Valparaiso University in Indiana.

Liz Scheid is pursuing her MFA in poetry at California State University–Fresno. She also is a graduate assistant on Fresno State's new literary magazine, the *Normal School*. When she isn't chasing her one-year-old, who hates to wear diapers, she spends her time revising and stealing lines from her favorite poets.

Wesley Stace was born in Hastings, Sussex, in 1965 and educated at the King's School, Canterbury, and Jesus College, Cambridge. Under the name, John Wesley Harding, he has released fifteen albums, ranging from traditional folk to full-on pop music. His most recent pop release, *Adam's Apple*, was called "the finest album of his career" (*All Music Guide*), "one of his best, a sharp collection of pop that cleverly weds sunny melodies to dark matters" (the *New Yorker*), and "a dazzling piece of popcraft that shows wide range and real heart" (*No Depression*). His first novel, *Misfortune*, was published in 2004 by Little, Brown and was nominated for the Guardian First Book Award, the Commonwealth Writers' Prize, and the James Tiptree, Jr. Award, listed as one of the books of the year in *The Washington Post* and the *Boston Phoenix*. His second novel, *By George*, was published last August.

Katrina Vandenberg's first book of poems, *Atlas*, was a finalist for the Minnesota Book Award. Her poems have appeared in the *American Scholar*, the *Iowa Review*, and other places; new work is forthcoming in *Orion*. She has received fellowships from the MacDowell Colony, the Fulbright Association, as well as the McKnight and Bush foundations. She lives in St. Paul.

G. C. Waldrep's collections of poems are *Goldbeater's Skin*, winner of the 2003 Colorado Prize for Poetry, and *Disclamor*. He currently lives in Lewisburg, Pennsylvania, and teaches at Bucknell University.

Diane Williams's most recent book is *It Was Like My Trying to Have a Tender-Hearted Nature*, just out from FC2.

" *Post Road* reminds me of that girl in eighth grade—the one with the chipped tooth and the precocious knowledge of drugs—who I admired in secret. It's the brilliantly strange literary journal that just might be your best friend, if you're lucky. "

PAGAN KENNEDY

1 YEAR: $18, 2 YEARS: $34   **WWW.POSTROADMAG.COM**

Post Road is pleased to announce the winners of our writing contest:

FICTION
"Chris Stops the Boys"
by Dawsen Wright Albertsen

Judged by Heidi Julavits

POETRY
"What We've Forgotten"
by Lorraine Healy

Judged by Wesley McNair

Chris Stops the Boys

Dawsen Wright Albertsen

Chris stops the boys before Scott's house. Scott stands on the stoop within the doorframe. He looks down the steps at Chris. He stares at her.

Chris ignores Scott. There is everything and nothing to say. She calms herself. She smiles. The boys stand still. She sighs. The boys smile. Their biweekly limbo holds them to that spot. She kisses each boy on his forehead and cheeks. She cups their faces so they look in her eyes as she says, "I love you, I love you, I love you."

The boys stare at her. They do not stir. They wait. She nods toward their father. She tugs their backpacks' straps.

Robert, the youngest, begins the stairs. William begins to follow Robert. Chris grabs William's shoulder. She turns him.

She whispers, "Remember what I told you."

Robert looks at them. William hurries to Robert. Robert waves to his mother. The boys turn toward their father.

Slowly they ascend the stairs. Chris thinks those are the steps to the gallows. Her executioner poses in polo and khakis.

The boys are quiet. They silently rise side by side. They step to their father. Scott pats them into the house. He says nothing to Chris. He glimpses her. He stares slightly above and beyond her. He grimaces and turns into the house.

William and Robert stand in the hallway. They stand at attention. Little stolid soldiers stop for father. The boys have returned. They wait.

Scott passes them. He walks into the kitchen. He counts to sixty. He does nothing but count. At sixty he returns. He stands before them.

The boys stare at his collar. They don't look at his face. His pressed collar folds perfectly. William thinks it is ridiculous. Why would anyone press a polo shirt?

Robert likes the line. He likes lines. He likes the iron. He wants to press his clothes.

"Robert, what did you do Friday afternoon?" Scott asks.

"Mom picked us up," Robert says.

"Then what, William?" Scott asks.

"We went to the museum," William says.

"What museum?" he asks.

The boys wait. They don't know who should answer. Scott delays. He stretches seconds to minutes.

"Robert, what museum?" he asks.

"Met," Robert says.

Scott shakes his head. He looks at his feet. He mumbles. He looks at William, then Robert.

"The Metropolitan Museum of Art," Scott says.

"Metropolitan Museum of Art," Robert says.

"What did you do there, William?" asks Scott.

"We looked at art," William replies.

"Art?" Scott asks. "What type of art?"

"Paintings," William says.

"And ...," Robert begins. He wants to tell his dad about the sculptures. Scott glares a warning at Robert.

"Not now, Robert," Scott says.

Robert grabs his backpack straps. He clinches them. Gently he yanks one, then the other.

"William, who was your favorite?" Scott asks.

William knows his father knows nothing and cares nothing about art. He wants to lie to his father. But Scott would check. Scott will check for truth and falseness.

"Don't have one," William says.

"And your favorite, Robert?" Scott asks.

"I liked it all," Robert says.

Robert's mouth cracks. He sounds, "Uuuuuh." He clinches his thumb. William notices his little brother. He nudges Robert. Robert does not ask his father's favorite.

William knows his father memorizes names and times. Scott records and begins calculating. An equation will explain their mother's weekend. If one variable is wrong, does not compute, then the boys might not see their mother for a month. William still wonders how his father gained custody.

"Robert, then what?" Scott asks.

"Mom took us home," Robert says.

"To her house," Scott says.

"Yes, home," Robert says.

"No, this is your home," Scott says, "she took you to her house."

Robert mumbles, "To her house." He yanks his backpack straps. He tells himself, *Mom's home*. He smiles.

"Mom's home," Robert says.

Scott stares at the boy. Robert looks at Scott's collar. He counts the three buttons below the collar. He looks at the logo. He hopes the tiny man falls off the tiny horse. He hopes the horse runs away.

"Then what, William?" Scott asks.

"We ate," William says.

"What did you eat, Robert?" he asks.

"I had chicken, broccoli, and rice," Robert says.

"And you, William?" Scott asks.

"The same," William says.

"Robert, what was for dessert?" Scott asks.

"There was no dessert," Robert says.

Robert easily and proudly lies to his father. He loves to lie to his father. This is the one game that only he plays. He has seen his father explode over ice cream. He can't fathom how his father would react to brownies and ice cream.

"William, what did you eat for dessert?" Scott asks.

"There was no dessert," William says.

"Then what, William?" he asks.

"We played cards," William says.

"What did you play, Robert?" he asks.

Robert smiles. He loves games. Card games are his favorite. Games with his brother and mother are better than lies.

"Go fish, rummy, and spades," Robert says.

Scott huffs. He looks at William. Surprise and disbelief contort Scott's face. He grimaces. He looks at Robert.

"You play spades?" Scott asks.

"Yes," Robert says.

"And who won, Robert?" Scott asks.

"We all won," Robert says.

"William, you and Robert beat your mother?" Scott says.

Scott has never seen anyone beat Chris in any card game. Chris is a card shark. Her grandmother was a card shark. Her mother is a card shark. Her brother was a card shark and cardsharp. Scott knows not his youngest has Chris's gift. Robert is a natural shark. William knows it. William loves his little brother more for it. He knows they, William and Robert, can beat their father at something.

"Mom let us win," William says.

"She let you win, Robert," Scott says.

Robert nods. He doesn't know if his father asks or states. A nod is safe. Robert knows nodding works. It seems Scott doesn't care if Robert understands anything.

"Then what, William?" he asks.

"I went to bed," Robert says.

Robert's face reddens. Guilt and fright hold the boy. Before he can emend the statement, his father asks, "What did you do, William?"

"I read, then went to bed," William says.

"What did you read?" Scott asks.

"*Huck Finn*," William says.

William thumbs to his bag. He shrugs and smiles. He waits for his father.

"They still teach that crap," Scott says.

"It's not crap," William says.

Scott glares at his son. He steps closer. He tries intimidating the boy with his stature. He tries imposing his will by towering. It is Scott's best hand. Imposition and intimidation are his trumps.

"It is crap," Scott says.

He breathes into William's crown. He steps backwards to see the boy's face. He pokes the boy in the hollow between his shoulder and pectoral.

"They don't teach it," William says, "but it's not crap."

"Crap," Scott says.

William grinds his teeth. He digs his toes into his insoles. His knees lock. He closes his eyes. He imagines. There hangs a portrait, a painting. A portrait of his mother lights his mind.

"Do you read that crap, Robert?" Scott asks.

Robert has never read a book. He doesn't know who or what Huck Finn is. Robert is smart, but he dislikes reading. He prefers games and numbers.

"Yes," Robert says, "it's not crap."

Scott leans forward to tower over both boys. A hand rests on each boy's shoulder. He huffs. His hands slightly tighten. He steps backwards. He looks at William, then Robert. His manner holds the boys resolute. He releases them.

Scott storms into the kitchen. He stares at the window. He grips the counter's edge. He is irate. He is sure they are lying. They lie to protect her. *She did this*, he tells himself. "She did this," he says to his reflection. Scott begins counting to 120.

The boys stand still. Each brother wants to touch the other with his hands. Robert wants to hold William's hand. William wants to ruffle Robert's curly brown hair and pinch his neck. They stand still. They wait. He will return. They stare forward. They stare where his pressed collar will float.

Scott stomps into the hallway. He stands before his sons. He smiles. He smiles an ugly smile. It is a forced smile. William calls it the Joker. Robert thinks it is the face a man makes before he does something very, very bad.

"Then what, William?" Scott asks.

"We ate pancakes," William says.

"Only pancakes, Robert?" he asks.

"And syrup and sausage," Robert says.

"Sausage, William?" he asks.

"Chicken sausage," William says.

Scott does not eat pork. It is not a religious observance. He hates pork. An irrational fear of hogs began in his youth. He doesn't want his children eating the animal.

"Then what, William?" he asks.

"We went to the park," William says.

"What park, Robert?" he asks.

"The park by Mom's home," Robert says.

"What did you do there, Robert?" he asks.

Robert thinks his father is stupid. Even he must know that parks are for play. Robert's eyes bulge. He yanks his backpack straps.

"We played," Robert says.

"Played what, Robert?" he asks.

"We played," Robert says, "swings and slides. The jungle gym."

Robert can't believe anyone is that dumb. Everyone knows parks mean play. Everyone knows play means anything.

"Did you play on the jungle gym, William?" Scott asks.

"No, I read," William says, "I read *Huck Finn*."

"You were outside and you read?" Scott asks.

Scott points toward the door. He shakes his head. His face scrunches. His forehead is a million wrinkles. He nods forward.

"Yes," William says.

William smiles. He knows that he is too old for swings and jungle gyms. But Robert played. So William kept to Robert. They played on the jungle gym. William almost laughs, remembering their swinging contest.

"Then what, Robert?" Scott asks.

"We walked home for lunch," Robert says.

"To her house," he says, "you walked to her house."

"Mom's home," Robert says.

"What did you eat, William?" he asks.

"Leftovers," William says, "chicken sandwich and salad."

"Robert?" he asks.

"Chicken salad sandwich," Robert says.

"Chicken salad?" he asks.

"I put salad on my sandwich," Robert says.

"You ate a chicken sandwich," Scott says.

Robert yanks the backpack straps. He does not reply. He doesn't know the difference between chicken salad and chicken with salad. He doesn't care. His feet hurt. He lightly steps in place.

"Then what, William?" he asks.

"Robert napped while I read," William says.

"Where was your mother, Robert?" he asks.

"I was sleeping," Robert says.

"William?" he asks.

"She read on the couch," William says.

"She was with you Friday and at the park," he asks, "the whole time?"

"Yes," the boys say.

"Did she have visitors?" he asks.

"No," they say.

"Then what, William?" he asks.

"We walked," William says.

"You walked," he says, "where'd you walk?"

"Around the neighborhood," William says, "we got groceries."

Scott surveys her neighborhood in his mind. She lives in a nice neighborhood. They lived there as a young couple. He searches for pitfalls. He finds nothing.

"Then what, Robert?" he asks.

"We cooked," Robert says.

Robert smiles. He loves helping his mother. Helping her cook was fun. The kitchen was a laboratory. Robert was a scientist.

"You cooked?" Scott asks.

Robert nods and smiles.

"Robert, you cooked?" he asks.

"Yes, we cooked," Robert says.

Scott stares beyond the boys. In the wall something does not make sense. His face twists and puckers. The boys wonder what he thinks.

"That was kind of early," he says, "wasn't it."

"No," Robert says.

"Seems it," Scott says.

Scott stares at the floor between him and the boys. No one moves. It is quiet.

The silence bothers Scott. William thinks about painting. Robert wants to play. He wants to swing. He wants to swing and jump over the fence. He is sure he could clear a fence.

Scott computes times and distances. Time isn't working. Scott plots Chris's neighborhood. He imagines their walk. A walk is fifteen minutes. A walk is no more than thirty minutes. How could it be dinner? There is no place to walk greater than fifteen minutes. He bites his lower lip. His eyes seem to cross. They cross from one boy to the other.

Scott imagines the walk. He repeats the walk. He tries imagining different walks. Scott fails. He imagines his walk. He can only imagine himself: he walks to the store; he walks to the bus, to the train, and to work; he walks to laundry and to home. It doesn't make sense to him.

"Where'd you walk?" he shouts.

Neither William nor Robert answers. They stand still. They lean into each other.

William imagines painting a portrait of his mother. She smiles. His eyes nearly pop from his head. He hears nothing.

Robert closes his eyes. He bites his cheek. He bites his tongue. He tastes the saltiness.

They anticipate an explosion. It is imminent. They wait. They wonder if he will go to the kitchen.

"Robert?" Scott asks.

Robert bites and waits. He is frozen. He swallows.

"Robert, where did you walk?" Scott asks.

Scott attempts a falsetto. The ugly smile crooks across his face. He leans toward Robert.

Robert feels Scott's breath. Robert sucks his cheeks. He tightly clinches his straps. He opens his eyes.

"I don't know," Robert says.

"What do you mean you don't know?" Scott asks.

"I don't know," Robert says.

"What don't you know?" he asks.

"Where," Robert says.

"William, where did you walk?" he asks.

"Around," William says, "we walked around."

"Where?" he asks.

"Around Mom's house," William says.

"Where around her house?" he asks.

"Here and there," William says.

"You don't know where?" he asks.

"No. Not every street," William says.

"Are you lying?" Scott asks. "Are you lying to me?"

"No," William says.

Scott thinks about his walks. He can name every street. He walks for minutes. Their walk confuses Scott. He thinks.

Scott doesn't know that the boys walk with their mother for hours. They walk slowly. They play games. They identify trees. They discuss school. They chat about all the world but Scott.

Scott mutters, "Visitation." He reminds himself that he has custody and he makes the rules. He is confident that they are lying, and they would lie only if she had told them to lie. Scott concludes that she lied, she, but why did she?

Scott storms to the kitchen. He stares at the window. He drums the counter. He begins counting to 180.

William ruffles Robert's hair. Robert looks at William. William nods. Robert grabs William's belt loop.

Scott moans. He groans loudly. He stomps his foot. He kicks the cabinet. He smacks the counter with both hands. He takes a pan from a hook. He raises it. He slams it on the counter. He hits the floor. He smacks the island. He beats the faucet and drops the pan into the sink. He stares at the windowpane. He sees only the glass.

The boys hear the noise. William removes his hand from Robert's head. Robert releases William's belt loop.

Scott strides into the hallway. He smiles the ugly smile. He nods to each boy. He shrugs. He wags his head. He throws out his arms. His hands shake. He shoves his hands into his pockets. His elbows tremble.

"What did you cook, Robert?" he asks.

"We made croquet and potatoes," Robert says.

"Croquettes, Robert, croquettes," he says.

"Croquettes," Robert says.

"What did you do, Robert?" he asks.

"I helped," Robert says.

"Yes, but what did you do?" he asks.

"I measured and put stuff in bowls and piles," Robert says.

"You didn't cook," Scott says.

"I did too," Robert says.

The boy does not know his father is trying to diminish his assistance, his enjoyment. Robert thinks maybe his father is teasing. Robert knows that he cooked.

"He helped Mom cook," William says.

"He sorted and piled," Scott says.

Robert frowns. He wants to scream. He wants to yell. He wants to hate him.

"What did you do, William?" he asks.

"I watched," William says.

"You watched?" he asks.

"Yes," William says.

"Did Robert use a knife?" he asks.

"No," William says.

"You weren't reading *Moby-Dick*?" he asks.

"*The Adventures of Huckleberry Finn*," William says. "I wasn't reading."

"Then what, Robert?" he asks.

"Mom cooked croquets and potatoes," Robert says.

"Croquettes," Scott says. "Crow-ketts."

"Croquettes," Robert says.

"Did you help?" Scott asks.

"No," Robert says, "Mom doesn't let us use the stove."

"What about you, William?" he asks. "Did you help?"

"No, I watched," William says.

"Did you talk, Robert?" he asks.

Robert says nothing. He is tired. His feet hurt. His legs want to bend. He wants his brother. He wants his mother. He wants him to leave.

"Robert?" Scott says.

"About school," Robert says.

"What about school?" he asks.

"If I like it," Robert says.

"Of course you like it," he says. "What else?"

"What I like," Robert says.

"All of it," Scott says.

William notices the wall. The boys have shuffled backwards. Their backs are at the wall. William palms it. His fingers begin painting behind his back beneath the bag.

"Then what, William?" Scott asks.

"We ate," William says.

"That's an early dinner," Scott says.

Scott walks from the boys into the kitchen. He has to think. Things must make sense. The time is wrong. The times are wrong. His sons are hiding something. He stares at the window. He notices nothing outside the window. The pane is all he sees. Scott counts.

Robert looks at William. William notices and smiles. Robert's eyes beg, *When?* William shrugs. He musses Robert's hair and tugs his ear. Robert shakes his head and smirks. He looks at the floor. He is tired. William thinks about painting. He fingers the wall. Both stare where the collar will return.

Scott finishes counting at 240. He walks to the boys. He wears the ugly smile. The boys' stolid faces wait.

"How was it?" Scott asks.

The boys do not answer.

"How was the meal, Robert?" he asks.

"I liked it," Robert says.

"Yes, but how was it?" he asks.

"Good," Robert says.

"What was for dessert, Robert?" he asks.

"Nothing," Robert says.

Robert steps in place. He wiggles and crosses his toes. He wants to stand in ice cream.

"How were the croquettes, William?" Scott asks.

"Very good," William says.

"Then what, William?" he asks.

"We walked," William says.

"Again?" he asks.

"Yes," William says.

"Where?" he asks.

"To the park," William says.

"Then what, Robert?" he asks.

"We walked," Robert says.

"Where?" he asks.

"Mom's home," Robert says.

William's left foot and Robert's right are snugly beside each other. Their respective shoulders and elbows are so fast and close one could mistake them as uneven conjoined twins. The boys stand as one, waiting for their father to record and compute. They wait for another question.

Scott shakes his head. He looks to the ceiling. He sighs. His arms are akimbo.

"To her apartment," Scott says.

"Yes," Robert says.

"Then what, Robert?" he asks.

"We played," Robert says.

"What did you play, William?" he asks.

"Cards," William says.

"Again," he says, "you played cards again?"

"Yes," William says.

"Kind of late," he says, "wasn't it?"

"No," William says.

"No," Robert says.

Scott stares at Robert. Robert steps into the wall. He looks at his father. He steps in place. Scott bites the corner of his mouth.

"Then what, Robert?" he asks.

"I went to bed," Robert says.

"What about you, William?" Scott asks.

"I read *Huck Finn*," William says.

"Are you going to finish that book?" he asks.

"No," William says.

"You were up late," Scott says.

"No, I wasn't," William says.

"What time did you go to bed?" Scott asks.

"No later than ten," William says.

Scott closes his eyes. His head tilts forward and backwards. His face scrunches. He gasps. The time is wrong. He turns toward the kitchen. He slaps the jamb. He storms to the kitchen.

Robert grabs William's belt loop. He looks at William. William smiles. He beams. Robert tugs the loop. William looks at Robert. Robert shakes his head. William shrugs. Robert's eyes plead. William mouths, "We're okay."

Scott counts. He keeps time by hitting the counter with the edge of his fist. Scott shakes his head at the windowpane. His reflection shakes its head. He hits. He counts.

He stops at 300. He rubs his face. Slowly he inhales and exhales. He pats his hair. He returns to the hallway.

The boys stand. Robert is still. Both look forward and stare at the collar. William taps and paints the wall. He smirks.

"Then what, Robert?" Scott asks.

"Waffles," Robert says.

"You had waffles?" he asks.

"Yes," Robert says.

"What else?" he asks.

"Not-bacon bacon," Robert says.

"And you, William?" he asks.

"The same," William says.

"Then what, William?" he asks.

"We packed," William says.

"Then what?" he asks.

Neither William nor Robert answers. Robert looks at the floor. William smirks and fingers the wall.

"William," Scott says.

"We came here," William says.

"What?" he asks.

"We came here," William says.

"That doesn't make sense, William," he says.

"So," William says.

"So . . . ," Scott begins.

William smiles. He shrugs. He grips his backpack straps. He tugs the straps like his mother tugs them. Robert tugs his straps.

Scott shoves his hands into his pockets. Fists bulge through the khakis. He shakes his head. He thinks, *Why are they doing this?* He looks at Robert. He looks at William. He mutters, "Why?" The boys do not stir. Scott twists and writhes. He appears tortured. Robert thinks his father will cry or hurt something.

Scott stomps his foot. Robert jumps. Scott stomps again. Robert backs into William's side. Scott kicks the wall behind him. Robert nudges behind William. Scott stomps the floor. William steps toward his father.

"We're going to bed," William says.

Scott gnashes his teeth. He flexes his body. He shudders. He looks at the boys. His head shakes. He stomps his foot.

"Go to bed," he screams.

William thinks. He remembers. Robert snored on the floor while he and his mother read on the couch. His mother pulled him near her down the couch. She hugged him. She stood and sat across from him on the ottoman. She grasped his knees. "No more fighting," she said, "I'm not there. It is you and Robert. You two. It will be you against your father. You against others. Even you against me. From now on, you are you and Robert. No more fighting. Okay?" William nodded.

The boys ascend the stairs. Scott stands frozen in the doorframe. William smiles. Robert holds William's belt loop. ✧

What We've Forgotten

Lorraine Healy

Maps are useless.
One can only get there

riding the trail of a dry,
fractious wind.

On the secret sea.
The one cartographers so feared

they placed it beyond
the lip of the world.

The one the wise
avoid dreaming about.

A place of slaked lime
and furnace sun,

cliffs like giants' bones bleached
to chalk. A place

of lead whites, velvet
ivory brush, which fools

the eye with blinding glee. Whose
eye, though? Who gets this far

into such vacuum of air,
into this mistake of salt

and soil hardened and boiled?
Meet me on this island, beloved.

Meet me where we are certain
to die and resurrect.

The island of no name, beloved.
The place where gods are made

to be crucified.

Marion Ettlinger

Adam Braver

In 1993, Marion Ettlinger got the gig of a lifetime. For its fiftieth anniversary issue Esquire *magazine was to feature fifty writers, and Marion, who was living in Vermont at the time, got the assignment. After about the first twenty shoots she realized the writer was her natural subject. "It wasn't like I was looking for it; looking to zero in or narrow in. It just came to me that I felt something right about, and something I wanted to do." Since then Marion's portraits of writers have become synonymous with American literature. Just thumb through her book,* Author Photo, *and you'll understand. Shot in black-and-white. In natural light. Timeless poses that could come right off the movie stills at the neighborhood movie theater. Look at her iconic portrait of Raymond Carver, staring menacingly at the camera, his eyes almost like storm clouds; this is not just a photo of Raymond Carver, this is a picture of the mind that wrote those beautifully troubled stories. In other words, in Marion Ettlinger's photography we don't just get portraits of a writer; we get portraits of the writer.*

1.

Adam Braver: What is it like to photograph someone whom you are in awe of? Does that change the relationship or the experience?

Marion Ettlinger: It means I'm filled with dread, you know. Scared out of my mind. It's not a good feeling. Still, I have to go forward. I'm never sure what the source of the fear is—maybe that I'm going to be annoying or boring. And, you know, I don't wish to annoy or bore people.

AB: But you're on the other end now, because there's a certain fear or anticipation in meeting you, for getting the picture taken. I know I felt it.

ME: That's been a big switch, and it's not particularly one I'm all that comfortable with. I'm used to people being apprehensive about being photographed. That is natural, of course. But for anyone to feel any apprehension or nervousness about meeting me or being with me seems absurd.

AB: From my experience with you, it seems that you work very hard at making a session feel natural, and not such a formal occasion.

ME: Well, thank you. I'm glad. It should be a collaboration. It's hard for me to take in that people are regarding me in the way that I regard the writers. Hey, it's a psychological problem.

AB: When we did the photos for the last two books, I remember being in your studio all day.

ME: I'll take the heart of anybody's day, if I can.

AB: In the course of a five- to six-hour shoot, is there a point where you can feel everybody starting to become normal or natural together?

ME: I think the apprehension goes away pretty early on. At least the first third of however many hours we're together. My apprehension pretty much goes away when the person finally materializes.

AB: So are you more likely to use pictures that come more midway and toward the end? Is it rare to use one of the first shots?

ME: It happens, but it's rare. Predictably rare. Yeah, the first stuff usually says, *We're starting this process, and we both know it's weird.*

2.

AB: I know you read the books in question before the writers come in. What are you looking for when you're reading in advance, especially if you've never met the person?

ME: I want to know about the inside of their head. Of course, I don't know if writers say, "Oh, yes. My book is the inside of my head." Is it, Adam?

AB: Perhaps the inside of one of a number of heads. And other places as well, I suppose.

ME: The gut, the heart, the brain. I feel like that's important information for me to have.

AB: And how do you take that information into a picture?

ME: If I have one opinion about this, I think a photo should have some intensity and drama. I'm a reader too. Why do I have to think that this person who gives me this incredible story should be sold as the friendly, innocuous neighbor? Maybe they are friendly, innocuous neighbors in real life. But I don't understand why, on a book, they need to be depicted as friendly. I don't think readers would run away, screaming, "Oh, no, no, no. A dramatic, intense person wrote this book!"

AB: I remember when you sent me the photos for *Divine Sarah.* I brought them to some party or another where my editor was. We laid them all out, and all the people there got involved, siding off, until they narrowed it down to two photos.

ME: "What to do? What to do?"

AB: The interesting part was that the women picked one picture unanimously, while the men picked the other.

ME: That's so fascinating.

AB: I was trying to sort out what each saw in it. Yet nobody really could say what it was. It didn't seem that one was particularly more masculine than the other, or more feminine than the other. And I wondered if it was different perspectives of what, as you put it, drama and intensity should mean.

ME: Reactions to photos are very individual and potent. How did it work out?

AB: I went with the one my editor was leaning toward. The so-called masculine one. Then I used the other for *Crows*.

3.

AB: What I always love about your pictures is the romanticism around them, in the same way there is with a 1930s movie still. Other than an occasional hairstyle here or there, the pictures could be taken anytime. They really have that timelessness to them, which I think one also wants from a writer and his or her book.

ME: Thank you for noticing that, because that is of deep importance to me—that sense of timelessness. And of course, wouldn't writers be concerned with that as well?

AB: Sure. I think all of us who are trying to write somewhat serious work, have this hope that somebody can pick up our work in twenty years and it will be no different than it was when it first came out. The photographs do the same thing. Together with the writing, they create a sense of perpetuity to the whole process.

ME: God knows I try. I love timeless novels from other eras—ones where brands and labels don't cloud our reading of the work. I wonder how they managed to avoid the fashions.

AB: It seems that in classic literature most of those so-called brands are very iconic images or products that have lived on. Recently I was rereading a story by Graham Greene or somebody like this, and it referred to a Brooks Brothers overcoat. But see, to me, there's a real iconography to that Brooks Brothers overcoat.

ME: Right. Right. Yeah. I want a Brooks Brothers overcoat, now that you mention it.

AB: Lincoln was wearing one the night when he was shot.

ME: No kidding.

AB: Yes. Yes.

ME: That blows my mind. I didn't know, Adam, that Brooks Brothers had that provenance, and that Lincoln—

AB: Wore it—

ME: As part of his ensemble.

AB: And I do not know this, Marion, from writing about Lincoln. I actually know this because I once had a Christmas job working at Brooks Brothers. It was in some promotional piece or training manual.

ME: Wow. Well, see, that's the value of being in the real world.

4.

AB: When we did the pictures, you used only natural light. And if I recall, your cameras were ones you'd been using forever.

ME: I respond to timelessness in all things. But, you know—I'm very low tech. I'm a technophobe with cameras, and that's going back a long time. I am the same about lighting. The first way I started to take photos is the same way I take photos now. That's part of my own limitations. Being stuck in time, or not being flung around by technology and the latest thing, actually has helped. The so-called classic quality of the photos is not a result of me saying, "If I just do it this way, it will equal timelessness." Looking at it retrospectively, it was an equation that was organic. It's who I am. I've got this camera. It works fine. I don't want to know from other cameras.

AB: It's interesting that you say "organic." Because at this moment there's probably someone developing technology to make pictures look like they have natural light, instead of using natural light.

ME: I'm sure there is. It's hard to maintain tradition these days.

AB: The courtroom sketch artist may be the only one left.

ME: But there's probably somebody developing a technology where we can take away the person to do the sketch and somehow make a digital impersonation of the sketch. Those sketches are amazing, like from some tabloid paper, bubbling up from the '20s.

AB: And yet they still show them on the evening news every night.

ME: They do. Believe me, if they didn't have to, they wouldn't. You can imagine the producers saying, "We have to show *these* drawings? What's going on here?" But don't you think there are people everywhere saying, "Oooh, look at that drawing of so-and-so. Doesn't he look guilty?" It's a very complex job. I'm just enthralled with court sketch artists. I really am.

AB: The other thing I love is how they always put the artist's name in the corner of the sketch. Right there on the nightly news.

ME: Yes. Praise the Lord.

AB: You would never see who shot the video.

ME: Right. Yeah, it's a drawing, goddamn it. No, it's an amazing . . . it's an amazing vestig[e]—I can't believe [it]. It's got to disappear. I'm convinced it's going to disappear. But let's hold it with love while we can.

5.

AB: Your famous picture of Capote, the one where he is in profile. It's such an incredible picture, especially when one knows his biography, after his so-called fall from grace. You can just read that all over his face in the picture.

ME: Truman was the person who taught me about what it was like to photograph someone I wasn't sure I wanted to be around. It's a bit of an anecdote. Do you want it?

AB: Of course.

ME: This was a part of the *Esquire* gig. And Truman consented to be photographed—but with the condition that the *Esquire* office would remind him three days before the photo shoot that it was going to happen, then the day before the photo shoot, and then the day of the photo shoot. But on the actual date *Esquire* couldn't get in touch with him. But they told me, "Go anyway. Just go." And so I did. And I went to his house. I knocked on the door and I got no response. It was utter silence. I figured maybe he was out, and I'd go away for some time, and then come back.

An hour or two later I drove up the driveway to his house. There was a car driving down the driveway. As our cars passed next to each other, I saw it was Jack Dunphy at the wheel. I rolled down the window and said, "Hi. I'm here to photograph Mr. Capote."

"Good luck," he said. He rolled up his window and drove away.

AB: That doesn't bode well.

ME: I was in the process of getting out of the car when the door of the house flung open and Truman ran out of the house waving his fists in the air like in a Farmer Gray cartoon, screaming at me, "What are you doing here? This isn't the right day. I knew they would fuck it up. I can't believe this." I just said, "Well, actually, yes, this is the right day."

"No, no, no, no, it isn't—you're screwing up my whole day. I don't have time for this. It's ridiculous. I can't believe they're sending me such an amateur to do this."

"Oh, yes, Mr. Capote, I know."

"I don't know what you're doing here. This is ridiculous." He looked ragged. There were these stories about how he had been wandering around in some town, a little disoriented. In some kind of weird phase. I don't know, but either way, he looked like hell.

"Okay," I said. "Let's go in the house and I'll look around to see where we can stage a good shot."

"I'm not going to let you in my house. Are you crazy? Why would I let you in my house?"

He was wearing a really grubby sweatshirt or T-shirt with some kind of logo on it. "Well," I suggested, "perhaps you want to go and maybe put on some other shirt."

"I'm not going to change. This is what I'm wearing. Okay?"

"Yeah."

"I'm wearing what I'm wearing. I'm not going to go change or anything."

"Well," I said, "why don't we go up on the porch? I see there's some—"

"It's dirty on the porch. I'm going to get all dirty if I go over there."

Then I realized, *Duh, he's just going to deny me anything that I request.*

AB: Or suggest.

ME: When I realized that, I started to freak out because I was really still new at this; and in a way, and I'm thinking, *Oh, my God, he is going to fuck this up. I'm not going to be able to do anything, and it will be his fault because he's fucking it up, but it won't matter whose fault it is, because it's going to be on me.*

AB: Was all this going through your head?

ME: Oh, yes. *It's just going to be my failure. My failure alone, my failure alone.* I was in between rage and tears, spinning in my head about how I couldn't believe this was happening. *I can't believe this is going on.* Finally Truman said, "Look. Either take my photo or get out of here. Get off my property."

"Okay," I said. I got my camera out, lifted it up, and asked him if he would take a few steps back, which he did, because there was some kind of a fence that seemed as if it would make a good background.

He did do that.

I started to photograph him. And the first pictures were of him glowering at me. Just glowering. I think to relieve myself of this gaze, of this glowering gaze, I asked him to turn in profile just so that he wouldn't be looking at me in this way.

AB: The pose on the cover of your book.

ME: He raised his head and lifted his chin. Suddenly he looked magnificent. And I saw it. I saw it.

I murmured words of encouragement as I took one roll of film. When I ran out, I told him I needed to reload.

"That's it," he said, and walked back into his house and closed the door.

And that's how that photo happened.

AB: Did you ever hear from him again?

ME: I stuck my pathetic business card into the limb of a tree outside of his house. But no, I never heard a word from him, ever. Ever, ever.

AB: What a lesson.

ME: Cooperation. Politeness. Delightfulness. Compliance. I thought all of the above were essential to getting a good result. And he taught me that when all of the above becomes lost, something much more interesting might happen. Something you wouldn't have done might happen. So I have always been incredibly grateful to him for teaching me that lesson. And who better to teach me that lesson than Truman fucking Capote. ✧

Mikhail Bulgakov

Robert Olen Butler

I first read Mikhail Bulgakov's *The Master and Margarita* on a balcony of the Metropole Hotel in Saigon on three summer evenings in 1971. The tropical air was heavy and full of the smells of cordite and motorcycle exhaust and rotting fish and wood-fire stoves, and the horizon flared ambiguously, perhaps from heat lightning, perhaps from bombs. Later each night, as was my custom, I would wander out into the steamy back alleys of the city, where no one ever seemed to sleep, and crouch in doorways with the people and listen to the stories of their culture and their ancestors and their ongoing lives. Bulgakov taught me to hear something in those stories that I had not yet clearly heard. One could call it, in terms that would soon thereafter gain wide currency, magical realism. The deadpan mix of the fantastic and the realistic was at the heart of the Vietnamese mythos. It is at the heart of the present zeitgeist. And it was *not* invented by Gabriel García Márquez, as wonderful as his *One Hundred Years of Solitude* is. García Márquez's landmark work of magical realism was predated by Bulgakov's brilliant masterpiece of a novel by nearly three decades. That summer in Saigon a vodka-swilling talking black cat and a coven of beautiful naked witches and Pontius Pilate and a whole cast of benighted writers of Stalinist Moscow and Satan himself all took up permanent residence in my creative unconscious. Their presence, perhaps more than anything else from the realm of literature, has helped shape the work I am most proud of. I'm often asked for a list of favorite authors. Here is my advice: Read Bulgakov. Look around you at the new century. He will show you things you need to see. ✧

Why the
Devil Chose
New England
for His Work

Stories by
Jason
Brown

"Stories so beautiful, faceted,
and durable, they feel excavated from
a mine. A collection of subtle gems."
—Aimee Bender

"Linked, gem-cut stories of troubled youths, alcoholics, illicit romances, the
burden of inheritance, and the bane of class, all set in the dense upper
reaches of Maine . . . delivered with hope, heart, and quiet humor."
     —*Elle*

 **OPEN CITY BOOKS**

November 2007

Suite for the Twentieth Century (for Carole Lombard)

Joseph Campana

1. To Be or Not to Be

Sometimes you laugh so hard
you think your face will fall
right off. So what if it does?
It won't hurt, it won't make
you any different. You're quiet,
the night is resting, and *To Be
or Not to Be* flickers on the
television like the cheap slogan
it is. The Nazis invade Poland
and everyone laughs. Nazis
close the theaters and drag off
a Jew, so everyone laughs:
they were only pretending
(as were the pretend Nazis who
dressed up just for the sake
of a daring rescue). Headline:
THE THEATER SAVES US AGAIN.
It was 1939 in the film but
1942 for everyone else: the
Nazis *had* invaded, and Carole
Lombard had just gone down
in flames selling war bonds.
Everyone laughs because
they know a secret. Hidden
at the beginning of the speech,
in the form of a question, is
a cue. Someone stands up to
leave. No one wants an answer.
We prefer props, like a skull
in the hand to focus a thought.
Who needs existentialism?
The war isn't over yet. It *is*
nobler to suffer, but no one

wants to anymore. There are
now others to do that for us.
Why not instead fool around
in the star's dressing room?
What happens on this stage,
what is said or understood, no
longer matters. We have rid
ourselves of the need for such
complication. Look: everything
glitters, everyone laughs. No
one here has a face left to fall.

2. My Man Godfrey

Sometimes everything you do
is funny, no matter how hard
you try. This week let's take
poverty and how you believe
you can empathize, providing
someone gives you a bum to
play with. For all your casual
glitter, you have never felt
anything to be your own. For
whole days you can't stop
thinking of the poor, of the
idea of the poor, who come to
seem like philosophers: "Alas,
poor Yorick!" and all of that. It
starts as a game you think you
can win: call it "the mousetrap."
At some later moment you come
to realize you are never as free
as you'd like to be, nor as daring.
Beneath those polished smiles,
lurking underneath your savoir
faire, is the saddest of longings:
to be safe in a world you treat
as your own playground, a world
in which either no one is safe or
no one is there at all. There's
the rub: security costs. Luckily,

all you can make is money, so
you know the ache of failing.
How can you stand to be wrong
when bodies pile up the skies?
You think you could be happy
bound in the smallest of spaces,
living in a dump, as long as you
had a picnic. How can you stand
to laugh when the joke's never
really on you? You think you'll
someday love someone enough
you won't need to keep him.

3. Twentieth Century

It's the twenty-first century,
which doesn't seem to mean
anything at all (or if it does,
it can't mean anything good),
so you watch a film called
Twentieth Century, in
which everyone is trying
to get away from the stage,
especially Carole Lombard,
who died in 1942: not in the
war but with her mother
in a plane crash near Las
Vegas. For now it's 1933.
There's still time to be funny,
only nothing is funny for all
the histrionic flare-ups, which
are what happen the farther
you try to get from theater.
Who doesn't want a gold
star, who isn't ready to learn
and to be invincible? But
everything falls apart, even
when John Barrymore takes
charge: one minute you're
modeling lingerie, the next
you're Joan of Arc, ready

to blaze out in flame, but
someone tapped your phones
and tails you to the market.
He looks just like someone
in a movie you've seen. So
you grab your things and
run and run and run, with
a repetitive clacking of
locomotion foreshadowing
a journey on a train. No
matter how closely you
studied your lines, how
carefully you traced chalk
markings on the stage, you
trip over your own feet. At
the end of the film a maniacal
director tricks you into a role
you didn't want: you signed
the contract, but we haven't
gotten there yet. Currently,
you're still on the train, the
train is called *Twentieth
Century*, and it moves without
seeming to move. There's a
madman painting its windows:
REPENT, FOR THE TIME IS AT HAND.
Can he have written this for you,
can he have known your terminus
to be Hollywood? Life's a big
scream, everything's a hit, you
realize, and the louder you are,
the more people cheer. Everyone
imagines a little world with stage
and curtain, a scattering of props,
and a quiet backstage where
they can pretend not to watch,
not to act, not to ask for a story.
There's always a story to tell,
always a tale of vice, which is
really the glamour of suffering
spectacularly for the pleasure

of others, as long as it doesn't
look like pleasure and as long
as it doesn't look like suffering.
Every play is a Passion play:
there's nothing new to learn.
The play isn't written for you.
The play isn't written at all.
But you want to be a player,
you want to strut and fret,
which is what we all want, so
we do end up where we belong.
The real problem is we're not
people anymore, people on a
train in a car where someone
left open the window. The wind
is too strong, someone's smoking.
The train shrieks *promise*. You
didn't mean to make one. You
waited in dark and dusty wings
to be called. No one does. Not yet.
There's nothing to learn that
isn't already behind you: no one
needed to teach you to scream.

4. Nothing Sacred

Fear and the wish come together,
both unbidden, as is the secret,
shameful urge to laugh. It's not
a dream, exactly, not a movie.
Maybe it's you. On the one
hand, there is the longing for
fame. On the other, certainty
and time, both of which poison
ardor. On the one hand, you
really aren't dying: it's a ruse
to prolong your exposure to
the possibility of renown. On
the other hand, you *are* dying:
who isn't? The world's dying
too, as if to keep you company,

only it happens so slowly you
pretend not to notice. At some
point you'll wish you weren't,
you'll wish it weren't, you'll
wish the ice caps would freeze
so polar bears might hunt again
in peace. First wish, then fear.
Then laughter without source
devours you from within. You're
in a strange city (aren't they
all?) and so is everyone else.
All the papers tell you you're
dying. You feel some notion
coursing through you. *Let it
be now, let it be real.* You're
burning up. You can't wait
to read what comes next.

Suite for the Twentieth Century (for Marilyn Monroe)

Joseph Campana

1. Niagara

The heart is not merely a
whore: it's also a murderer.
Every small town breeds
them by the dozen. And if
what you see is unclear, it's
because you've crossed a
border and the mist rises
to greet you. Welcome to
oblivion—see how small
it is? Marilyn Monroe goes
noir, fulfilling all your
sociopathic fantasies: at
last, America stripped down
in a cheap hotel. How can
it be said there is a wrong
variety of love when there
is so little love at all? Who
is it you really want to kill?
Everyone comes to the falls
to die or to marry, but to
return to the real problem,
which is neither a husband
nor a lover nor the endless
torrents of obscurity, how to
speak of the unpacking of
the heart? The problem's not
the words but the unpacking.
What if the unpacking of
the mind is both endless
and futile? Once it was all
you could believe in. Each
night thought carried you
out in darkness to what

must have been the great
cascade into which all
minds flow like barrels
into a great ocean. Fear
respects no station: take
Hamlet and every small-
town girl. What if the mind
is the small town that never
gets any bigger and the act
of unpacking the heart is
more virtuous than action
but still meaningless? It's
a wonder you didn't kill
sooner. It's a wonder you
got yourself anywhere at all.

2. The Misfits

Will you see it come for you?
Will it be a flashing sign,
a streaking star, your own
private dog-and-pony show?
Or will you sag into a mirror,
never noticing? The end is
always the end. Everyone
told you so. Everyone saw
it coming before you did.
The burden of living again
is the same as the burden
of living on, and it is borne
in the flesh as its weight.
Don't try the old smile.
Don't pretend to be a little
shy, a little simple, a little
coy. Beauty doesn't move
that way. Beauty was never
enough. It won't make wild
horses run faster. Don't look
at them, don't sing: "Let me
start again. I know I can. It
can begin again and over and

over again." Don't ask what
happens when the horses stop.
Don't ask what the guns are
for. Don't ask this of me—I
could never say no. I couldn't
bear to stop watching you
run yourself into the ground.

3. We're Not Married

One morning you wake up and
you are not what you think you
are. Someone had to tell you so:
you swore it was only the rain.
As long as there's a letter, as
long as there's a contract with
a seal and behind it a lawyer,
a justice, and a governor, you'll
be fine. They all have the same
name: Bush. This is the least
of your problems. To say you
don't know what state you're
in, though you recognize hewn
marble for a whited sepulcher.
To say there are no real unions
here: practical heresy. Each day
familiar voices, seeming to echo
around you, sell you the same
story: happiness is everywhere
and will cost you all you have.
The payments will be small. In
exchange you receive a series of
discrete items designed either to
keep you asleep or to keep you
clean. You'll take whichever you
can get. One morning you wake
up grateful you did wake up this
time, and suddenly everyone is
blond and so pure you all wear
crowns and sashes. Imagine you
could spend each night with a

different person, every night
wearing a different clean face.
"I'm not married," you cry, "I'm
not married," because you have
no idea what it is not to be one.
Imagine the devastation, imagine
solitude a kind of victory. To say
it was a choice, to call it a second
chance, to know what it is to be
with other people: for this you'd
not get married all over the place—
New York, Chicago, Hollywood,
London, Paris, Rome. In truth,
no one will let you, no one will
take you, no one will teach you
not to be what you have been.

4. Bus Stop
It doesn't matter how you came
to me, not at all, I don't care how
many wheels dragged you to what
you are now, how many skies
opened up to rain you down over
a thousand buses, how many skies
you tore yourself out of to drop down,
a thousand suitcases springing open,
and you were nothing I anticipated
finding: not there, not green, not
whistling out of a film, and there
is some particular thing happening
to people stuck in snow, when the
whole world drags its ruthless
engines to a halt because the ice
is not a thing to be roped down and
held away, and you are perhaps
nothing I can keep, whether here or
in some other desperate concentration:
a small room, a small fire spitting
out smoke like roughened cargo,
which is what it feels like, such

improbability, and what a trick it is
to hold on long enough to find out
we've survived the night and now
you know you've seen me beaten
down low so wrecked to see you,
getting to me however it was you
got yourself across, and there are
lines you trace and I could trace
them too now and they are deeper
every time, which is what we call
direction: that sense of being not
where you are or being where
you are but not yourself until you
move a little further down the line,
and I'd have put down all my winnings,
all my chattel and change to see you
open that door as you did and you
the sun I wasn't ready yet to see.
There will be another time, another
rodeo, and I'm the one to be had for
a song, for a little spot of coffee
someone held for me: like a ticket
for a trip to a house in a blizzard
with the light driving on, with
the light sparking on, with the light
someone's striking on for me to stop.

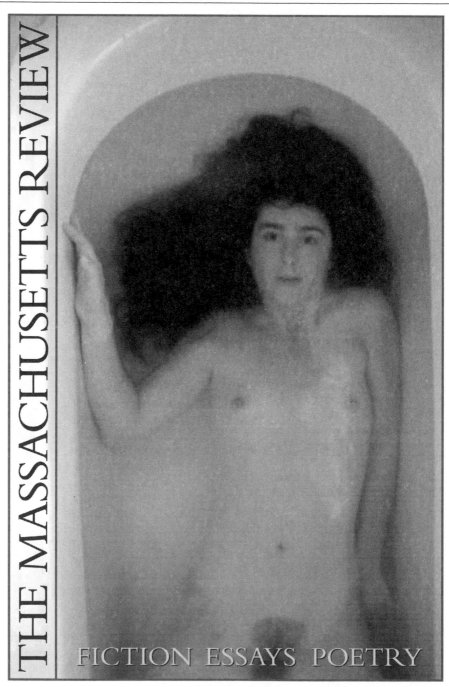

THE MASSACHUSETTS REVIEW

FICTION ESSAYS POETRY

A QUARTERLY REVIEW *of* Fiction, Poetry, Essays, and Art, *since 1959*
massrev@external.umass.edu | www.massreview.org

Birthday

Kim Goldberg

I was born in 1969—Year of the Rooster, of Woodstock, of electric Kool-Aid, of Country Joe booming *There's three hundred thousand of you fuck-ers out there, I don't know how you ever expect to stop the war if you can't sing any better than that!*, of Captain America getting shotgunned off his hog at the end of *Easy Rider*, pile of sunny-side-up fragments left to sizzle on the skillet of some hate-filled southern highway—or rice paddy (no, those movies came later, we were still living it then), I was born on the day I quit high school, on my fifteenth birthday, crashed out the vacuous dou-ble-doored vagina of Marshfield Senior High in Coos Bay, Oregon, take your stinkin' hall pass and shove it you dork-face fascists, the fucked-up world needs me today not after graduation, I'm my own teacher now, if I meet the Buddha on the road I'll be killing that self-righteous little prick (but I just ended up shooting a bunch of drugs and swiping various TVs and a car or two, which somehow seemed revolutionary at the time, but it worked out okay because it gives me something to write about in my twi-light years).

I was born in 1954—Year of the Horse, of America's top court ordering desegregation, of an eight-pound space rock beaning an Alabama lady listening to her radio (the country ain't safe for no one these days!), of an eight-pound baby shooting into the sacred heart (or an edifice so named) of the corporeal world between a shapely pair of legs (or more likely was yanked in since I was born breech, but it worked out okay, I mean I don't have any visible impairments or anything).

I was born in 1970—Year of the Dog, of *Apollo 13* (which was a dud), of *Lunokhod 1* (which wasn't), of blood-spattered Korea fronting for Vietnam in Altman's *M*A*S*H* (because we were *still* living the other one), year of lights-out at 9:00 in Villa Saint Rose, some nun-run Guantánamo for wards of the state, the year I hauled my bell-bottomed paisley ass over the twelve-foot wall one night, shredding a forearm on razor wire, beating feet to I-5, getting off at Eugene, getting lost in the lotusland of deadheads and yogurt and acres of bean sprouts, scoring fake ID to keep me off the radar till I turned eighteen (which worked out okay, although the name Smith wasn't very creative for a future writer, so that's when I decided it's best to figure out your aliases before you spark up).

I was born in 1954—but earlier than the other one so it was still Year of the Snake, of the navy's first nuclear sub, of atomic tests on Bikini*BABOOM*Atoll, of the puke-sweet stench of electrocuted flesh still clinging to the air like a spring thunderstorm washing the nation clean of those commiejewspies the Rosenbergs, I was born to the shapely vowel sounds of a leggy young woman speaking Middle English from four centuries ago, a young bride full of hope and cultural programming and Dr. Spock, reading all seven books of Edmund Spenser's *Faerie Queene* to the unborn first child inside her, tuning unformed ears, weaving harmonic resonances into spongy fetal tissues, smooth as a parabola, rhythmic as amniotic tides, perchance to yield a poet (and that seemed to work out okay too, although there are those who say the prose poem is not really poetry).

I was born in 1913—Year of the Ox, of some Danish guy flaunting his quantum model of the atom (which led to some harsh radioactive shit later on), year that they locked up Gandhi, that my grandfather Solomon Goldberg strode down the gangplank and onto Ellis Island, scarcely more than a teenager, nothing to his name but a torn topcoat and pocketful of Yiddish—and a dream that became his own chemical company until World War II, when the US Army recruited him to translate design plans on fighter planes to give the Russians (who were our allies back then and sort of are again now), that was the year I was born, for had Sol not hopped that steamer from Lithuania and brought his childhood sweetheart, they both would have ended up in the mass grave with the rest of the tribe thirty years down the line, along with their son Philip Abraham, currently known as my astrophysical father (so this one definitely worked out okay).

I was born in 1972—Year of the Rat, of *Life* magazine's death, of Nixon's contaminated re-election, year that *The Godfather* tommy-gunned its way into our heads (since Coppola wasn't ready to make *Apocalypse Now* because we were *still* still living it), year that my family pulled up tent pegs and moved to Canada to save my brother from Vietnam, *this boy ain't made to kill or be killed* said the Faerie Queene with the sacred heart (which worked out okay for everyone because people in Canada are super polite and have very few guns and smell nice too, maybe because it's colder—I even took up hockey).

I was born in 13,700,000,000 BC—Year of the Quark, of the gaseous outpouring, of the time-warped contractions of the universe unformed, the first fart in the first billionth of a second after the Big Jack-off, it was pretty confusing for a while, like some over-amped flashback with streaking lights and kick-ass tidal waves of blackness all slamming into each other in a cosmic mosh pit (Stanley Kubrick got it more or less right so I am assuming he was swirling around in there too), and then a shitload of head-banging boredom for what seemed like eons (and probably was) at the bottom of a wormhole with nothing to read but some half-baked frequencies, just a bunch of fuzzy squiggles not even trying to pull themselves together, kind of like being stuck in juvie at Coquille where they stuff you in a five-by-eight box for weeks and only let you out for forty-five minutes a day to play pool or thumb *Reader's Digest*, I mean how fucked up is that? (but I got through it somehow, this stellar cumshot, so I guess it worked out okay, in fact I really like stargazing now and I know most of the constellations, but that could be because my uncle is an astronomer—it's tough to get a handle on causality). I was born, and it worked out okay. ✧

Whatever Happened to Harlan?
A Report from the Field

David Hollander

After running out on *L.I.E.*, the novel in which he briefly played the protagonist, Harlan Kessler headed west. Not like, *far* west. He didn't point his old clunker (Volkswagen station wagon, circa 1974) toward the Pacific, disappearing in a cloud of diesel soot. He didn't entertain romantic notions of salvation-via-the-road. No, when *L.I.E.* was over, when he was left with nothing but his denim jacket, his battered Stratocaster, and half a pack of Marlboro Lights, he abandoned the teetering geometry of slipshod Long Island housing developments for the steaming vortex that was Brooklyn. He went west, that is, *but only thirty miles west*, where he landed in the vicinity of Red Hook, on the waterfront, because water was apparently his inescapable legacy. Long hair flowing, teenage agony dimming to the slower, burning agony of adulthood, he found a splintered one-bedroom with his girlfriend, Sarah DeRosa, who'd also had enough of *L.I.E.* and was more than happy to flee her cocaine-dealing stepfather and all the trappings of her life on *Wrong Island*. (Never mind that Brooklyn was and is physically part and parcel of that very same island. It's perception that counts, and for our young couple—just turning twenty and on the lam from their *shithole past*, as Harlan liked to say—the perception was clearly that they had moved on, and were beginning another chapter in their previously fictional but now all-too-real lives.)

It so happened that, during this same period, and at the beginning of what would become a painfully long interregnum between novels, the writer of *L.I.E.*, a middling experimentalist whose name is at the top of this story, also settled in Brooklyn, though in a slightly tonier district known the world over as Park Slope, where multimillion-dollar brownstones glowed beneath dappled sunshine, and where every woman seemed to push a stroller loaded—like a warship's line of cannons—with several screaming infants all in a row. Hollander had received 50,000 dollars for the sale of *L.I.E.*, which given his history of half-assed manual labor and part-time temp work, was a fuckload of money and more than he could really fathom. Random House was printing some twenty-odd thousand copies of his first novel, a huge advance sat like a fat Buddha in his just-opened checking account, and he was officially retiring from the plaster-and-Sheetrock industry. His Fourth Street apartment might just as well have been on Easy Street, so sure was he of his future. He was a *someone* now, a young literary celebrity. How could he ever have resembled that Harlan Kessler character, who was such a clueless, improvident screwup? Life was opening up, not unlike (he would think later) a lesion, or a mine shaft.

Now, if you haven't read the book (and odds are overwhelmingly in favor of your having not read the book), a brief synopsis may help. Essentially, *L.I.E.* is *an autobiographical coming-of-age story* centered around Harlan, who (along with a group of disenfranchised and miscreant punk rockers) spends most of his time looking for a way to spend his time. The hook, though—and here's where Hollander thought himself to have been quite clever—is that Harlan is growing increasingly aware that he is a *character in a book* and that any autonomy he seems to possess is illusory. He's at the whim of forces he can neither control nor comprehend. His escape from the novel in the culminating chapters is in many ways an assertion of the free will he has been denied as a fictional character. The rest of the book's cast—oblivious to the fact that they are a book's cast— are left to shrug their collective shoulders over the fact that Harlan and Sarah have vanished. Inadvertently, Hollander had unleashed these two upon the very same real world that he himself inhabited, and in which he was currently flaunting fifty-dollar bills and doing saucy interviews with *New York* magazine.

(The ISBN of the *L.I.E.* paperback is 0-345-44100-1. Not that the author of this story is pressuring you to buy it or anything.)

Harlan and Sarah didn't last long on the outside. Although Hollander had pitched them as hopelessly inseparable, the fact is that they didn't have much in common other than their desire to get as far away from the novel as possible and to have a fresh start outside its confines. Sarah transferred to Pratt (where she got pretty serious about printmaking, specializing in intaglio; she loved the scraping sound of awl on copper, the little bronze flecks that would collect beneath her fingernails). Harlan joined up with a band called *Tyrannosaurus Wrecks*, a hard-driving rock outfit with a sense of humor and a penchant for strange time signatures. Our young couple started wanting things other than each other, and the apartment in Red Hook—which crouched at the water's edge—simmered with quiet resentment. Sarah would return from class in the evenings and sneak up on the crumbling brick structure, pondering her future while an angry sun set the low-lying warehouses ablaze before dousing itself beneath sizzling black surf. Harlan would usually be leaving, heading out to band practice in a nearby practice studio, or to his job at a local indie-label record store, where he was slowly discovering hipness. A few months into their cohabitation, and already Sarah felt herself fading from his vocabulary. She met another boy, a painter from Pratt with whom she shared studio space, and soon after she stopped coming home to the waterfront. "You saved me," she wrote to him in a letter that he still keeps at the bottom of his dresser, handwritten on crinkled loose-leaf. "Without your love, I never could have become a full person." Harlan cried as she moved her things out of the apartment. But he'd had a gig that night, and the show went on, and he took his anger out on his guitar and goddamn it, he totally kicked ass (though really, the variety of *math rock* his band was playing was completely devoid of anything remotely akin to anger, *which he knew*, but he liked pretending that the guitar was an emotional release and not the foreign and impenetrable object he truly felt it to be). And between the easy good looks of twenty-years-old, and the fact that *Tyrannosaurus Wrecks* was beginning to garner some momentum, he found that the girls were interested in him. And what's more: they were *hot*. Hotter than Sarah. He was young and smart and full of verve. Things were looking up for our Harlan Kessler.

Meanwhile, David Hollander was making some unfortunate discoveries about money and fame, namely that he possessed neither. He had squandered the initial portion of his advance on the partial repayment of his student loans (when he could have been buying *things*—a car, maybe, or something even better . . . like *two* cars!), which actually outweighed his total book advance by some ten thousand dollars. Not realizing (because of flaming, feckless ignorance) that there would be heavy taxes due on these monies, he quickly found himself in trouble with the Internal Revenue Service. The irony here was that in *L.I.E., A Novel*, Harlan held down a job for this very agency, mocking the boondoggle of government employment with ferocious mirth, certain that the bureaucrats were powerless to hold him accountable. Hollander was, perhaps, getting his just deserts. "When will I start receiving royalties?" he asked his agent, hoping that the answer was, *Right fucking now.* "Royalties are based on sales, David," came the perplexed reply. "Well, I have sold *some* books!" And the agent: "Yes, but you're not even *close* to making back your advance. At the current rate of sales, *L.I.E.* would have to be on the market for nearly seven hundred years before you even broke even." David's silence was met with confused sympathy. He hung up the phone and sat in the dank bedroom of his basement apartment, picking splinters from the tarnished hardwood floor. "I am a published novelist," he repeated, rocking back and forth on the heels of his dingy socks. "I am a published novelist!" he shouted, and his housemate—a dreadlocked hippie girl named Hyacinth—shouted back, "Keep it down, would ya? I'm doing yoga!"

Tyrannosaurus Wrecks was written up in *Spin* magazine. They were the centerpiece of a big feature on the New York music scene, which was thriving despite the industry's focus on more exotic locales (the place du jour for the record executives was Chapel Hill, North Carolina, where a band called the *Squirrel Nut Zippers* was just breaking loose, leading a swing revival that would last about as long as *L.I.E.*'s misbegotten hype), and this publicity had a tremendous impact on the band's desirability. A manager was hired, a cross-country tour was scheduled, and Pete Puma, the band's devilish drummer, started referring to Harlan as "the world's greatest young guitarist." He introduced him that way at each show, and Harlan would stomp on every effects pedal at his disposal and play a twelve-bar *noise solo* that bled irony as if his amplifier were a corpse that bled irony. Or something like that. Two years earlier, on his fictional Long Island, he'd worshipped guitar solos with grave seriousness (his hero, after all, had been Joe Satriani, perhaps the greatest noodler of the 1980s, when noodling was at an all-time high), but he now understood that they were, well, *kinda stupid.* Hipster irony became central to the *Tyrannosaurus Wrecks* gestalt, and their shows were one part kitsch, one part showmanship, and one part bizarre rock and roll. The tour was a blast. Harlan had never known, while muddling through *L.I.E.*, that such joy was possible, or that his life could feel so wet, so rich, so heavy with possibility. On stages lit deep indigo and hellfire red, beneath the strontium-90 glow of a hundred different clubs, he became—for moments at a time—that very thing which he'd been dreaming about for many years: he became *substantial.*

David Hollander's parents had, by this juncture, stopped talking to him. He should have expected it. In the novel he did not even go so far as to change their names. His father remained Bob. His mother remained Alice. They became *Harlan's* parents, granted, but kept many of the same characteristics as their source personas and were treated with something well short of kindness. Hollander had portrayed his father (again, through the mouthpiece of the pseudo-fictional Harlan) as a selfish, gluttonous tyrant, known to family and friends simply as Fatso. He'd outed his mother's extramarital affair and gone so far to refer to her as "the Kessler Whore." He hadn't worried about their rejection while writing the book, for two reasons: First, he thought they would never in a million years read the fucking thing, because he had never spotted either of his parents holding a book, and they might have been illiterate for all he knew. And second, they really had it coming, as far as he was concerned. He hadn't even *lied* about anything. His mother *was* an adulteress! His father *was* a fatso! But it turned out, to Hollander's own surprise, that he loved these parents, and that he had taken their (admittedly lackluster) support for granted. Love, it now occurred to him, could exist in a life's negative spaces. (Think of this as the acquisition of wisdom, something that nearly always comes too late, as the wise among you will surely acknowledge.) At a reading out on Long Island, at a Border's Books, beneath wan and flickering fluorescent lights, his own reflection wavering in the dark glass of the storefront, he read aloud to a small audience that included his own father. Afterwards, during the brief Q and A, an elderly woman in a pink scarf asked, "Are your parents proud of you for writing a book?" Hollander blushed, then turned to his father and asked in turn, "I don't know. Whaddaya say, Dad?" His father rose, spit on the *industrial-weight carpeting*, and strode out, with his second wife in tow like an aluminum can. "Shame on you," this stepmother said as they tore past soon-to-be-returned stacks of his novel, piercing the Long Island night, perhaps never to be heard from again. (Check in from time to time and he'll let you know.)

At a gig at Manhattan's Knitting Factory, Harlan met a woman. His band's set was over, and a small collection of devotees had filed backstage to inform them of *how fucking great* the show had been, how they *completely kicked ass!* Harlan was already over this variety of postcoital praise and was busy coiling up black cords and arranging equipment for transportation back to their Brooklyn practice room when she approached him, smiling. She was not dressed like a groupie, and anyway they didn't really have groupies, not yet, but she wasn't even dressed like Harlan's *idea* of a groupie. She sported a stylish black skirt and a white blouse and high-heeled shoes. She wore cat-eye glasses, and her lipstick was a bright ruby red. She was maybe thirty years old—exotic to our young musician—and she held a business card in her hand. "Hi, Harlan?" she asked. She smelled like strawberries. He caught Pete Puma's eye, who gave an approving nod, as if to say, *She's all right, man, go for it!* "That's me," he grinned, pushing hair from his sweaty face, "what's up?" She explained that she worked for a major media company beginning an Internet experiment, "live streaming programming," she said, and they were looking for talented, good-looking, intelligent young people to run various thirty-minute shows. "We saw the write-up in *Spin*," she smiled. "We loved the way you answered questions, really funny, really natural." Harlan was wondering, *Am I going to sleep with this woman tonight?* and his libido pulsed. "We thought," she continued, as musicians and their kin crowded through the small backstage area, the air hot and humid, "that you'd be great to head up a show for us. You'd have total creative freedom. We'd love to talk to you about it if you're interested." Harlan stacked one amplifier atop another, flexing. He pushed his hair back one more time. "That sounds really cool," he said. "What are you doing tonight?" Her name was Wendy, and later on, when she was in his bed in Red Hook, glowing with sweat, she confessed that she'd *wanted to fuck him* the moment he took the stage, which was weird because she usually wasn't into younger guys. There was something about him, she said. "You seem like you're from someplace else. Has anyone told you that before?" Harlan grinned his seductive grin: "I used to be a character in a book," he explained. "It was a real bad scene." Wendy, unreserved and insatiable, only laughed, grinding her hips into him, moving in for round two.

The critics of the novel, meanwhile, kept asking what the deal was *with all the book's unnecessary italics,* to which Hollander found himself fabricating answers in both actual interviews (which, after a month or so, had stopped coming) and *in his mind,* where he often drifted on burnt-marshmallow clouds, wondering how this whole publication thing might have gone differently. He started looking for teaching work—he'd aggressively quit his job plastering brownstones, and between the publication of *L.I.E.* and the fact that he'd acquired a master of fine arts degree in fiction writing, he figured he'd be a good university candidate—but the best thing he could find was an adjunct position teaching freshman composition at a state school, where they claimed to be paying him thirty-five dollars an hour (based on his time in class), but where his *actual* pay, after calculating in prep time and grading and office hours and transit, came to something much closer to *three* dollars an hour. His weekly wage was less than half what it was when he was slapping plaster on wire lath. And of course, gone were the easy good looks of his twenties. He felt the future rearing up on its hind legs, teeth bared, giggling maniacally at his supreme buffoonery.

Harlan took Wendy's offer to run a program on the Net. And they started dating, too, and were really into each other, and Wendy didn't believe in monogamy and encouraged him to *bring home other girls* and demanded to hear the dirty details or, better yet, *to watch*. The show itself was successful by industry standards (it revolved around Harlan's interviews with people from the New York art scene, musicians and painters and even a writer or two, all of whom seemed to thrive on self-deprecation and irony, which fed into the show's slacker paradigm). Harlan called the program *The Belly of the Beast* and used it to promote *Tyrannosaurus Wrecks'* self-released CD and their upcoming gigs at every possible turn. Between the *Spin* article and this new soapbox, Harlan and his band were in ever-higher demand, booked up solid and making some actual money—sometimes a thousand a night or more. They agreed to headline several shows during the annual CMJ festival—two in Manhattan and two in Brooklyn—and all the festival's buzz swarmed around them. At a practice leading up to these dates Harlan actually stopped the band midsong just to say, "We are so fucking awesome!" His two bandmates—Pete and Mitchell—laughed and agreed. They loved Harlan. He was, as Pete liked to say, "so real, you know? No bullshit." The CMJ ad campaign read, at Harlan's suggestion: *Prepare to be Wrecked!*

There was a reason, David Hollander was discovering, that so many writers are afflicted by drink. Between the teaching work (which he loathed—his students were at best clowns, at worst criminals) and the attempts to write in the evenings (attempts now burdened by the weight of *L.I.E.*'s immense failure and by the knowledge that said failure would *track him forever*), he found himself entering a period of radical self-loathing for which the only palliative was alcohol. Becoming more of a cliché every day, he would visit his most local tavern (a place called Great Lakes, where placards depicting these freshwater monstrosities hung in gargantua from dark blue walls, and where the green track lights were kept dim enough to permit the development of film) and sit patiently, pretending to write in a black-bound journal. Sometimes he *would* write, but these scribblings fell well outside the parameters of literature and were adorned by unreassuring marginalia. "I am a published novelist," for instance. Or, "Don't try suicide, 'cause nobody gives a damn." Within this dark hipster watering hole, cigarette smoke forming complex strata and inebriated glee climbing and falling, Hollander sat and tried to look complicated so that some woman, *any woman*, would speak to him. But they were all too young, and he was already too old (how had *that* happened?), and the best he could manage was to coax a smile of pity from these pretty, sweet-smelling creatures. His second book, which he'd ambitiously entitled *The Key to All Mythologies*, would be finished in 300 years at what was his current rate of progress (and 400 years after that, he mused, he could begin collecting royalties on *L.I.E.*). He felt thwarted and clueless; he was a cistern accumulating liquid anger, and each day he became fuller, heavier, hotter. When his housemate, Hyacinth, ladled out New Age encouragement ("Be here now! Live for the moment!"), he imagined jabbing an ice pick through her fleshy white throat.

L.I.E. had been blurbed by best-selling author Sheri Holman (*The Dress Lodger*, Atlantic Monthly Press, 2000), who called it "achingly funny and mordantly sad" and "a soul map for modern suburbia." Around this time Hollander began thinking about "soul maps." His own would include a tar pit, countless black-rimmed sinkholes, and some sort of perpetually burning forest into which deformed children were dropped from airplanes. (But Sheri Holman was really nice to say that stuff, and it was much appreciated, and he wrote her a letter of thanks that he regrets never sending, just to set the record straight.)

"Hey, Sarah," Harlan said into the telephone, "you should come out to the next show. It's right here in the borough—CMJ set it up for us." Sarah was living near Pratt now with Ernest, the aforementioned painter. It had been over six months since the breakup, and Harlan and Sarah were slowly finding their way back toward friendship. "Ernie can come too," Harlan said. "I mean, it's tough for me to see you with another guy, but I know I've gotta get used to it." Sarah thought it over. "Maybe . . . ," she said. "Let me ask him." She cradled the phone between chin and shoulder and mixed cake batter in a glass bowl, the sunlight streaming through her Clinton Hill loft, making her feel very much like the young urbanite she was becoming. Sarah had no real intention of going to one of Harlan's gigs, watching the girls fawn over him, seeing this new chick Wendy she'd heard about . . . it was too much too soon. But she did enjoy teasing him. "Tell you what," she said, "I'll come if you cut your hair." It was an old joke between them from back in the days of *L.I.E.* Harlan giggled on his end. She knew he was tossing those long locks around at that very moment. "Sarah," he said. "Don't you know the story of Sampson?" And her reply: "Oh, I know all about him. Another pretty boy with a chip on his shoulder." They bantered this way for a while. They did love each other after all, and they had shared a unique experience, parlaying their time as fictional characters into what was, for all intents and purposes, a real-world existence. Sometimes Sarah missed the people she knew from *L.I.E.*, but mostly she felt tremendous gratitude, for Harlan, for Ernest, for art, for music, for a world of shapes and colors and light and air, a world in which every breath was inscrutable and sublime.

So it was that on a typical Thursday evening Hollander found Great Lakes filling up atypically fast, and with a crowd even younger and hipper than the one to which he'd resigned himself. He was drinking heavily. He'd started at the start of Happy Hour, when he was at his most Unhappy, and after a brief and reliable period in which his spirits rose to catch a glimpse of the light, he found himself plummeting back into the familiar dark pit of despair. He knew this pit from its well-marked location on his *soul map*. It was not unusual for the bar to have live music, but it was usually reserved for weekends proper, and as Hollander ordered a gin and tonic— his belly was already bloated with beer—his ire rose. This was *his* fucking bar. Couldn't he even go out for a few drinks on a weeknight without being reminded that the world still possessed joy? He uncapped his pen, preparing to unleash some wicked sentences regarding *the supreme stupidity of hope*, trying to remember an old Schopenhauer quote ("Never a rose without a thorn, but many a thorn with no rose," something like that), when the PA system sprang to life, noise and electricity conducted between packed, sweating bodies. David looked to the stage. There was a drummer—stout and young with spiky red hair—standing behind his kit, holding a microphone. To either side, crouched down over their instruments, a guitarist and bassist tended to private agendas. The drummer wasted no time. "Ladies and gentlemen of Brooklyn!" he shouted. "I give you the world's greatest young guitarist, Mr. Harlan Kessler!" And then came noise— scrapes and echoes and some strange digital phasing sound that seemed to herald the landing of extraterrestrials—as Harlan tortured his guitar, obviously aware of how awful it was, and clearly loving this interface with a crowd cognizant of the gag. David looked at the young man, the long hair, the thin face, the eager smile, the black Stratocaster and the black boots and the denim, all the torn denim. He thought, *Holy shit.* And then he thought, *That's Harlan.* Then he thought, *That's my Harlan.* And then he swallowed the rest of his drink and watched the set, entranced. He existed within a bubble of privacy. His barstool was the axis around which our worn-down planet spun, and he felt pinned to this perch, as if by some reversal of the principle of centrifugal force.

In *L.I.E.* Harlan's band had been the Dayglow Crazies. They had played three-chord rock to a group of friends in the drummer's basement and written a few originals and swum in the same stagnant pond as a thousand other Long Island dreamers. Anyway, Harlan always knew that within the confines of the book he would be begrudged no success. But now, ending another set with *Tyrannosaurus Wrecks*, climbing off the stage to find Wendy, and then finding her sugary tongue in his mouth, feeling all the hands on him, all the people eager to absorb some of his fledgling celebrity, he felt anew his supreme good fortune; his life was among the best of all possible lives. He pushed through soft bodies, toward the bar, Wendy's hand on his ass and his torn T-shirt soaked through, the PA system blasting the Ramones as the next band set up, smoke drifting in cumulus formations through the green light, simulating cosmic phenomena, nebulae and pulsing quasars. He turned to say something to a fan he recognized, and was blinded momentarily by a red strobe mounted to the ceiling. When he spun forward again, he was met with the unexpected. A second passed before he realized he'd been punched hard in the mouth, and with the shock of the unforeseeable came a sizzling rush of adrenaline.

He stumbled backwards, his teeth swimming in blood. The guy was on him again, *some older dude*, it was all happening fast, and Harlan raised his hands to hold off the next punch. But the pugilist had Harlan by the shirt and they went down to the beer-soaked concrete together, Harlan underneath, squirming, pinned to the ground, aware of the huge crowd, already calculating whether or not his image would suffer or benefit from this strange turn of events. "I made you!" the assailant was screaming. He had Harlan by the neck now, throttling him. "And I'll unmake you too, motherfucker!" Harlan managed to pull the bony fingers from his soft throat—fingers strangely similar to his own—and he looked the man in the eye. Already they were being pulled apart, but now Harlan was actually groping, attempting to hold the man tight, to keep him there for a moment. The music and the crowd and the flurry of profane exclamations were all swallowed by the immensity of his recognition, and suddenly it was as if they were alone, just the two of them. Harlan shivered. "It's you," he said as Hollander was overtaken by several sneering onlookers, first among them Pete Puma. Hollander was pulled to his feet, and Harlan rose too, watching as they dragged his assailant to the door, the crowd parting, cheering this righteous ejection. "I know who you are!" Harlan cried out over their applause, blood spraying from his mouth, pooling in the corners of his lips. "I don't forgive you!" he screamed. Wendy was there, attending to him. There were people offering to follow the asshole home and teach him a lesson, but Harlan waved them off: "It's cool," he said, recovering his bearings. "Don't worry about it." And Wendy: "You sure, babe? You're shaking." And it wasn't cool, not really. His former overlord was a flesh-and-blood man, some loser in his thirties with a bad haircut and an angry streak, nothing special at all. Somehow he'd always expected . . . more. This epiphany may have been the true onset of adulthood for Harlan, who felt for the first time in his short life the burden of nostalgia; no matter how special his entry into this world may have been, he was simply here now, and he was aging, just the same as everyone else. "Let's get a drink, huh, Wendy?" He smiled, hiding his eyes from her. "You handled that really well, babe," she said, grinning, and he led her through his admirers, to a well-stocked bar, thinking inexplicably of Sarah, and of all the things he'd left behind, all the things he could never revisit.

As for Hollander, he went home bruised and bloody, after being kicked mercilessly by several pairs of anonymous boots, thrown into the street, the black sedans of various local car services slowing, his face illumined in their headlights. He could see himself as *they* saw him, one of the world's downtrodden, a curiosity, an object of interest but not a man exactly. The three-block journey to his half-submerged basement apartment was impossibly long. He limped. He shuddered. The air tasted like his blood. His fingers trembled as he unlocked the gate to his building, the streetlamps bathing him in crisp blue light, rendering him a phantom, his own ghost, *here and not here*. He walked in, and Hyacinth, unseen, called from the kitchen: "Great timing! I just made some lentils!" He let himself into his room and closed the door. He pulled the black-bound notebook from his pocket and sat hunched over on his bed, sobbing. The tears stung wounds he had yet to explore. The time had come, he realized, to face a whole new set of demons. The old ones, it turned out, were doing just fine. "I am a published novelist," he choked. And again: "I am a published novelist." He was repeating these words quietly between gasps when Hyacinth knocked and asked if everything was all right. ✧

Farewell

Laura Didyk

Good-bye to the pink sun I saw rise that night over a field in Freedom, Indiana.

Good-bye to the pink sun I took a square of and dropped under my tongue.

Good-bye to believing everything is made of leaves and sickness and fire.

Good-bye to boxes of wine, to 40s, to joints saved for a week in a playing card box until the exact perfect moment.

Good-bye to lines of I don't know what up my nose.

Good-bye, Southern Comfort and Jim Beam.

Good-bye, Boone's and Carlo Rossi.

Good-bye, 151 and Mad Dog.

Wild Turkey, you were my one and only.

Good-bye to puking outside of vans, behind buildings, in the toilets of crowded and overheated motel rooms, on my lap in a dealer's Audi 5000, all over his new leather seats.

Good-bye, dealers everywhere.

Good-bye to the grass I slept in behind the Motel 6, and the cop's club that nudged me awake, and her husky voice telling me, "The party's over."

Good-bye to whole days of my life I don't remember.

Good-bye to the man in the parking lot at the Oakland shows who lifted the shopping cart over his head and yelled, "I am the king of America."

Good-bye, revelation inside Terrapin Station.

Good-bye to the campground in North Carolina where I hid behind a van and watched my sixty-year-old friend Honeybee run from the cops with one busted sandal he'd glued five times since we left Indiana. Good-bye to the thick bag of Mendecino we went through hell to get that the cop threw onto his dashboard like a pair of sunglasses. Good-bye to Honeybee's scraggly hair that swung back and forth over his shoulders as the cop pulled his arms tight behind his back and cuffed him.

Good-bye to glitter, to shimmer, to stray rainbowed hearts meeting my breath in the air.

Good-bye, nineteen years old.

Good-bye to strychnine in the stomach on a curb. *I can't get up, I can't walk anymore.*

Good-bye to the dreamy guy in Jersey with the straight teeth and peppermint breath who looked like he just stepped off a jet. Good-bye to how he stood, inches from me, tugging gently the front of my dress, pupils filling his eyes, colors winding from his mouth in a slow stream as he tried to explain that he knew me. He knew me somehow.

Good-bye to the handful of flawless, double-pointed crystals the size of pills I mined on a plot in Herkimer, New York. Good-bye to the seven-foot Native American man named John whose plot it was, who let us dig. Good-bye to promising myself as I stood there, crystals in hand, shaking them like dice, that I'd be young forever.

Good-bye to cowboy coffee and Dumpster doughnuts and sunburn, to beating the waitstaff at Denny's to the leftover food on the tables—the french fries, the chicken sticks, the cheese.

Farewell to the very clean, very straight ex-boyfriend of mine from the college I'd quit and left behind for my new life whom by mistake and utter coincidence I turned to in the parking lot with my palm out and said, "Spare change." He wore Bermuda shorts, Top-Siders with no socks, and a red polo shirt. He majored in bio-chemistry. He made my stomach hurt the way he looked at me. Like he was saying: *What I thought you'd become, you became.* Like he could see the germs on me, the bugs laying their eggs in neat, orderly rows under my skin, which they were, like he was calculating the distance of the arc between my dirty bare feet and his well-scrubbed hands.

Good-bye to the two hundred different kinds of lice that lived in my dreadlocks, on my scalp, on everyone's scalps around me.

Good-bye to Walter and his homemade tattoo machine, to those ridiculously tiny tattoos that always turned out looking like moles.

Good-bye to Justin and his gray backpack and the mini Clorox bottle inside it that he watched over like a hound. Good-bye to the side trips behind buildings. To his long ponytail I'd watch from behind as he bent forward, as he tied and tightened and filled and plunged. Good-bye to the look in his eyes right after.

Farewell to the one drug I never tried.

Good-bye to roadside dilation tests and walking the line and road blocks and sniffing dogs.

Arrivederci to my entire free life flashing before my eyes.

Good-bye, vials and sugar cubes.

Good-bye, Wharf Rats and Spinners and Krishnas. Good-bye, Family and Cali boys.

Good-bye to the eternal parking lot where what we called each other didn't seem much to matter.

Good-bye, Dave TV and his peanut butter and banana sandwiches. Good-bye to the fifty cents per sandwich I made selling them. My regards for making me a partner, my gratitude to capitalism, alive and well on the fringe.

Good-bye to the ground scores: a quarter sheet; a ticket I gave away to an Asian guy named Louie who stood with his finger pointed to the sky waiting for a miracle; two marbles wrapped in copper wire that smelled like patchouli and cigarettes; a tie-dyed shirt I traded for two Budweisers; and a fluorescent pink whistle I blew into, not caring whose lips had touched it. It said MAGIC on the top. It said BLOW. So everywhere I went for an entire day in a city I can't remember, I blew.

Good-bye to the shirtless brother who got hit over the head with a skateboard next to the McDonald's in San Fran until his head cracked open, because the kid with the skate and the mohawk said the tabs he sold him were bunk. Good-bye to those around me who yelled, "*Shanti, shanti,* brother. PEACE, man!" and pulled the kid off. Good-bye to that kid, who held his skateboard up to the sky as he walked away and said, "FUCK peace," shrugging the ripped side of his army coat back onto his shoulder.

Good-bye to thinking love can heal all wounds.

Adios to the Deer Creek shows, where I ate two tabs of acid and a palmful of mushrooms and felt nothing except during "Franklin's Tower," when a thick red line split my body in half lengthwise—my right side was pain, my left side pleasure. I didn't know which one to choose. They were both ugly and both beautiful, and neither one was true. Good-bye to having to decide. ✧

Portraits in Plasma

Judith Page

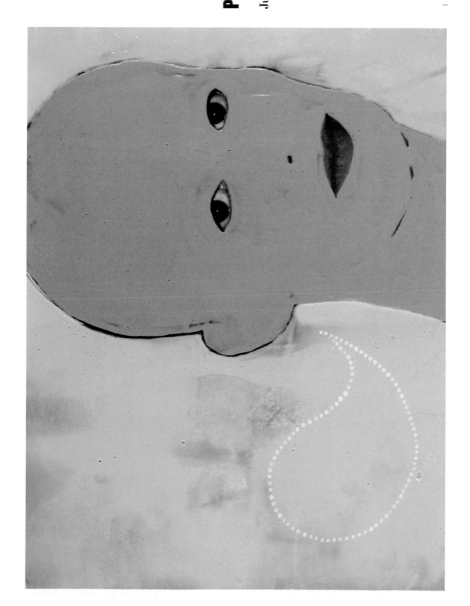

Obsession/Revelation

In describing his approach to recording the history of Imperial Rome, Tacitus distinguished himself from his contemporaries, who primarily recounted the glory and the grandeur of their times, by focusing his attention on the sometimes brave but more often appalling individual acts that constituted the memorable and the catastrophic. To concentrate one's creative

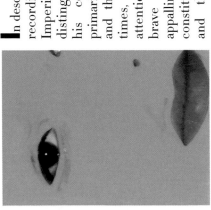

energy in difficult territory is not necessarily a rational decision nor a popular one. It is something that one just does—with joy, trepidation, curiosity, and without question.

I have obsessively focused my creative energy for the past twenty years on the human condition, exploring such subjects as the transcendence of death through regeneration, the abuse of power and the plight of the powerless, the struggle between physical necessity and spiritual values, and the fluidity of history—coagulating, dispersing, and reconstituting, I consider myself a visual historian, recording and interpreting the spirit of my times. Through the exploration of specific issues, I search for patterns, for the aberrant, for the profane, for the divine, for that elusive propellant that hurls us from one moment to the next.

My art has consistently included the presence of the figure—not surprising, considering my focus on the human condition. The form, however, has swung between representation and abstraction, and between painting and sculpture. Many works combine both these approaches, and for the past ten years my art has also included collage, drawing, photography, sound, and text. My most recent body of work consists of portrait paintings of acquaintances, friends, and family that are influenced by such diverse sources as Roman portrait sculpture, the El Faiyûm encaustic portraits, Mexican vernacular art and artifacts, and contemporary television programming from *Extreme Makeover* to the evening news.

My portraits begin as photographs and, through the addition of a gel-like paint, become both reliquary and visionary. The reliquary aspect of the paintings comes from the fragments of the original photographs—eyes, mouth, teeth, or bits of skin—that one can glimpse through the layers of paint. They are like the bone fragments that one might view in a sculptural reliquary of a saint. The visionary aspect of the paintings involves the intuitive addition of paint over the photograph. Occasionally this action takes place in a passionate explosion; more often the process is deliberate and meditative. This blend of photography and painting allows me to reveal more about the character of the subject than the photograph itself—an expressive vision rather than a depiction.

Portraits in Plasma is an ongoing installation that consists of a selection of these portraits, most recently shown—in the format of a television viewing room—at The Aldrich Contemporary Art Museum. The variations in meaning of the word *plasma*—from its origin as the Greek word, *plassein*, meaning "to mold," to its contemporary use in reference to television (green translucent quartz), as a gaseous medium, to the fluid part of blood, and as a substance extruded from the body of a spiritualist during a séance—are all relevant to the content of these portraits. I want *Portraits in Plasma* to embrace the essence of each subject by stripping away the superfluous and allowing the subject to transcend the mortal, perpetually dissolving and evolving before the viewer's eyes, a vision both profane and divine.

—Judith Page

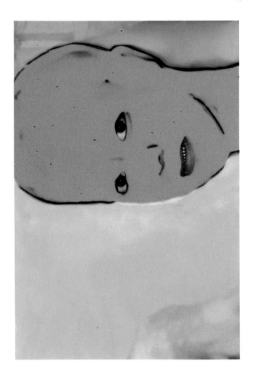

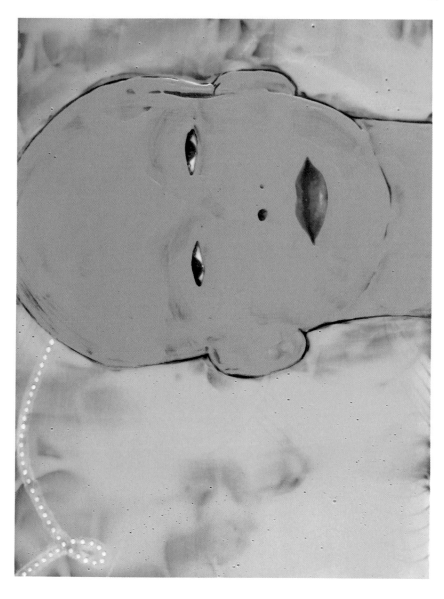

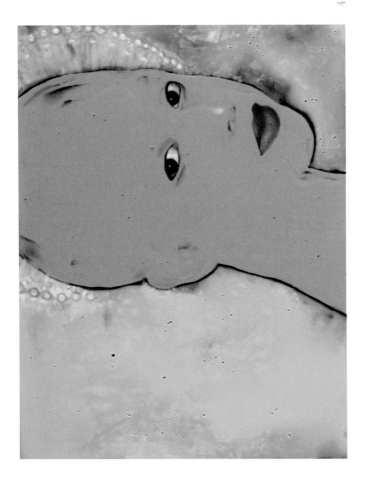

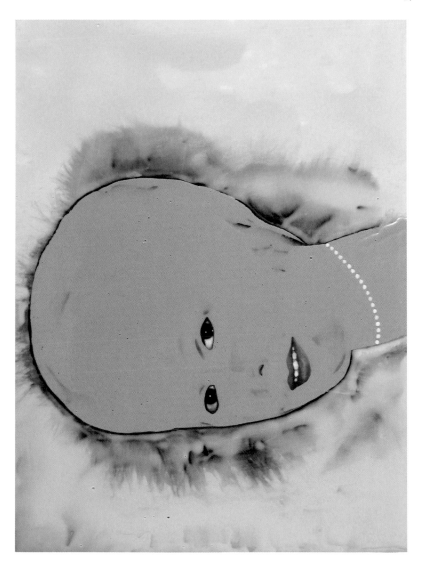

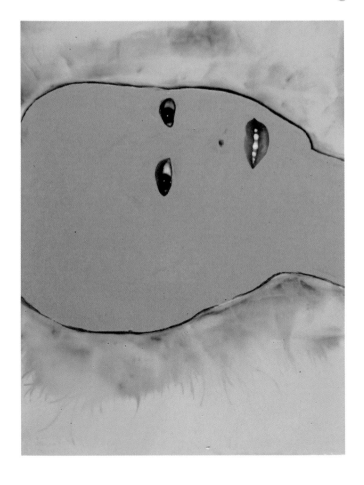

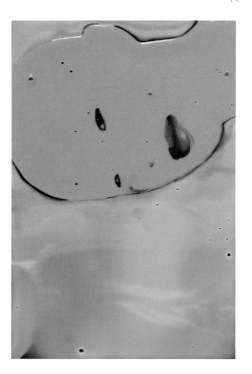

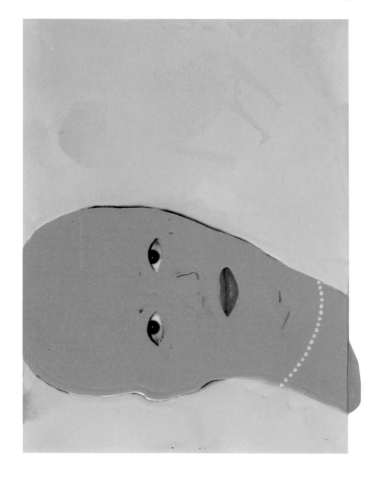

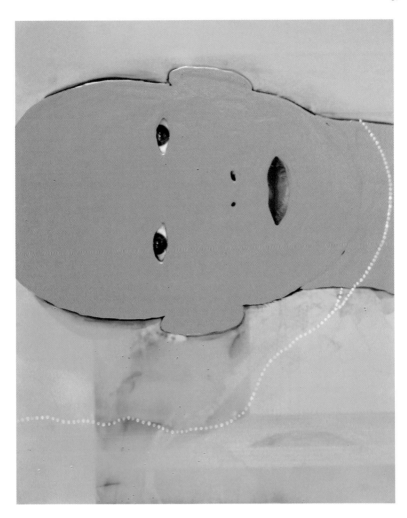

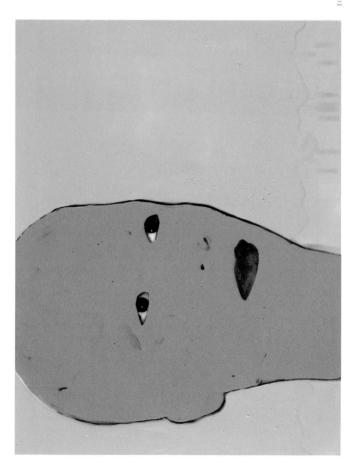

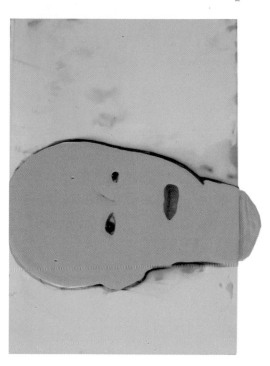

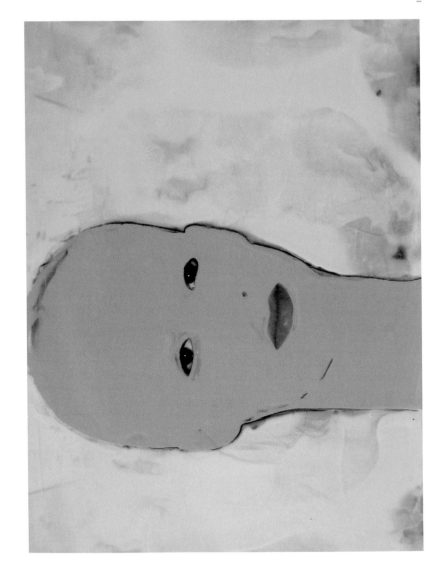

Judith Page: Portraits in Plasma

1. *Lucy* (9-5-06). Tar gel, acrylic, photograph on canvas, 12 x 16 in., 2006–2007.
2. *Amanda* (12-27-06). Tar gel, acrylic, photograph on canvas, 4 x 6 in., 2006–2007.
3. *Robin* (8-27-06). Tar gel, acrylic, photograph on canvas, 12 x 16 in., 2006–2007.
4. *Maria* (12-1-06). Tar gel, acrylic, photograph on canvas, 9 x 12 in., 2006–2007.
5. *Jane* (6-18-06). Tar gel, acrylic, photograph on canvas, 12 x 16 in., 2006–2007.
6. *Jane* (7-28-06). Tar gel, acrylic, photograph on canvas, 9 x 12 in., 2006–2007.
7. *Ted* (12-23-06). Tar gel, acrylic, photograph on canvas, 4 x 6 in., 2006–2007.
8. *Sarah* (3-21-06). Tar gel, acrylic, photograph on canvas, 9 1/2 x 12 in., 2006–2007.
9. *Robin* (12-30-06). Tar gel, acrylic, photograph on canvas, 11 x 14 in., 2006–2007.
10. *David* (12-30-06). Tar gel, acrylic, photograph on canvas, 9 x 12 in., 2006–2007.
11. *Lucy* (3-16-06). Tar gel, acrylic, photograph on canvas, 4 1/2 x 6 in., 2006–2007.
12. *Sarah* (7-27-06). Tar gel, acrylic, photograph on canvas, 4 1/4 x 6 in., 2006–2007.
13. *Lucy* (3-25-06). Tar gel, acrylic, photograph on canvas, 12 x 16 in., 2006–2007.
14. *Lucy* (12-30-06). Tar gel, acrylic, photograph on canvas, 4 x 6 in., 2006–2007.

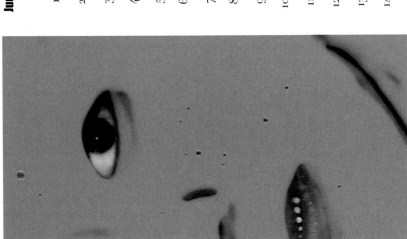

DIGRESSIONS ON SOME POEMS BY FRANK O'HARA, by Joe LeSueur

Allison Lynn

First, there's the title. When it comes down to it, a title should let the reader know what lies ahead. So calling this book *Digressions on Some Poems by Frank O'Hara* is genius. Because this book contains digressions. On poems. That are by Frank O'Hara. It's not only genius, it's remarkably appropriate, since O'Hara himself was nothing if not direct when it came to naming his poems—and when laying his life on the page as it happened. So let me just say that I love this title. Which may unfairly bias me to what comes after it.

Of course, what comes after is much more than simple digressions. Written by Joe LeSueur, Frank's friend, roommate, and occasional lover in the years that spanned 1951 to '66, each chapter uses a poem as the launching pad for describing Joe and Frank's life on the day it was written. These reminiscences don't just illuminate O'Hara's poetry—they evoke an entire expansive, bon vivant, bohemian, flagrantly gay (even when straight) slice of New York City life from that time. And oh what a time it was! New Year's Eve at John Ashbery's pad, drinks at the Cedar Tavern with Franz Kline, trips to the Hamptons with Jasper Johns, afternoons whiled away in romantically ratty apartments where Bill de Kooning and Cy Twombly might drop by for dinner!

Writing more than three decades after Frank's death, LeSueur is appealingly honest about the fact that his memory may not be perfect. But where's the fault when most of the remembrances are so frightfully innocent? Like the gay bar that Joe and Frank liked to frequent, their shared life was "more limp-wristed than S&M or pseudo-macho, and it was about as wild as a high school prom of years past."

Paul Bowles remarked, about his own journal, "I suppose the point of publishing such a document is to demonstrate the way in which the hours of a day can as satisfactorily be filled with trivia as with important events." The same could be said of LeSueur's book—and that's part of its draw. In an era when memoirs seem determined to prove that incest, addiction, and dog ownership are the only worthy subjects, it's refreshing to read one that simply aims to bring to life a time, a person, a way of being that, some fifty years later, is history. Which isn't to say this book is fluff. On the contrary, in recording his version of these days for posterity (LeSueur himself died as *Digressions* was on its way to publication), LeSueur allows all of us to be a part of a formative era in the American arts scene.

So in the end, this isn't a memoir for lovers of O'Hara's poetry, though they'll certainly get a kick out of it. It's a book for people who love New York, have a thing for lost innocence, or just crave a bit of art-world gossip with their coffee. It's sweet and nostalgic and, as it meanders (true to its brilliant title), can get a bit bogged down (though entertainingly so) with who was sleeping with whom, and who went to what opening.

I began reading *Digressions* in my apartment, not far from the Cedar. I finished reading it a few days later while in East Hampton. In the final pages LeSueur talks about Frank's burial in Green River Cemetery, which was just a few miles from where I sat with the book in my lap. The coincidence was too much. "I'll be right back," I said to my friends, who were stretched out on lawn chairs next to me, and without another word I got in my car and drove to Frank's grave. Part of what motivated me was certainly the emotion that Joe conjures for O'Hara, a good friend, a magnetic personality, an eager accepter of the limelight, a poet and art curator with a reverence for both James Dean and Rachmaninoff. I was wildly moved before I even found Frank's headstone. But there was more to it than that. Having spent much of the week with LeSueur's book, I found its world had somehow usurped my own. I think I needed to see Frank's grave to prove to myself that *that* world, the book's, was really gone. And also, I guess I have a bit of Frank in me: I hate to miss the party. In reading the book, Frank and Joe had become my friends too, and I wanted to be close to them.

Standing at O'Hara's grave, I asked myself: If I happen to get run over by a dune buggy (believe me, it could happen), is there anyone who will be able to look at my work and say, "I remember that passage. It was a late-summer day and our AC was on the fritz, so we walked over to Tavern on Jane, still in our pajamas, to watch the Yankees play, and the bartender had just gotten his Sharon Shannon CD in the mail, and when we left, it was still light out and we were drunk and happy and we came home to write"? Probably not. Frank O'Hara was very lucky to have Joe LeSueur. And so are we.

Which is to say: if you, too, hate to miss the party, don't worry. Thanks to Joe LeSueur, we all have a chance to attend. ✧

Tiny Monuments: A Look at Snapshot Photography

Hannah Lifson

> Thanks to the photograph, yesterday is no more than an endless today.
> —*Carlo Rim, "On the Snapshot"*

For the past year I have been organizing one man's private collection of snapshots. When I find time, I work out of his apartment, where I sit for hours and pore through piles of dusty, sometimes ripped, warped, curled, and cracked snapshots, sorting them into categories with names like "Women in Furs," "Men on Poles and in Trees," "The Ends" (this means people shot from behind), "Double Exposures," "Action Shots," "Knowing Looks," "Nudes," and many more, determined by both the content and the mood of each snapshot. I then place the snapshots in clear plastic baseball card holders and store them in red cardboard boxes from IKEA. I would estimate the collection, conservatively, at ten thousand snapshots.

From the moment I began this project of organizing snapshots, I felt inspired to write about them.

Among other things, the collector's taste tends toward, in his words, the "Magritte-like happy accident" snapshots—photographs where something unexpected happened, either in the taking or in the developing process. The result, almost always unintended by the snapshooter (or photographer), often has elements of the miraculous, magical, even the occult. As anyone who has ever picked up a camera knows, things don't always turn out the way we expect them to. I have found in this collection, for example, dozens of snapshots in which everything is in focus except one person's face, obscured entirely in a blurry mess. Some are chemical accidents; some incidental, particular to the moment captured. Or maybe an unexpected object, person, or light entered the frame at the very moment when the shutter opened and closed. In the best of these snapshots the end result is a thrilling mistake, like a fortuitous splatter on the canvas, a drop in the developer, a misplaced stitch. These accident shots take on a modernist quality, in that they "make strange" the ordinary. Often discarded by their owners for their muddled images—in other words, their inability to describe their intended subject clearly— "mistake" photographs are accidental hymns to the unpredictability of life itself.

In addition to these mistake shots, the snapshots in this collection are full of compassion; the pictures, often lyrical, illustrate the moments that make up a life. Within the broader categories I have noticed a large number of what I call "People at Play" snapshots: a man sticking out his tongue; a woman hiking up her skirt suggestively; a group arranged in a humorous, acrobatic feat, such as the human pyramid or the old contortionist trick (one person sits on another's legs in such a way as to make two people appear as one smaller person with a small torso and big feet). Like still images of slapstick comedy, these pictures make us smile as we imagine the laughter brewing in the performers' and photographers' chests. In this collection there are also moments of surprising tenderness—a kiss, an affectionate glance, a mother and her child—as well as strange, unsettling ones: a stern look; a stark, foreboding cloud hovering over a vast field; a lonely child. Mood, movement, tone, rendering, light, and edges are defining features in each and every snapshot.

The term *snapshot* generally implies a photograph taken by someone with no particular training or knowledge of photographic technique. If you look up *snapshot* in the dictionary, you will see that it is a term borrowed from hunting, originally meaning "to shoot without aiming." When George Eastman invented the Kodak camera in 1888, soon followed by the Kodak Brownie in 1900, he marketed the handheld camera as an everyman's tool—a relatively inexpensive piece of technology (the Brownie sold for $1.00) accessible to the so-called average American with little to no previous knowledge of the way photography works. As the well-known slogan went, "You press the button, we do the rest!" By removing the hold that studios and professional photographers had on the medium, Eastman directly influenced the *way* people photographed and, consequently, what photographs looked like.

It is nearly impossible for me to understand what it must have been like when photography was new (and available). Imagine the novelty of discovering you can capture and record what you see in front of you, and later return to it as a reminder of a specific time in your life: a friend's wedding, a trip to the beach, a new car, a picnic in the park with your lover. This revelation speaks to our instinct to document our existence—to record, or *mark*, in some permanent way time on this earth. When Henri Cartier-Bresson first discovered the Leica camera, which gave him the mobility and ease of photographing on the move, he "prowled the streets all day, feeling very strung-up and ready to pounce, determined to 'trap' life—to preserve life in the act of living." (Note the hunting imagery in Cartier-Bresson's statement: "prowled," "ready to pounce," "determined to 'trap' life.") This ability to "[fix] forever the precise and transitory instant," as Cartier-Bresson described it, is unique to photography as a medium, and common to all who take pictures, professional and amateur alike.[1]

Distinct from the realm of professional and commercial photography—photojournalism, advertising, fashion, art—snapshots are spontaneous,

---

[1] *Cartier-Bresson,* Decisive Moment, *4–5.*

familiar, without pretense. Unlike early photography, which usually took place in a studio with considerable forethought and direction, snapshots appear casual and loose. Usually taken to commemorate certain moments and experiences in a person's life, they possess the quality of having been made with little to no preparation. They are not intended for museum walls. (It is only in retrospect, as years passed and photography became an appreciated art form in and of itself, that snapshots have found their place on the walls of various art institutions.)[2] Thus, snapshots can be risky, instantaneous, hectic, and even boring. We all know the difference between leafing through a friend's family photo albums and attending an exhibition of photographs. Nevertheless, most of us possess an innate desire to document our travels, interactions, activities—what we consider meaningful, or simply emblematic, moments in our lives.

Since its arrival, eBay has transformed the market for snapshots, and collectibles in general. Before eBay, snapshot collecting was a physical, tactile, and personal process. One had to *go* to the flea market, seek the estate sale, visit the secondhand store, and contact a dealer. Once there, the collector touched the snapshots, turned them over, understood them as objects, not just pictures. Now sellers post their snapshots on eBay with such colorful item descriptions as "Three Boys Riding a White Lion—Snapshot—1944," "1930s–40s Photo Snapshot, Woman Pole Sitter," and "1960s Vintage Photo Snapshot Drunken Man, Bottles." A relatively small community, snapshot dealers and collectors know what sells and what doesn't; they know that Linda in New Mexico loves snapshots of babies with puppies, that Isaac in New Jersey collects snapshots of people in costumes, and so on, and they try to advertise accordingly. My collector checks eBay on a regular basis, but it has not replaced his other methods of collecting. Some dealers he knows personally, while others he knows strictly as their eBay personalities and will probably never meet. A digital scan of a three-dimensional image is, at best, a close approximation of its actual state, so when the snapshots arrive, they are often met with a moment of surprise—sometimes pleasant, sometimes less so.

This said, snapshots are not merely family talismans, to be discarded or sold at an estate sale, at a flea market, or, most recently, on eBay.

---

[2] *The exhibition the Art of the American Snapshot, 1888–1978: From the Collection of Robert E. Jackson was on view until December 31st, 2007 at The National Gallery of Art in Washington, D.C. Some other institutions that have featured exhibitions on snapshots include the San Francisco Museum of Modern Art: (Snapshots: The Photography of Everyday Life, May 22nd – September 28th, 1998) and the Metropolitan Museum of Art (Other Pictures: Vernacular Photographs from the Thomas Walther Collection, June 6th – August 27th, 2000).*

Snapshots are pictures that exist within a frame, chosen and composed by their photographer, inhabited by their subject matter. (The border of a snapshot is a hot topic within the world of collectors. One collector told me that when printers stopped developing snapshots with narrow white borders, they ceased to be "snapshots" and became "images.") They are, at their best, small works of art by an artist we have come to know well: Photographer Unknown. Snapshots represent a collective creative outpouring. Perhaps more so than any other medium, they are our culture's collective art form. A collection of snapshots is like a visual diary with entries from thousands of anonymous diarists (and the abundance of "trick" shots or humorous gag shots tells us that people like to play).

For the snapshooter, subject matter is paramount. As I mentioned, the collector and I have divided the collection of snapshots (which are mostly American and European) into categories based on their content. Since most of the snapshots date from the 1920s to the 1960s, during the rise of photography as a hobby, there are certain subjects—such as small-town parades, lonely wooden train tracks that lead away from country railroad stations, blimps, zeppelins, automobiles, children in pushcarts, and men on telephone poles—that now appear quaint and old-fashioned. Generally speaking, however, people took pictures of one another more than they did landscapes, objects, or abstract forms; thus, to my eye, most snapshots take human beings and the things we do as their subjects.

As Cartier-Bresson wrote in his seminal piece on photography, *The Decisive Moment*, "There is subject in all that takes place in the world, as well as in our personal universe." And so, like an artist, a snapshooter chooses his or her subject: "We cannot negate subject. It is everywhere. So we must be lucid toward what is going on in the world, and honest about what we feel."[3] Thus, some of the best snapshots describe exactly what the snapshooter intended: a lover, one's parents, one's children, a parade, a trip to the beach. No subject is too small, too insignificant to photograph. My father, a photography instructor, often advises his students, from beginning to advanced: "Everything is subject! Photograph anything and everything!" As Cartier-Bresson wrote, "In photography, the smallest thing can be a great subject. The little, human detail can become a leitmotiv. We see and show the world around us, but it is an event itself which provokes the organic rhythm of forms."[4] Thus, we understand the reason for our categories such as "Children in Pushcarts," "Women in Furs," "Automobiles," "People in Life Preservers," and other equally small, quotidian subjects.

---

[3] *Cartier-Bresson,* Decisive Moment, *6.*

[4] *Ibid.*

"Here I Am!" Pictures

There is one substantial category of snapshots I have not yet defined, at least not officially, and that is the simple, posed photograph, usually full-length, of one person or a small group—family or friends—looking solemnly at the camera, in front of a backdrop of no particular note, such as a front yard, a hedge, or the entrance to a nondescript city building. The solemn, full-length pose: the straight shot. I want to call them "Here I am!" pictures. Belonging to the same tradition as portraiture, carved initials on a classroom desk, and scribbled graffiti on a bathroom wall, these snapshots feature people that stand erect before the photographer, who will document their experiences—and, therefore, their existence—with visual proof. You can just hear the accompanying narratives: "See, here I am in front of Aunt Susie's house in Charleston," "Oh! Here we are, about to go to Caroline's wedding, all dressed up!" "There's the Eiffel Tower—it looks smaller in the photograph," and so on. You can hear them, and imagine them, because you have been such a narrator yourself. Snapshots not only commemorate significant moments; they also ratify an individual's experiences, preserving each one as proof of a life, we hope, well lived.

Pictures of Strangers

Nonetheless, this is not enough to explain the urge to collect snapshots. Why do we bother looking at pictures of strangers? Is it a historical exercise? It can be, but since most snapshots have unknown provenances, historical inquiry cannot be the primary joy or purpose of collecting them. (And, I should add, my collector is not a historian.) Is it a sentimental experience? Yes, but since the people in these snapshots are strangers, whose identities will never be known to us, the nostalgic, sentimental element goes only so deep. It certainly does not account for my collector's ten thousand photographs. Also, as acknowledged by scholars and amateur photographers themselves, snapshots are rarely collected for their monetary value, and the market for them, although growing, is essentially insignificant when compared with that of fine art photography. My collector has never paid more than $150 for any given snapshot; most cost him $5 or less.

Form and Composition

So the answer must lie somewhere in the definition of photography itself. For despite its lack of artistic intention, a snapshot is, primarily, a photograph. Apart from subject matter, snapshots are compositions within a frame, generally rectangular or square, printed on a sheet of photographic paper. Their composition—arrangement of shapes within the given frame, determined by the photographer, subject matter, and outside influences (weather, light, movement, camera, distance), because photography is simultaneously inclusive and exclusionary—gives them their individuality and form. As Cartier-Bresson wrote, "One does not add composition as though it were an afterthought superimposed on the basic subject material, since it is impossible to separate content from form. Composition must have its own inevitability about it." Even the snapshooter, in all of his or her amateurism, chooses when to take the picture, and it is this "decisive moment" that creates and defines a photograph. This composition—planned or circumstantial—determines the quality of the snapshot *as photograph* (there is, as Cartier-Bresson termed it, a "geometry" to picture taking).[5]

In addition to composition, snapshots have form. By *form* I mean that each and every snapshot has a specific, rhythmic order that gives each shot its individuality, its "thingness." It is a record, yes, but a visual one. Now, certainly not all snapshots possess what Cartier-Bresson called a "geometric pattern," and some do border on the "formless and lifeless."[6] These, however, are usually not the snapshots in a collector's collection. As any collector or dealer will tell you, some snapshots are better than others. Some shots are more coveted simply because there are few like them (World War I pictures and those of gay couples are some of the rarer subjects that come to mind), while others (such as the common shot of one person standing in a front yard) often remain in the pile, glanced over and rejected by the collector's discerning eye. But within our box of "People in Cornfields," for example, there are snapshots that stand out from the rest because their form—their composition, geometry, rhythm, and order—moves, arrests, and transports, in the way that only art can.

We come to snapshots as strangers investigating found objects, rescued treasure. Since our response to them is intrinsically tied to the manner by which we first discovered them, snapshots' anonymity—their very "foundness"—is their form.

The Snapshot Aesthetic

The term *snapshot aesthetic* surfaced in critical circles during the 1950s to describe the work of Garry Winogrand in particular, as well as that of Joel Meyerowitz, Lee Friedlander, and other greats. Influenced by photographers such as Walker Evans and Robert Frank, Winogrand's work departed from mainstream photography's emphasis on clear representation and neat, well-balanced composition. He photographed public spaces familiar to all of us—lobbies, airports, public parks, squares, street corners, and zoos—in unfamiliar, astounding ways. To conservative

---

[5] *Ibid, 8*

[6] *Ibid.*

critics Winogrand's photographs seemed untidy and strange, maybe because they appeared too "messy" or "real"—not the stuff of fine art photography. Winogrand, however, dismissed the comparison of his work to the snapshot, noting, in his words, snapshot photography's inextricable obsession with subject matter. When I examine a small selection of my favorite snapshots from the collection and hold them next to a book of Winogrand's photographs, I both understand the association and appreciate his insistence on the distinction.

By "snapshot aesthetic" the critics and scholars of photography pointed to snapshot photography's attention to the real and the actual, as opposed to the ideal, the composed, the fabricated, of which we see the former, in its finest form, in Winogrand's photographs. Instead of "snapshot aesthetic," let's say that Winogrand and his peers photographed the artlessness of life—typically the domain of snapshot photography—in a new, artful way. Winogrand is famous for having said, "The photograph *isn't* what was photographed. It's something else. It's a new fact."[7] Thus, even though snapshots record a moment in a life, they are indeed facts—objects—in and of themselves.

Pathos

When content and form are in concert, snapshots resonate on both an aesthetic and an emotional level. In these familiar shots of anonymous families, friends, lovers, and children we will never know, we sometimes experience pathos, for the images can remind us of moments in our own lives. Despite the technological advances made in photography since the invention of the Kodak Brownie, people still take snapshots in much the same way as they did fifty years ago. If you walk through Times Square, you will see dozens of the "Here I am!" snapshots in the making—a woman taking a picture of her boyfriend in front of a Broadway marquee, a mother photographing her children in front of the Disney Store, a man holding up his hands to point to the larger-than-life billboard above him. The backdrops seem banal and ordinary to the passerby, but the impulse is universal: to document an experience visually and prove that we were there.

So, when looking through piles of snapshots, we cannot help but to identify with the strangers who appear in them, as we recognize familiar scenarios, settings, and memories. Usually taken with some affection for the subject, snapshots are often imbued with feeling and largely avoid Edward Weston's stark warning on the more unfortunate of photographs: "Recording unfelt facts by acquired rule results in sterile inventory."[8]

---

7 *Winogrand,* Man in the Crowd *(unpaginated).*

8 *Weston,* Photography, *61. Written for 40-Print Exhibition, at the Museum of Fine Arts, Houston, May 4, 1930.*

The empathy of seeing a teenager's awkward moments captured in a snapshot, for example, reminds us of our own. The snapshot situates this awkwardness in a specific, untouchable past, where all the adolescent angst of that moment exists merely in our mind, and it is up to the viewer to choose whether or not to access it. A good snapshot is anything but sterile. In these tiny monuments to quotidian life we observe the continuity of human experience.

Since snapshooters are never entirely in control of their medium, snapshots contain an element of chance. (Think of the endless list of things that have affected you—and therefore the outcome of the photograph—while you've tried to take a picture: the glare of the sun, something moving in the background, a car going by, an automatic flash.) Unlike studio photographs, snapshots do not enjoy the privilege of a controlled environment; they take place in the "real" world: messy, unpredictable, and flawed. Thus, snapshots are moments of order imposed on an otherwise disorderly world. The events they depict cannot be recreated or revisited. As soon as the shutter opens and closes, the camera captures the moment *as it was*, and the snapshot becomes an entirely new thing—an object—separate from the moment of its creation. With age, the edges may fray, the surface can crack, its colors may change.9 (And it should be noted that black-and-white photography is, in itself, an abstraction of reality.) And so, the ontology of a snapshot is never fixed, while the image it depicts is, as Cartier-Bresson put it, "a simple, factual testimony."10

Much like a poet reading his or her poetry, snapshots create order where previously there was none. A few months ago I sat in my father's apartment, thinking about all the things I had to do. I was scattered, nervous, distracted. Then my father asked me if I wanted to listen to something. The next minute Ezra Pound's booming, imposing voice blasted through the speakers, filling up the living room with the sound of his poetry: rounded vowels; sharp, staccato consonants; scratchy breaths; and static from the recording. All of a sudden there was order. I forgot about my list of things to do and sat listening. When the record finished, there was silence again, and the mess of my life came back to me. Like poets reading their own poems, snapshots are our visual narratives of our life's work: whom we knew, where we went, what we saw, what we did there, and what we looked like at various moments throughout our lives.

---

9 *Most of the photographs in the collection I work with are black-and-white; however, there are quite a few color snapshots, as well as older cyanotypes.*

10 *Cartier-Bresson,* Decisive Moment, *7.*

Poetry of a Collective Past

Snapshots can be tiny windows into the past, brimming with emotional and visual significance. For instance, the nudes in the collection I work with are largely amateur. We can therefore assume that they were taken by the subject's—usually a woman—lover in a moment of affection, attraction, and desire. They are often humorous, as the woman in the picture strikes her sexiest pose, but the humor is of a generous, loving nature. Equipped with all the tender mishaps and un-Hollywood imperfection of real relationships, they speak to the desire in all of us to find someone and capture that person, as Fred Astaire sang to Ginger Rogers, "just the way you look tonight." They illustrate the meaning behind W. H. Auden's verses in "Alone":

> Whatever view we hold, it must be shown
> Why every lover has a wish to make
> Some other kind of otherness his own:
> Perhaps, in fact, we never are alone. [11]

For, as the snapshot makes clear, the woman in the picture is never alone; at the moment we see her, she is intently aware of the person behind the camera, who is framing her within the bounds of the shot, subtly and permanently joined to her at that very moment, and for as long as the snapshot survives. Snapshots allow us to connect to a continuous, shared experience by providing us with visual, photographic records of life in the distant and immediate past. So snapshots are vessels for the imagination. But why does our imagination need such vessels? There are plenty of other kinds of documents that act as fuel for our mind's wanderings.

William Butler Yeats's 1933 poem "A Dialogue of Self and Soul" contemplates the nature of the imagination—belonging to the mind—and its relation to the soul. The speaker of the poem, an aging man "[l]ong past his prime,"[12] wonders, perplexed, why his imagination leads him down the winding narratives of ancient history. In one of his wanderings he arrives at the image of "Sato's ancient blade, still as it was, / ... / Unspotted by the centuries" (10–12) and loses himself momentarily in imagined associations of "[t]hat flowering, silken, old embroidery, torn / From some court-lady's dress" (13–14). Lest he linger too long in his daydream, he moves from an examination of the self to one of the soul, asking:

---

11 *Auden, "Alone," lines 16–19.*

12 *Yeats, "A Dialogue of Self and Soul," line 18; hereafter cited in text.*

My Soul. Why should the imagination of a man
Long past his prime remember things that are
Emblematical of love and war?
(17–19)

In other words, what is an old man doing conjuring images of
swords, court ladies, and ancient blades, "[s]till razor-keen, still like a
looking-glass" (11)? What are we, in the year 2008, surrounded by Web
sites like Flickr and our own prolific digital masses (or messes), doing
looking at snapshots of strangers from 1921?

The answer, beautifully examined in the poem, addresses the power
of imagination in its purest form. Above all else, it is a transporting faculty;
ignoring the limitations of reality, imagination takes one to a place acces-
sible only in the mind. Thus, the speaker in Yeats's poem is able to recall,
with the aid of his imagination, a time in which he himself never lived. In
the quiet of his thoughts he accesses "things that are / Emblematical of
love and war" (18–19), understanding that the "ancestral night" (20) has
the power to "[d]eliver from the crime of death and birth" (24). Imagining
the past—and Yeats implies a *collective past*, not simply his speaker's
life—sates the pain of earthly existence by providing us with images and
stories of ancient struggles and romances, connecting us to our ancestors, known and unknown.

This process can be fraught with pain and frustration. Why, one
might ask, should we relive the growing pains, hard-learned lessons,
rejections, regrets, and mistakes of life, someone else's or our own? Once
over, wouldn't we rather forget them entirely, content to live in the present alone? On the contrary, "A Dialogue of Self and Soul" ends in a statement on the necessity of the imagination. The speaker, wondering, "What
matter if I live it all once more?" (43), wonders why he would endure
"[t]he ignominy of boyhood; the distress / Of boyhood changing into
man" (45–46).

Witness, here, the determined answer: he will revisit even the most
painful memories conjured up by his imagination:

I am content to follow to its source
Every event in action or in thought;
Measure the lot; forgive myself the lot!
(65–67)

The poem ends in triumph; faced with the imperfect "lot" of life, having found forgiveness for himself and others, our speaker will gladly live
it all again:

When such as I cast out remorse
So great a sweetness flows into the breast
We must laugh and we must sing,
We are blest by everything,
Everything we look upon is blest.
(68–72)

Like the speaker in Yeats's poem, lost in imagined fantasies, when I look at snapshots, I find myself wandering in make-believe worlds far from my immediate reality. Sometimes the contrast of the black and white on the paper makes me imagine a time when color pictures didn't exist; other times it's a boxer's arm, photographed so well that it appears as if drawn with a careful hand, and I'm lost in the contours of his musculature; still other snapshots make me pause, take me who-knows-where: a cornfield, a strange home, the beach in winter, a rowboat on a lake—perhaps imagining "things that are / Emblematical of love and war" (18–19). They might sting of some personal memory—or lack thereof. Like any work of art, they are at once intimate and strange, familiar and unreachable. By showing us the imperfect, unpredictable, messier, impulsive moments of life, a vast collection of snapshots such as the one I know shows life as it is *lived*: the very stuff of life. It expands our collective visual memory, giving us avenues into which our imagination can, and should, escape. ✧

Works Cited

Auden, W. H. "Alone." In *Collected Poems*. Edited by Edward Mendelson. New York: Random House, 1976.

Cartier-Bresson, Henri. *The Decisive Moment*. New York: Simon and Schuster, 1952.

Rim, Carlo. "On the Snapshot." In *Photography in the Modern Era: European Documents and Critical Writings, 1913–1940*. Edited by Christopher Phillips. New York: The Metropolitan Museum of Art/Aperture, 1989.

Weston, Edward. "Statement." In *Edward Weston on Photography*. Edited by Peter C. Bunnel. Salt Lake City: Peregrine Smith Books, 1983.

Winogrand, Garry. *Man in the Crowd*. San Francisco: Fraenkel Gallery, 1999.

Yeats, William Butler. "A Dialogue of Self and Soul." In *The Collected Poems of W. B. Yeats*. 2nd ed. Edited by Richard J. Finneran. New York: Scribner, 1996.

Further Reading on Snapshots

Frizot, Michel, and Cedric de Veigy. *Photo Trouvée*. New York: Phaidon Press, 2006.

Johnson, Robert Flynn. *Anonymous: Enigmatic Images from Unknown Photographers*. New York: Thames and Hudson, 2004.

Kimmelman, Michael. *The Accidental Masterpiece: On the Art of Life, and Vice Versa*. New York: Penguin Press, 2005.

King, Graham. *Say "Cheese"! Looking at Snapshots in a New Way*. New York: Dodd, Mead, 1984.

Levine, Barbara. *Snapshot Chronicles: Inventing the American Photo Album*. Princeton, NJ: Princeton Architectural Press; Portland, OR: Douglas F. Cooley Memorial Art Gallery, Reed College, 2006.

Nickel, Douglas R. *Snapshots: The Photography of Everyday Life, 1888 to the Present*. San Francisco: San Francisco Museum of Modern Art, 1998.

Walther, Thomas. *Other Pictures: Anonymous Photographs from the Thomas Walther Collection*. Santa Fe, NM: Twin Palms Publishers, 2000.

SPIN, by Robert Charles Wilson

Yael Goldstein

A few years ago I decided that I loved science fiction. This was a bold decision to make, since I had yet to actually read anything that qualified. But I had developed a yearning for a certain kind of book, a book dense with psychological truth and lit by incandescent prose, where the laws of nature bent and twisted in subtle, scary ways, and in the process revealed thrilling facts not only about the characters, but about all of humankind. I figured the genre was just about saturated with these things. Then I spent three years trying to find one.

I'm not saying I didn't find some good stuff in those three years. I found some good stuff. I even found some great stuff, if *Dune* counts as stuff. But I didn't find what I was after. In fact, the more I read, the more precise and elusive this what-I-was-after seemed to be.

I discovered, for instance, that the book had to be set in the present or very near future. It could not involve time travel. It could not involve evil trans-universal corporations. It could not involve space aliens, especially not space aliens in leopard-printed unitards. In fact, it could not involve unitards at all. It had to be about real, normal, fully human, unremarkably wardrobed people, the kind of people you'd meet in a Richard Russo novel. It'd be Margaret Atwood–esque, but with more-interesting science; it'd be like the issue of a drunken night of passion between Margaret Atwood and Richard Feynman as raised by Richard Russo. I had secretly started to suspect that I would never reach my own potential as a writer until I found it. I had started to despair.

Then about six months ago my friend Dave called. He was excited, but he usually is. "I think I've found it," he said. Dave is a science fiction writer himself and had been my primary source of recommendations all along. The book he was recommending now was *Spin*, by Robert Charles Wilson. I didn't think it sounded all that promising—now I can't imagine why—but still, I started it as soon as I got home from the bookstore. I didn't put it down again for another ten hours. I read all night, and would have read all week if I'd had to. This book was it, my nerdy grail.

It is a delicately realized love story, an incisive exploration of the human mind's reaction to terror, a gripping portrait of the phenomenology of religion, a paean to the pursuit of pure knowledge—and also a totally awesome adventure tale about what happens on Earth when the stars suddenly go black. The latest discoveries in cosmology give rise to essential and elegant plot points. Complex calculations about the passage of time are not only lucidly lovely, but—I swear—exciting. I was actually laughing from sheer joy through the last forty pages.

When I finally closed the book, giddy and exhausted, and exhaustively satisfied, there was a part of me that wanted to roll over with a self-involved grunt and let science fiction show itself out. But instead I let it stay and cuddle, and it's still hanging around. Which is to say, I'm still reading sci-fi, just not as urgently. Sometimes I wonder now whatever was so urgent about finding a book like *Spin*. I tend to trust my literary cravings like a pregnant woman trusts her yen for peanut butter. Cravings know what's good for you, even if you don't. I still don't know what vital narrative nutrient I got from *Spin*, but I think it must have something to do with Robert Charles Wilson's definition of science fiction. My new literary hero calls sci-fi "literature that imaginatively inhabits the idea of human contingency as it relates to time, space, history, consciousness, and perception." I think it's true that what I'd wanted out of my nerdy grail was some kind of an exploration of human contingency and its flip side, human necessity. Or, anyway, of what seems to arise necessarily from the givens that themselves arose accidentally from our evolution, our history, and the evolution and history of our universe. And what could do this better than a sci-fi book that holds most of its fictional world recognizably constant? Frankly, when I think of it that way, I wonder why everyone isn't looking for *Spin*. ✧

Cretaceous Moth Trapped in Amber (Lament in Two Voices)

Katrina Vandenberg

What a shame I have nothing to give you but midnight, my story
Little moth caught forever in the last moment of before,

of five French soldiers with identically shaved heads,
when the dusk was thick with incense and crickets

the one who spit in my hair, the one who slapped me,
and great northern evergreens wept puddles of resin

the one who kissed my mouth as the others watched.
on the forest floor. What were you stammering toward

Their green nylon jackets, their laced boots, their laughter,
the night you got stuck, a moon lost in thought

the glass wall of the lit phone booth they pushed me against.
as it cast its glistening net over tree frogs, over the mites

I got away. But when I reached my unlit street
punctuating the laddered webs of orb weavers,

and they were still following me, I had to choose:
over the orb weavers about to be lodged in resin

break for the host family's door? Or light back
themselves? This is the story now under glass,

to the phone booth, to the main drag, where
honeyed and see-through: a palm of red gold beads

yellow headlights kept slipping by? I wanted
traded for swords and furs in the Viking town

home. I chose the glass box, though I feared it a trap—
of Dublin. And in millions of years

if I chose or thought. I moved toward the lights.
>   *the moon has not changed; it is still perched*

Today I know that saved my life.
>   *in its starry web, dropping its sticky strands.*

But you know what I am saying, moth.
>   *The world has not changed; there is still a great deal*

It could just as easily have been different.
>   *of getting caught in it, you must choose.*

Palinode for Being Thirty-four

Katrina Vandenberg

I am at an age now where I would like to take back
what I said: last summer, I did not crouch
with a group of college students on a pilgrimage
under a tomb in Saint Brigid's cathedral in Kildare

to see a hidden stone carving of a sheela-na-gig, naked
and parting her legs to show her gaping vulva.
And the students were really more of a careless sort,
not inclined to take notes. The boys were not

uncomfortable. One did not mock-moan,
"Oh, Sheela, Sheela!" as he rubbed his knees
and righted himself. No, none of it was as I said,
I did not make love with a boy with HIV

for the first time at their age, never once
believed that if a condom broke, I could die.
Ask my mother, and she will tell you
I have a flair for the dramatic. I am sorry

I misled you about the carving's moronic grin,
the black hole of her womb, her fierce
and glinting eyes. The students did not buy
Cadbury bars and Orangina whenever

their tour bus stopped. They tended
toward the dour, crying and eating apples.
The cathedral does not have a pit in which Brigid's nuns
tended her fire for a thousand years, sacred

in a land of rocks and rain. Brigid's fire
still burns. Actually, it is the students
who are a thousand years old and remember
Brigid with her crosier, the good old days

in her school yard when they played with fire
and found life sweet, took notes in French class
on how the French phrase for *orgasm* means "little death,"
that feeling of falling someone might learn

under another body and like it so much
she would not give it up, whatever the danger.
Finally, none of the students were beautiful. When
the girls' jeans rode low enough that you could see

their incandescent skin, their gluteal cleavage
would not have reminded you of perfect peach clefts.
I did not remember what it was like to be
their age while under a tomb, on my knees.

William Faulkner's "The Bear"

Allen Morris Jones

I was introduced to William Faulkner by my own personal Iago, a high school English teacher who, despite pushing fifty, favored stiletto heels and miniskirts. She had a penchant for playing favorites and liked to flirt with the cockiest football players. She threw erasers at the kids who pissed her off. We had our many differences of opinion, and I spent half my sophomore year with dusty yellow rectangles across my shirt. All these years later, though, I can somehow go maudlin over the old crone, and only because she was the one to hand me a copy of *Go Down, Moses*, because she assigned "The Bear."

An experience no less poignant for its banality—a young writer discovering Faulkner. But here was the book that changed it all. That dropped the scales from my eyes. It was like riding motor scooters your whole life, then being tossed the keys to a Harley. It was like picking out "Chopsticks" before hearing Prokofiev. This, this was what language could accomplish. The taste and sound and feel of words rubbed together until they smoked; the passion of poetry that wasn't really, after all, poetry; the story that wouldn't stop; the author's utter arrogance in the face of his art; the characters that believed in themselves.

If you haven't read it (and I remain astounded by the number of my peers who've missed it, or who have turned up their noses at its superficially plebeian accessibility), "The Bear" is the story of young Ike McCaslin, a child born into Mississippi aristocracy, whose greatest desire is to go on the annual hunt in the Big Woods, to join the men as a man, and to pursue—as these men have always pursued—the enormous and uncontainable, the indestructible bear. Nine-toed and nicknamed Old Ben, he's one of Faulkner's very few overt literary symbols, a stand-in for Mississippi's vanishing wilderness. Kill the bear, kill the wilderness.

> It did not emerge, appear: it was just there, immobile, fixed in the green and windless noon's hot dappling, not as big as he had dreamed it but as big as he had expected, bigger, dimensionless against the dappled obscurity, looking at him. Then it moved. It crossed the glade without haste, walking for an instant into the sun's full glare and out of it, and stopped again and looked back at him across one shoulder. Then it was gone. It didn't walk into the woods. It faded, sank back into the wilderness without motion as he had watched a fish, a huge old bass, sink back into the dark depths of its pool and vanish without even any movement of its fins.

In not quite a hundred pages all the traditional and expected Faulknerisms are present: Language that walks the line between pomposity and perversity. References arcane enough to make you run for an old *OED*. Family trees that branch out into a Talmudic intricacy. The racial epithets that, anachronistic though they are, still make you squirm. A section that, when read in the right mood, might be a lost chapter from *Finnegan's Wake*. But it is also—next to perhaps only *The Sound and the Fury*, or maybe *As I Lay Dying*—Faulkner's most accomplished melding of art and narrative. A revenge tale, a cautionary conceit. And most of all, a really, really goddamned good hunting story.

After Ike learns to track and find the bear (it's necessary for him to leave the artifacts of civilization behind), after his mentor, Sam Fathers, has found and tamed just the right dog to bring the bear to bay—a feral, muddy-eyed creature named Lion—the boy finally stands witness to the success of the hunt and, simultaneously, the loss of everything he's come to love: "Then the bear surged erect, raising with it the man and the dog too, and turned and still carrying the man and the dog it took two or three steps toward the woods on its hind feet as a man would have walked and crashed down. It didn't collapse, crumble. It fell all of a piece, as a tree falls, so that all three of them, man, dog and bear, seemed to bounce once." There are no absolutes here, no reassurances. Just a mirror, as Stendhal called it, a mirror walking down the road.

For a Montana kid who aspired from the get-go to some measure of literary accomplishment, for someone raised in a family of outdoorsmen—a boy who had indeed been out bear hunting—who was just starting to wrestle with the moral vagaries of the chase, with the ambiguities, uncertainties, failures, triumphs, and inevitable, elegiac sense of loss that comes from hunting and killing an animal you find beautiful, there could not have been a more timely or important fiction.

In the years since, I've gradually made my peace with the painfully too-obvious truth that I will never, not in my entire life, ever write anything half so good. ✧

Little Orange Bottles

Jeremy Rice

1.

My girlfriend and I are leaving the university at around five in the afternoon. We're tired, stressed about homework, already thinking about dinner, when the cell phone jumps and squeals in my lap. It's my older brother, Kyle, his voice loud, filling my head. "Jeremy. Do you know about Mom?" My blood freezes. Kyle tells me how he went to visit her the day before, drove the hour and a half from his apartment in Hendersonville, North Carolina, to our parents' isolated cabin on the Tennessee border. She wasn't expecting him; they have no phone connected, so he couldn't call beforehand. She was alone. Our father was working a sixteen-hour shift at a group home for the developmentally disabled. "She was going to OD, man," Kyle says, voice cold and clear. "I came in and she had the pills all lined up on the table. Said she'd been planning it for days." I think of Kyle in his khaki shorts, his short hair, veins in his forehead moving as he chews gum. What did he do when he got there? Did he shout? Did he cry? Was he embarrassed? Did part of him want to just walk away and get back in his car? He tells me she had already started eating the Xanax, had taken eight milligrams: enough to fuck her up, but not enough to hurt her. She let Kyle drive her back to Hendersonville, to the ER. From there they transferred her up to the third floor, the psychiatric ward. I think of the car ride. Did they talk? Did she sleep? Did he put on some music, something soothing? Was he scared? "It's a good thing I came when I did," he says, "Or else . . ."

"Yeah, good thing," I say, but I can hear the echo of my voice, and it's hollow. I pinch the phone to my ear so hard it hurts, and I think about the pain, see my earlobe turning pink. I think of Kyle, probably sitting on the edge of his bed. Did he have to prepare to make this call, pace his bedroom, sigh, and smooth his pants? Is he holding a drink against his knee? Or a mug of green tea? Maybe he popped a Xanax himself to calm down.

"It's visiting night tonight," Kyle says. "Can you come?" My girlfriend, Maggie, driving the car, is looking at me strangely. I breathe for a few moments. "I'm sorry. I just can't. I've got too much work."

I hang up and clench my fists and my body. For whole minutes I can't talk, can't tell Maggie, who stares at me, what happened. I go home and sit in the rocking chair, body still clenched, tell Maggie I don't want to talk about it. She doesn't know what to do: hugs me, rubs my shoulders, looks stunned and helpless. I tell her I don't want to talk, and I make myself a drink, and another, and another, and I go to sleep.

2.

I can't remember exactly how old I was. Around eight or nine, because that's when I played basketball for the recreation league, and I remember I had a game that night. I remember cold, slicing rain. And that our car brakes were shot. We lived near the summit of a three-thousand-foot mountain, and to get to the gymnasium in the town below, Dad drove the blue Pontiac like a bullet down the mountain, whipping around curves at sixty, his right hand yanking and releasing the emergency brake between our seats—the only way to slow the car.

Everybody else had already gone to bed when Dad and I returned home—my mother; my older brother, Kyle, who would have been about eleven; and my younger brother, Alex, who would have been about five. I didn't have a bedroom—I slept in the den until it flooded one winter, destroying most of my clothes and my baseball card collection—so I curled up on the couch in the living room, a hideous, scratchy green-and-orange thing that had been made in the seventies. The slats of the couch were broken, and jagged springs bit into your back if you lay on it wrong. I padded it with egg carton foam.

I don't know what time it was when Dad woke me up, his leathery hand touching my back. I remember he looked scared, his brown eyes hard and wide in the dark, and I felt scared in reflex. Dad was the one who made me feel safe, who sat me on his knee and scratched my head with his fingertips, who made me hot tea with lemon and played chess after dinner, who came home from work mutt tired yet still summoned enough energy to play H-O-R-S-E with me on creaking knees. I didn't always feel safe with Mom, who spent more time in the hospital than at home; who had totaled the car; who one day would slip love notes into my lunch box with homemade brownies and play Uno for hours on the floor, and the next would sit on the porch, gray faced, like a statue, smoking cigarette after cigarette, swatting away my questions like mosquitoes. Now, for once, Dad looked uncertain.

"Your mom's making strange noises," he said. "Snoring real loud, like a buffalo." He looked over his shoulder in the direction of the bedroom. "She usually doesn't make noises like that."

I don't know why he woke me, what he expected me to say, and I don't know if I said anything.

"I'm just going to sit up in here for a while," Dad said, and I smelled coffee brewing in the kitchen, then felt his presence in the armchair beside the couch as I drifted back to sleep.

I woke again in a cold terror. Blinding blue and red lights flashed against the plate glass windows in the living room, flooded over the carpet and my blankets. It took me a moment to realize that I was not dreaming, and I sat upright against the arm of the couch, clutching a blanket over my chest. Then loud, strange voices and thudding boot steps filled the house, and I watched them wheel my mother outside on a stretcher. I can't remember my father saying anything, but his face was twisted horribly and he was moaning like a dying animal.

I don't remember much of the following week. I know I visited my mother in the ER, her ashen body still and slack, suspended in a spider-web of plastic tubes and wires. I listened to the doctors. She had taken a "cocktail" of medications, they said, between seventy and ninety pills: she had outlined them in detail in the note. They didn't think she would make it, and if she did, we better prepare for brain damage. It was the lithium, they said, that they worried about.

I also remember going to school that morning, sitting through homeroom. I wonder what I was thinking. Was I still seeing the sharp blue lights clattering against the living-room window? Or was I replaying my basketball game, dribbling and driving and leaping toward the basket? They took me out of class and dropped me in the counselor's office. Miss Livingston. She had a soft voice and laugh wrinkles around her eyes. Bright red lipstick slathered over her warm smile. A plastic bucket of Starbursts perched on the edge of her desk. I remember she told me I was in a safe zone, that I could do anything I wanted in there and not be judged. I could cry if I wanted to. I could stick my head out of the window and scream as loud as I wanted to. Sometimes, she told me, even she liked to stick her head out of the window for a good scream. I nodded and smiled and sucked on the orange Starburst in my cheek. I felt bad. I wanted to cry and scream, like the kind lady expected me to, but I was too scared. I just sat there numb, wishing they would let me go back to class.

Later my best friend, Blake, a small, hyper kid with Brazilian ancestry and jet black hair, asked me why I had been in the counselor's office. I didn't want to tell him, but I figured I had to. You're supposed to tell your best friend everything. "My mom tried to kill herself last night," I said, my eyes on the carpet. Blake looked at me with awe and disgust. Eventually he told the rest of the class, started the rumor "Jeremy's mother is a psycho." Then everybody looked at me with awe and disgust, and at lunch I had to sit and sip my chocolate milk by myself.

3.

Xanax comes in four basic types: your white oval tablets (0.25 mg); your peach oval tablets, scored once (0.5 mg); your blue oval tablets, scored once, known by recreational users as "footballs" (1 mg); and—the jackpot—your white rectangular tablets, scored three times, fondly known as "sticks," "monkey bars," and "totem poles," and a benzo fiend's wet dream (2 mg). At age sixteen I had bottles and bottles of every form of Xanax, plus other beautiful narcotics such as Klonopin, Ativan, Restoril, and Valium. But Xanax—or "Zanies"—was definitely my drug of choice.

It was also my mom's drug of choice. She took them PRN, which meant whenever she wanted to, which meant, often, all day long. At Thanksgiving dinner that year, a stuffy, opulent event held at my mother's sister's mansion every year and attended by my mother's entire family, Mom popped about six milligrams' worth on the car ride over. By the time we got there, her cheek was plastered to the car window. She wobbled around, mumbling incoherent greetings to her wide-eyed, tight-faced relatives, who clucked their tongues and whispered in the kitchen, before she toppled onto the couch and began snoring deeply. My father had to drape her semiconscious body over his shoulder and lug her to a back bedroom to sleep through the entire dinner. We told the family she had a touch of the flu and felt like lying down.

So maybe I started taking Xanax to have a sort of connection with my mom, the way you order Beefeater Gibsons because it is your father's drink—even though everyone knows your father is an alcoholic.

Or maybe I started taking them because it was just so easy. The pills were literally handed to me. Whenever my mother would have suicidal thoughts, or a psychotic episode where voices told her to hurt herself, my dad would strip the medicine cabinet, toss all her meds—bottles and bottles and bottles and bottles—into a plastic grocery bag. He would knot the loops of the bag and hand it to me, saying, "Hide this." No one ever asked for the meds back. Every time Mom was admitted into the hospital (on average about twice a month), her doctors would administer her meds and change her prescriptions. Once discharged, she would start fresh at the pharmacy. The old pills would never be needed. By the time I was sixteen, I had probably ten knotted grocery bags, all stuffed with little orange bottles. I kept them all in a duffel bag under my bed.

For the virgin Xanax taker, 0.25 mg is enough to make the edges of your thoughts blurry and—if you take it at night—enough to put you to sleep, probably in less than an hour. One mg is enough to make your whole body relax, make your thoughts float away, and put you to sleep as soon as you lie down and close your eyes. And 2 mg—again, this is for the first-time user—is enough to have your thoughts replaced by a pleasant, quiet hum, and your body embraced by a sheet of cool, gently lapping water. You'll fall asleep on your back, the pillow soft as down on your cheek, and wake up twelve hours later—from heavy, heavy, dreamless slumber—in the exact same position, feeling as refreshed as if you were emerging into the spring after a winter-long hibernation.

I think maybe I started popping Xanax because of the silence it provided at night: the erasing of my dreams—of the swirling blue and red lights beating against the plate glass—and the erasing of my thoughts, my guilt. At this time I often wrote in my journal about my mother:

I can't imagine myself going on if she'd offed herself. Though at the same time I can't help but feel guilty knowing that there are times when every second of her life is pure unbearable agony, and any lesser person would have killed themselves long before, but the one thing keeping her from going all the way, forcing her to withstand this personal torture, is her indescribable love for her family. That's a lot of fucking pressure. In theory (in my own way of thinking) her suicide WOULD be justified; the very basic right of all people is to take their own life. At the worst times it's like we're stringing her out simply out of our own selfishness. Then at the better times it's evident that we're doing the right thing, and I'm sure she'd agree—for her sake of living, not just ours. I would die without her.

That year my dad was seriously considering leaving her. On the ride to school, after Mom had been hospitalized following a half-assed overdose, Dad confided in me, "It's never going to stop. You watch: she'll kill herself as soon as you and Alex are grown."

So she was only living—living in misery—because of me? What the fuck do I do with that? I quoted Kurt Vonnegut to myself: "I never asked to be born." So why did I have this responsibility? Should I tell her "Don't do it for me"? "Do what you need to do—don't suffer for me"? A chalky, bitter pill wiped away those questions like a wet rag run over a chalkboard.

I started by taking 0.25 mg a night, then 0.5 mg, then 1 mg. Then I was taking 0.25 mg in the morning before school; leaving class to go to the bathroom in the middle of the day to slide half a totem pole down the crease of my tongue, pressing the distinctly Xanax bitter taste to the roof of my mouth before swallowing, and staring at the chipped mirror in front of me to wait for my reflection to dull; and 1 or 2 mg at bedtime. You build tolerance fast. Within a year of taking the drug, it was not uncommon for me to consume as many as 6 mg in a day.

The drug's effect on me is evident in my journal. I shifted from anger and despair to numb indifference. At one point my best friend said he had been talking to our teacher about me and that they were really worried, scared that, if the idea struck me one day, I would drop out of school in a second. I wrote that night, "They're worried about me. That's pretty funny. Why are they worried? Well, I guess I'm slipping. My grades are abysmal. My apathy is bigger than ever. Well, whatever. I don't care." As my Xanax use increased, my grades decreased. In chemistry my grade slid each quarter—98 to 86 to 72 to 54—as I cared less and less. One time I wrote my name at the top of a test and turned it in blank, without even bothering to look at a single question. That night I wrote, "I'm getting pretty bad."

I always had an urge to write fiction, and I often jotted story ideas in my journal, though I rarely got around to finishing any drafts. One night I penned the following synopsis:

I've been working on this story I'm writing about a miracle drug that cures all emotional/psychological afflictions w/o any side effects. The drug is so great that eventually everybody pretends to have some sort of disorder so they can have it prescribed, and the doctors are willing to comply w/ the façade because the drug has no dangers. Naturally, eventually the drug can be bought cheap over the counter and basically everybody in the world is on it. It's considered a necessity, a staple, like milk and bread. And everybody is happy, and peaceful and basically all war is ended and conflicts are resolved reasonably. Then production of the drug has to cease for whatever reason and everybody just curls up and dies.

I remember being excited enough about the story to actually scribble six or seven pages of a rough draft. Thinking about it now, I wonder what was most appealing about my fictional drug: the somalike peaceful contentment, or the eventual curling up and dying.

4.

Early in my senior year of high school my English teacher, Walt Cottingham, assigned short class presentations on dilemmas. The idea was to introduce a problem without a clear solution, and conduct a brief class discussion on the topic. We were to begin the presentation with some piece of media—a movie clip, newspaper article, or song, for example—that related to our dilemma.

I decided to present the dilemma of suicide. Jack Kevorkian was in the news, and I figured I could incite a heated debate in the classroom, as surely some people would strongly believe in a person's right to die and some people would strongly oppose that right. I brought in an R.E.M. CD to play the song "Everybody Hurts." I considered the song to be a silly and fun take on suicide and hoped it would lighten the mood of the presentation.

But when I popped the CD into Cottingham's little boom box, and Michael Stipe's voice wafted through the classroom—"When the day is long and the night, the night is yours alone, / When you're sure you've had enough of this life, well hang on. / Don't let yourself go, everybody cries and everybody hurts sometimes"—I found my head growing heavy and my eyes tearing up. As I looked around the room, I saw my classmates were not snickering or nudging one another, but frowning down at their desks, or looking at me with strange, creased expressions.

My voice quaking, I talked about assisted suicide and opened the discussion to the class. Naturally, we quickly moved to the subject of suicide for people who are not terminally ill patients. Almost the entire class participated. One quiet and isolated girl talked about her tenth-grade boyfriend, who had died from a gunshot wound. The police ruled the death to be a murder, though they never had any convincing suspects, and the girl believed without a doubt that the gunshot had been self-inflicted. One shy boy who had few friends and spoke with a stutter revealed to the class that his best childhood friend had shot himself when he was twelve. And another girl, a good friend of mine, told the story of a family friend, a woman with two kids, who had attempted suicide by jumping from a bridge. She survived but was now crippled forever because of the fall, and she was more miserable than ever. My friend—high voice moving fast, bright pink rising through her face—contended that it would have been better if she had died in the fall. Her kids would have gotten over it eventually, she said, but now they had to live with a suicidal, crippled mother, and that was worse.

Thankfully, the bell rang at the end of my friend's story, because if forced to speak, I would have burst into tears. My presentation had lasted the entire fifty-minute class period; all other presentations had been between five and ten minutes. As I followed the class silently shuffling out the door, Cottingham handed me a slip of paper that read:

> Grade—A. Good song & topic. Nice segue to assisted suicide. Lots of good follow-up questions. I hope you're OK—I worry about you sometimes when you seem depressed. You have exceptional gifts, but with those can come burdens.

When I was blinking back tears in front of the class, I had been thinking of my mother, but I knew that everybody thought I wanted to kill myself, that my presentation had been a wild plea for something—help, guidance. Just like I was back in elementary school, my classmates acted strange around me. They stuck their heads together and murmured, shook their heads and bit their lips.

A couple days later Cottingham asked if I would talk to him after school. We sat in his classroom, portrait of Churchill on the wall, the desks in familiar disarray. He told me he took special interest in me as a student and a person. He started talking about himself, his battles with depression as a younger man. After a while I began opening up to him, sharing my secrets about my mother's illness and my own thoughts of death. I told him everything that I couldn't tell anyone else, especially not my own parents. After we had sat together for nearly an hour, he gripped my shoulder. "The best thing I can tell you," he said, "is to find passion. Find passion."

Coincidentally, or not, it was that same week that my parents confronted me about Xanax. They didn't ask if I was taking it; they asked if I was selling it at school. I guess they wanted to stop my use without having to probe my motivations for using. Mom told me she was missing twenty pills from her bottle in the medicine cabinet. I knew she was lying. I stole directly from the cabinet sometimes—she had unlimited refills and took anywhere from one to six pills a day, plus she had no short-term memory, so her ability to keep track of them was laughable—but I had a reasonable supply stashed in the pencil pouch of my three-ring binder, so I hadn't skimmed any from her in a long time. Still, the confrontation terrified and humiliated me. I lied and said I hadn't taken them, and in my head I swore off them forever. The next day I pressed a sandwich bag filled with my entire collection of pills into the palm of a shocked and ecstatic friend (who that night at a party mixed way too many pills with alcohol, suffered terrible hallucinations, and freaked out the entire party before blacking out).

A large part of me was relieved to have to give up Xanax. For a long time I had been worried about the severe memory loss that habitual medicating caused (I still have a very limited memory of that entire period), and how it required higher and higher doses to achieve the same affect. Also, I no longer had an easy ticket out. In the back of my head I had always kept the knowledge that I had enough chemicals to eliminate myself, quietly and painlessly. I could have chosen to simply go to sleep and stay asleep. Recently I had been playing a fantasy through my head almost every day: of walking to this small stream on our property, swallowing a handful of Xanax, and slipping into the water, bobbing on the surface for a while, my arms outstretched, before closing my eyes and letting the water's cool arms wrap around my body.

Later I found out that my older brother, Kyle—who had for some time been a benzohead himself—had narced on me. One of my friends had told him that I was taking a lot of Xanax, and, fearing for me, he told our mother.

5.

The next visiting day following Mom's latest overdose is Saturday. I twitch and pace all day, unable to concentrate on anything, then my girlfriend and I drive to Hendersonville to see her.

I could walk the path from the parking deck to the third-floor psychiatric ward with my eyes closed. I've taken those same steps hundreds of times. Smiling and looking away from the other visitors going up the elevator. Pressing down the call button outside the locked door. "We're here to see Kathy Rice." Nodding hello at the nurses—they all know my name, smile at me like grandmothers: "I remember you when you were *this* tall." I think about the time I came to visit on my thirteenth birthday and found that Mom had told all the patients and staff about the occasion. HAPPY BIRTHDAY streamers drooped from the cafeteria walls, and the smelly, confused, giggling, weeping, shit-smeared, heavy-breathing lunatics shuffled to me one by one to shake my hand and press sweaty one-dollar bills into my palm. I choked down a waxy slice of chocolate cake, my face scarlet, wishing I could drop through the floor.

Mom has a single room this time, thank God. We sit on her bed, over the starchy blue bedspread. The rooms are all the same: fake-wood furniture with smooth, rounded edges, non-glass mirrors that warp your reflection, windows that look out on the parking lot and are crisscrossed with wire inside the glass so the patients can't break through. Dad and my brother Alex are both working and can't make it, so it is just Mom, Maggie, Kyle, and me. They've given Mom Thorazine, and her speech is slurred, her movements clumsy, but she doesn't cry. Her hair is gray and wiry, her forehead indented from where she has banged it against the wall, her arms badly scarred from razor blade swipes. She holds my hand. Her small, curled hand is soft and warm, and it shakes in mine. Kyle talks about work and his girlfriend. I talk about school and my plans for summer. We laugh a little. Someone in the hall bellows in a thick country accent, "I want to go punch somebody!"

"Why?" a woman screeches back at him.

"Because it's fun!"

Mom says she's reading a book of Zora Neale Hurston short stories. She says they're good. She can't remember what they're about right now, but they're really good. "Look," she tells me. She has photos of all of us taped around her desk. "I like how in all of yours, you're smiling. Alex is always making faces, and Kyle has the same blank stare, but you're smiling in every single one."

Before we go, she stares at the pillow clutched in her hand and says, "You know I didn't really want to"—her voice is weak—"off myself, right?" We all look at the floor, nod a little but don't answer. She always tells us this. I wonder if she is just trying to make us feel better, or if she really believes the overdose was an accident. Probably she can't even remember.

6.

It's been a couple weeks since the call from Kyle, and I'm still out of whack. Maggie is worried. I mope around the house, skip class. At night I feel like crying but I can't, so I drink too much, watch TV, smoke weed. I think about my mom in the hospital. Even though she's just a shell of the woman she used to be, she's still too good to be stuffed in that hot, fluorescent-lighted ward with those crazies in stained sweatpants. I think about Kyle. I wonder if he's sleeping okay, if he dreams about Mom, sees her over and over again slumped on the kitchen table, gripping a mound of chalky tablets, the silt of medicine crusting her lips. I wonder again what I would have done if it had been me who had gone to visit her. If it had been my eyes that had caught her, wretched and alone, counting her piles of poison. Would I have been calm, in control? Or would I have screamed and grabbed her hair, slapped her face, yelled "How dare you"? What would her eyes have told me: *Please, Jeremy, help me* or *Please, turn around, if you love me, turn around?* And would I have loved her enough to obey?

My mom is proud of me. She tells me every time I see her. She's the one who taught me to write. Even before kindergarten, when Kyle was in first grade and Alex was too young to speak, we would spend hours at the table together, filling notebook pages full of notes back and forth, about how much we loved each other. Walt Cottingham would be proud of me too. For the thousandth time I think about how I should send him a few of my short stories, show him how I've found passion at last.

I look over my old journals, read that I hadn't cried in six years, and fresh tears warp the paper. I read my dad's words, "You watch: she'll kill herself as soon as you and Alex are grown." I read the word *Xanax* over and over and over, and I feel its cool fingers tugging at me from the past.

Maggie has problems with anxiety, and her doctor prescribed Ativan. She doesn't take it much—maybe two or three times a month when she's nervous about a presentation for school, or if she has trouble sleeping. Ativan is no Xanax, but it is a benzo. It turns your thoughts to warm static, makes your eyelids heavy. The little orange bottle filled with tiny pills sits right next to my head every night, on the bedside table. It would be so easy to pop the cap, swallow a couple, and embrace the silence.

Instead of picking up the bottle, I pick up a pen and open to a fresh page in my notebook. I fan my old journals around the table and think of my mom in her hospital room, curled in her bed with Zora Neale Hurston, stroking her stuffed cat, or sitting on the edge of her bed maybe, looking at our pictures, smiling back at me. For a moment I slide my palm over the fresh white page in my notebook. The paper is blank and silent—painless. It won't do. I hunch my back, grip my pen, and stab the paper like an injection, batter the page, sully the cool silence with hot words. ✧

The Promise of Failure, or Why You Should Drop Everything You're Doing and Read Richard Yates's REVOLUTIONARY ROAD Right Now!

John McNally

In 1988, Richard Yates was scheduled to teach a summer workshop at the University of Iowa, but he was too sick and had to bow out at the last minute. I had signed up for that workshop, but I hadn't read anything by him. Truth be told, I'm *glad* I hadn't read his work. What I didn't know then was that Yates's first novel, *Revolutionary Road*, would become my favorite novel, and I'm not sure I would have recovered from the blow of being offered to take a course by the man who'd written my favorite book, only to have the offer cruelly snatched away from me. (Okay, I *would* have recovered—I'm being melodramatic here—but you get the idea. It would have sucked.) But some part of me is also grateful that I never met the man either. After reading *A Tragic Honesty*, Blake Bailey's magnificent Richard Yates biography, I got the distinct feeling that Yates, like so many of his protagonists, was a train wreck whose personal disasters often sucked in those around him. While reading about Yates's life, I found myself saying, as I do so many times while reading *Revolutionary Road*, "Oh, no, don't do that! Don't say that! Don't go there!" And yet, like his flawed characters, Yates would inevitably do or say the very thing I'd hoped he wouldn't, at which point disaster would ensue.

In short, *Revolutionary Road* is the story of Frank and April Wheeler, a couple in their late twenties, with two kids, who believe that they've sold short their life's dreams and decide, with disastrous results, to remedy that.

The first time I read *Revolutionary Road*, I was twenty-three years old, with my first university teaching position, writing my first novel, and living with the woman I would eventually (in less than a year) marry. Oh, yes, the brightest of futures lay ahead of me! I read *Revolutionary Road* and loved it, but what most attracted me to the book was Yates's wry (and subtle) humor, the ways in which he would nail characterization in just a few words, and the freshness of his similes. It was a great book—I saw that instantly—but I had barely begun to scratch the book's surface.

Three months into my first marriage I was already bracing myself for divorce. Something—I wasn't sure what—had gone terribly awry in our relationship, and I knew (or sensed) that the end was near. My first novel was starting to accumulate rejections, and in a moment of grief and confusion I turned in my resignation to the English Department, even though I had nothing else lined up. My employment would effectively cease in May, once the semester was over. It was at this point in my life that I read *Revolutionary Road* for the second time.

I still appreciated all of the same things I had admired the first time around, but this time I had to keep catching my breath, afraid that I might break down and start weeping while I read the damned thing. In other words, Frank and April's failures hit a little too close to home. It wasn't necessary for me to live through what I was living through in order to appreciate Yates's novel, but what I saw now that I had failed to see previously was how perfectly (how brilliantly) Yates captured life's downward spiral, which could come as fast as *that* (something Yates himself knew well). And what I realized, upon this reading, was that *Revolutionary Road* was the great American tragedy, no less so than *Death of a Salesman*. More so, I believed. Could this be that elusive Great American Novel that everyone has been searching for? I happen to think so. Yes. (There. I said it.)

I'm forty-two now, and I have read *Revolutionary Road* many times since that second revelatory time, and I am no less astonished by this book's perfection. Every word is the right word; every semicolon is perfectly placed. You feel the spirit of Yates hovering over the story, but you never feel his presence in a clever or self-conscious way. He hovers over the novel as Charles Dickens or Gabriel García Márquez hover over theirs.

Revolutionary Road, more so than any other novel, is the book I press into readers' hands and say, "You *must* read this." It's also the book that, more than any other, I use as a litmus test. We all have one of those books, don't we? The one upon which we judge the people we've given it to, based on their reactions to it? I don't *mean* to use it as a litmus test; it just happens. *Do you like this novel? Will we be friends?* I'm not an elitist (if anything, most of my tastes are pretty lowbrow: Stooges, anyone?), but when someone tells me that they didn't much care for this book, I find it hard to look them in the eye afterward. (In all honesty, this has happened only a few times—once with a colleague where I teach, and once with a fellow writer, who told me he "couldn't relate to characters living in suburbia," as if the criterion for fiction is that the reader must first "relate" to it in order to find the beauty and worth in it. I mean, the fact that I wasn't in Vietnam shouldn't diminish my admiration for Tim O'Brien's *The Things They Carried*, should it?)

I've never been good at giving the hard sell for anything. Perhaps the best thing I can do here is end with one of my favorite passages. It's from the opening chapter, in which an amateur theater group rehearses for a play that they threw themselves into, months earlier, with the highest of hopes:

> Clumping their heavy galoshes around the stage, blotting at their noses with Kleenex and frowning at the unsteady print of their scripts, they would dis-

arm each other at last with peals of forgiving laughter, and they would agree, over and over, that there was plenty of time to smooth the thing out. But there wasn't plenty of time, and they all knew it, and a doubling and redoubling of their rehearsal schedule seemed only to make matters worse. Long after the time had come for what the director called "really getting this thing off the ground; really making it happen," it remained a static, shapeless, inhumanly heavy weight; time and again they read the promise of failure in each other's eyes, in the apologetic nods and smiles of their parting and the spastic haste with which they broke for their cars and drove home to whatever older, less explicit promises of failure might lie in wait for them there. ✧

The Doctors

Kirsten Menger-Anderson

I didn't know my father was sick until the hospital called. Dad threatened his cleaning lady at gunpoint. He accused her of cheating on him, stealing his credit cards, ruining his career.

I didn't even realize he owned a gun.

"What's his present condition?" I am still in my nightclothes, drinking a late-morning coffee. On Thursdays, I usually do rounds or lab work, but I took the morning off because I haven't taken a day off in months. My daughter, Arabella, earnestly examines my lower calf with my stethoscope. She finds an old razor nick, presses it. Outside, July heat forces the pigeons to the speckled shade of our fire escape.

"He's calm now. Sleeping. Is he on any medications?"

"I don't talk to my father much."

Dad has awoken by the time I arrive. The pale blue hospital robe exposes the loose skin of his neck and upper shoulders. He looks thinner than I remember, and he hasn't dyed his hair, blond ends and gray roots.

"Elizabeth," he says. His eyes meet the space between my nose and upper lip. He tries to pull his blankets higher, but they are taut, tucked tightly around the foot of the mattress.

"Feeling better?"

"I need my glasses."

"I'll pick up whatever you need."

"I'm fine," he says.

I sit down. "Have you had any tests?"

"They're doing an MRI tomorrow." My father smiles, waves a hand to convey the dismay already betrayed by his face. "At least it was the cleaning lady and not a roomful of surgeons."

"Dad," I say.

"They're sending a specialist."

"Do you want me to stay?"

He shakes his head. "Pick up my glasses, today's paper, a change of clothing, my travel kit, and two pastrami sandwiches on pumpernickel with pickles and slaw. Come back at seven, that way I won't starve."

"Two pastrami—"

"One's for you. Keys are in my pocket."

My father's pin-striped button-down and corduroys are folded neatly on a narrow table by the window. No one has sent flowers. As I feel through my father's pocket, I realize I may be the only person—aside, perhaps, from the cleaning lady—who knows where he is.

"Did you want me to call anyone?"

"No," he says quietly. "No calls."

Ever since college I've told friends that my dad and I don't see eye to eye. I tell them we never have, though I don't think that's entirely true. I understand my father more now that I'm older. Age has afforded me insight into a man so concerned with appearances he's forgotten what a face can hide.

Years ago, and not long after my mother moved out, Dad invited me to the Catskills, famous for golf and trout fishing. I was twelve and a half, and I beamed despite the strange, sharp pain in my gut. At the time I thought it was grief—that my body was still tied to my mother's in some odd, inexplicable way, and that she'd return when she heard I was dying. The prospect of a trip alone with my father—a first—to the exotic and mountainous land of the Catskills, no less, made me reconsider. School had started, but the days were still warm enough for swimming.

"Pack your bags!" Cheer discolored my dad's voice, and he smiled, but not a smile I recognized from the dinner table, where he shared stories of the day's successful boob jobs. "We're taking the company car."

The company car was new—a luxury my dad's practice could afford because the beauty business was good. He showed me pictures: a wide, white, boxy thing he described as a Mercedes.

We had to go to the clinic to pick up the car. Before we could leave, Dad saw a few patients. I sat in the lobby reading pamphlets about face-lifts and the joy of feeling young. I'd taken two Tums, but my stomach still hurt. When Dad emerged from his office, I didn't say anything for fear of jeopardizing the trip.

"No talking or radio until we leave the city," Dad said, and I agreed without question.

"No music, period," he declared an hour later. I didn't mind. I'd never been in the front seat of a car before. I could see everything—the road before us, and behind us through the outside mirror. Dad sat straighter than I'd ever seen him, so I sat straighter too. I counted the mile-marker signs at the side of the highway; I held my breath between exits; I tried to predict the next toll and prepare the correct change. Then I saw it.

"A rabbit! Look! Dad! A rabbit."

The rabbit bolted forward into our lane, the slow lane. I heard the clunk of bone against metal, and I'm sure my father did too, but all he said was, "Don't yell like that."

"We have to go back." I watched the rabbit in the mirror, already behind us, violently twitching, covered in blood.

"I can't stop on the highway."

My dad never looked away from the road, and we didn't stop until we reached the hotel, where my father had a conference and I found the pool, cold beneath a yellowing scum of blown leaves.

The next day I got my first period. I spent the afternoon folding toilet paper into thick rectangles or curled up in bed thinking about blood—the rabbit's, mine, one bloody mess where I had no one to talk to and nothing to do.

I later learned Dad skipped the keynote dinner to sit with me in the hotel room. All I remember was his insistence that he understood how hard everything was on me and that I'd get better with time. I didn't tell him about the cramps or the blood. He understood my troubles, he approved of them; I didn't want to disappoint him by admitting that something as trivial as womanhood confined me to my bed. Not until I got to college did I learn that my father has never had a driver's license, that the day he drove his girl-woman daughter to the country, he had little more experience behind the wheel than I.

The doorman at my father's building doesn't recognize me. When I introduce myself, I feel curiosity, or perhaps pity, in his gaze. He notes the deep furrow between my eyes and the overbite that leads many to believe me stupid. For the first time I am conscious of the fact that I did not iron my blouse or trouble with my hair, which is not even parted properly.

I have not been to my father's apartment since Christmas, the one holiday we celebrate together—perhaps because Dad wears his Santa suit and we can all pretend he is someone else, someone who cares so much about us and what we want that he keeps lists. Pink-faced and round, Dad wears a fantastic white beard and black gloves and carries a sack of gifts that makes Arabella squeal.

"Ring the bell if you need help with anything," the doorman says before the elevator door closes between us, and I am left alone in front of my father's door.

The apartment, a luxurious two thousand square feet with views of Central Park, has a peculiar smell: souring milk, molding peaches, ripe French cheese. A dark, sticky residue—spilled soda or a thick after-dinner liqueur—covers a wide stretch of the usually spotless hardwood floors. My father has covered the windows with taped newspaper, two weeks old and already yellowing. Even after I turn on the lights, the flat remains dim, foreign without the view of skyline that grounds it in New York.

I set down my purse. The answering machine blinks eight new messages. A cane rests against the wall beside a pair of podiatric shoes. The clock on the wall reads 1:28 A.M.; the one on the bookshelf reads 6:28 P.M. I reach for the phone. The dial tone startles me, as if I expected the line to be dead.

When I was young, my father forbade me to enter his bedroom. When he and Mom were at work, the door remained locked. I'd put my ear to it, listening for signs of a child—a secret child, one they loved more than me, one they played with, one they praised for her accomplishments.

In high school I picked the lock. My dad kept a few boxes of porn videos, some handblown glass vases, a pack of cigarettes. A series of graphic before-and-after face-lift photos hung on one wall—portraits of my mother from before she left us. She looked happy, almost radiant, even in the ones where her face was still bruised and recovering. By then I hated her. I hated that my mother could put on a new face and leave me with nothing but the fading memory of fine wrinkles. Her old face belonged to me, but it no longer existed.

I didn't move anything in the room, and I locked the door behind me, but Dad knew I'd been inside. He grounded me for three weeks, and when I "had the impudence" to ask why, he made it four.

Today the bedroom door stands wide open, the bed unmade, the curtains drawn. I find a half-used package of adult diapers; a collection of prescription medicines, all from Dr. Steenwycks; a letter in a hand I don't recognize until I realize it is my father's—shaky, distorted, falling apart. How long has he been sick? How long has he hidden here in his rooms? The last time I visited my father, he said good night with a hearty "Ho, ho, ho."

I sit on the corner of my father's unmade bed and read his unfinished letter. The note is addressed to his twin, my uncle Jack, a man I've seen only in pictures. Last I heard, he was in Florida serving time for driving drunk without a license, but that was years ago. "How are you feeling?" my father asks. He inquires after my cousins Evany and Stan; he mentions he will be flying out to Hawaii in mid-June (more than a month ago). I wonder if he made the trip. I imagine my father bent over his unfinished letter. I cannot reconcile the frail man in the hospital bed with the one I knew growing up. I cannot prevent the isolation, the emptiness, of his deserted bedroom from infecting my thoughts, or the tears from forming and falling.

I return to the hospital just after seven. Not even dusk breaks the midsummer heat. The nurse tells me Dad has mistaken her for his wife. My training and years of study are as useless as graduation robes. His illness, his apartment, this entire day, have proved me inadequate.

"Dad," I say. I have his clothing and toiletries in a grocery sack, and the sandwiches—two pastrami on pumpernickel, just as he asked—in another. "It's Elizabeth."

I pull up my chair beside him. "Elizabeth, your daughter."

I feel large—a parent in a child's seat, a grown-up trying to hide beside the bed because I can no longer slip beneath it. I take my father's hand.

"Elizabeth." Though he speaks my name, my father's eyes show no sign of recognition. He squeezes my hand so tight it hurts.

"Have you been self-prescribing?" I ask.

"Have you?" I ask again. "Damn it, Dad. You can't just . . ."

But my dad isn't with me. His eyes are open, but he is looking past me, through me, to the shadow beneath the silent television fastened high on the wall. My father, the plastic surgeon. I don't think he ever really looked at me. When I refused to take over his practice, Dad joined a Christian charity and began sending monthly checks to a six-year-old boy named Guillermo; according to the article in *Plastic Surgery Today*, which pictured my dad on the cover, he never leaves home without the boy's snapshot, the child's big brown eyes the doctor's only hope for "the future generation." Only in the last four years—since Arabella—have we begun to speak again.

I use Dad's hospital phone to call the lab. The new tissue samples are ready, waiting.

The best thing about my lab is that I have access to it at all times. I can spend the day caring for my dad, and the night examining tissue from spontaneous abortions or blood from children with congenital anomalies. I can care for the health of the passing generation and the coming one. I can do everything.

Still, as I sit beside my father's bed, I cannot imagine going anywhere but to my own bed. We are working on the Sunday crossword puzzle, which I clipped from yesterday's *Times*. I read clues and letters. At first Dad asks me to repeat them: "What was that—*S*, blank, blank, what?" Soon he stops pretending. I don't ask him to count backwards from five, but I doubt he can do that, either. Otherwise he is lucid. When I offer him the paper, he shakes his head.

"I see everything double," he says. "Even with my glasses."

At four o'clock his doctor arrives. He is just my age, balding, and—judging by the way he carries his chart (extended before him like an offering to the gods)—officious and petty.

"How are we today?" he asks.

"We are fine," Dad answers.

"I'm Elizabeth." I extend my hand. "Stuart's daughter."

"James Cranston," the doctor says. "I have the MRI results."

Dr. Cranston, clipboard at his side now, turns to me and smiles. "We did an MRI Friday morning. It's a standard test—"

"I know," I say.

"My daughter's a doctor," my father says. "A *medical* doctor."

I stiffen. A *medical* doctor. I am a new graduate again, and my dad, expectant smile as wide as his fist, makes his offer: "You'll take over my practice when I retire." Pride still rings in the words I spoke then: "I'd rather help people."

"A family of doctors, eh?" Dr. Cranston smiles. "Runs in the blood or something?"

My father snorts.

"What did you find in the MRI?" I ask.

Dr. Cranston turns from me to my father. "Good news and bad news," he says. "The MRI is completely normal."

I don't get to the lab until eight. The room feels too bright and so cold that the blood does not flow to my fingertips. Two of my colleagues are still working.

"Sorry to hear about your father."

"Thank you," I say. The woman's name is Kathy or perhaps Karen—a young doctor who's been with us for just over a year. Her team has a conference abstract due in just under a week, and they are still collecting and analyzing data. "How's the research coming?"

"Getting there," she says. "Not as conclusive as we'd like."

"Nothing ever is," I say. "If you need me, I'll be in the FISH room."

I like the FISH room because I always have it to myself. Only two other doctors in my group study chromosomes using fluorescent in situ hybridization, and both are on leave—one in Germany, the other in Russia. The room has no windows, and the desk is slightly too low for writing—perfect for microscope work.

I remember, suddenly, to call Harold.

"Hi," I say. "How's it going?"

"Fine. Good. When are you coming home?" He sounds tired. Behind him hums the air conditioner, a clunky wall unit we haven't made time to replace. Our apartment needs time: pantry shelves for the tinned fish Harold brings home from his import store; bookshelves for my medical journals; closet shelves for Arabella's old clothes; new paint; new floors; small things like drain plugs, a knob for the silverware drawer, batteries for the remote.

"I'm coming as soon as I can. How's Arabella?"

"Asleep. She diagnosed me with mumps at dinner."

"She did?"

"Mumps. Can you believe it? The child's only four."

"She's a smart one," I say. "I'll call before I head home."

I don't call. When I view the invisible, time speeds up. Law of microscopes: You can't cheat time and vision. Pull chewing gum long, and the width diminishes; stare at a slide long enough, time vanishes. One dimension gives way to another, one choice excludes another. When I look at a screen test, a glow of blue with red and green dots, human chromosomes, I feel pure joy. I don't leave the lab until 2:30 A.M.

The next morning I bring a bagel with lox and red onions and a decaf coffee to the hospital. Dad complains that the drink is too hot, that the room is too hot, that people are watching him. He believes that the television is actually a video camera, that his room is bugged, and that our conversation is being monitored.

"Anything else?" I ask.

He taps the side of the bed so I'll lean closer.

"They are weighing my turds," he whispers.

When I return that afternoon with the sandwich he ordered, he's more himself. I can tell by his eyes; the hazel has deepened, as if sanity is expressed in color.

"I brought you dinner." I can't tell if resentment sounds in my voice. I hope not. I want to help my father while he is fragile. I want to rise above our differences, to prove to him, to me, that it doesn't matter what he thinks of my decisions, my work. That we are family.

"Any news from the doctors?"

"It's not vitamin B toxicity." He shrugs, but his movement is jerky. "Tell me something nice. How was your day?"

"Good," I say. I don't tell him how tired I am, or how Harold lost his temper this morning, or how I haven't spent time with Arabella or my friends in days. "My paper came out in *Science*."

"*Science*. That's an honor. Bring me a copy. Give your old dad something to do."

"Sure," I say. My father has never expressed interest in my work; now he can't even read it. I study the lines around his eyes, the crease in his forehead, the stubble above his lips. I search for resentment, the old anger, but notice nothing except how changed he is, how foreign.

"I'm having trouble swallowing," he says. "Just the paper next time— just your paper."

I go home before I return to the lab. I want to have dinner with my family, but I should have called first; they aren't home.

Harold has taken Arabella out for a movie and milk shakes—I don't hear about the fun until the next day.

"You missed out," Harold tells me. He's making breakfast: poached eggs for us and raisin oatmeal for Arabella.

"I know." I think of my mother, her second face, the smooth one that showed neither anger nor pain unless emotion thrust her lips apart and colored her skin a hot red. She threatened to leave if my father said yes to another conference; she threatened many times, but only when he wasn't home.

"How about tonight?" I say. Already I'm anxious, worried that I won't have time to see Dad and make my first morning appointment.

"We eat at five."

Five. Midafternoon. Midworkday. Arabella looks up from the table, sticky orange pulp around defiant smile.

"We're having spaghetti," she says. "Daddy promised."

Just after noon my father calls me at work.

"Elizabeth, I need to talk to you. Can you come in?"

"I have . . ." I have already stopped by the hospital once. I have an appointment at two and another at three thirty, and dinner at five. Yet my father's tone, the fact that he called, alarms me. "I'll be there as soon as I can," I say.

When I arrive at the hospital, Dad raises his bed so he can sit with me. He folds his hands over each other but cannot hide their tremble.

"I only have a few minutes," I say. I still carry my purse and I make no move to remove my jacket, though I do sit down beside the bed. I woke too late to shower this morning, and my hair slips from a hasty bun.

"Doing research?"

"I'm meeting with a mother. Her first child has Down syndrome, and now she's pregnant again. She has a narrow window—"

"And she wants to know her chances?" My dad laughs. "Is that what medical doctors do now, hand out chances?"

"It's not like that."

"I know." A trickle of saliva runs down the side of his mouth. "They think I have Creutzfeldt-Jakob."

My throat tightens, and I clasp my hands because the pressure of my skin against itself calms me, allows me to collect my thoughts. I know prion disease—an exotic and elusive illness, sometimes familial, sometimes not, known for rarity and speed. One day my father woke and couldn't remember the word for breakfast; perhaps two weeks later he began to lose his balance, then his muscle control; he bought diapers; he pretended his health did not trouble him. Within a year, probably within the month, he'll be dead. There is no cure.

"They can't know without a biopsy," I say.

"They'll do that when I'm dead."

I shake my head, but he speaks before I can. "The chance you'll develop it is very slim."

He doesn't have to tell me that my daughter and I might carry a mutation, a single gene passed through generations, a gene that might one day express itself, or not. Most likely, in my case—in my hypothetical case—it will remain unexpressed, a dark thing inside me that threatens but never explodes.

"I can't make this look any better," Dad says.

I reach for his hand; his fingers are moist, cold. I can't tell him everything will be okay; he knows better. "I'm sorry."

"I have most everything in order. The will—"

"Dad, I can't talk about this now. I have to get back—"

"You have work. I know." My father's words have begun to slur, so that they seem to run together, to form a continuum. Beside him on the nightstand is my paper. The pages are open, as if he has only just set down the work.

"I'll come back first thing tomorrow," I promise.

"Go on, then." He tries to dismiss me with a wave, just as he did when I was a child and he wanted to work or slip into the forbidden bedroom. He waves me away to my work, to my choices, but his hand falls beside him. He lacks the strength for anger or hope, approval or sorrow, though I listen for one of those, one in particular, in his voice.

"Go on, then," he says again. "Go on and save us." ✧

To write from the thinking-heart, come to the heart of writing.

The Low-Residency MFA Program in Creative Writing at Lesley University

- Fiction, Nonfiction, Poetry, and Writing for Young People.
- Residencies in Cambridge, Massachusetts: a literary center.
- An interdisciplinary component that nourishes student writing.
- Graduate Assistantships and a Literary Ventures Fund™ (LVF) scholarship available.

Announcing: A partnership with the journal *Post Road* and LVF, offering residency publishing modules and opportunities for internships.

For a list of recent graduates' publications and accomplishments, please visit our website: www.lesley.edu/info/pw

Faculty Mentors:
Steven Cramer, *Program Director, poetry*
Anne Bernays, *fiction and nonfiction*
Wayne Brown, *fiction, nonfiction, and poetry*
Jane Brox, *nonfiction*
Teresa Cader, *poetry*
Rafael Campo, *poetry*
Pat Lowery Collins, *writing for young people*
David Elliott, *writing for young people*
Thomas Sayers Ellis, *poetry*
Tony Eprile, *fiction*
Laurie Foos, *fiction*
Indira Ganesan, *fiction*
Susan Goodman, *writing for young people*
Alexandra Johnson, *nonfiction*
Rachel Kadish, *fiction*
Hester Kaplan, *fiction*
Justin Kaplan, *nonfiction*
Michael Lowenthal, *fiction*
William Lychack, *fiction*
Rachel Manley, *nonfiction*
Elaine Mar, *nonfiction*
Cate Marvin, *poetry*
Kyoko Mori, *fiction and nonfiction*
Anita Riggio, *writing for young people*
Don Share, *poetry*
Christina Shea, *fiction*
Janet Sylvester, *poetry*
A.J. Verdelle, *fiction*

Recent and Upcoming Visiting Writers:

David Ferry	Sue Miller
Louise Glück	Tom Perrotta
Robie H. Harris	Joyce Peseroff
Emily Hiestand	Robert Pinsky
Richard Hoffman	David Rivard
Marie Howe	Lloyd Schwartz
Lois Lowry	Maurice Sendak
Gail Mazur	Tom Sleigh
Roland Merullo	

LESLEY UNIVERSITY   Let's wake up the world.℠

MFA in Creative Writing
www.lesley.edu/info/post

A SPORT AND A PASTIME, by James Salter

Noy Holland

First I thought: *Better not.* Because I'm smitten. Or I was smitten twenty years ago, in Paris, in my twenties, and it has lasted, the way a crush will last between people who exchange not a word, the way a cliff above a river seemed a thousand feet high—seemed, and seems so still—until you go back to the river and see it, see the drop is mild and measly, no hazard in it and no drama, and now the shoreline is crammed with wrappers and balled-up socks, and Johnny Stevens won't burst from the bushes to tickle you, tickle you blue.

It is hazardous, truly, to return to a book held in lofty esteem after such a long time away. To return is to invite disillusionment. Worse: grief. A little deathly, unbudgeable loss. I'm superstitious about it, at least about the few books I find privately, indelibly emblematic of a cherished era. James Salter's *A Sport and a Pastime* is for me such a book; I carried it in my back pocket (the Penguin edition is just the right size for this) while traveling through Europe in my twenties, off my feet in love. Certain paragraphs, I read—in bedrooms, in trains—again and again; I found them thrilling. The book hummed in my hands.

Would it hum, still, in the kitchen of my gracious New England home, in my forties, among grocery lists and God's-eyes and the first-in-the-fair watercolor of my daughter's homely War Bonnet? My husband has waked up for months now, taken a look at the daily planner, and intoned, "Violence, violence, violence," shaking his rumpled head. "Busyness is akin to violence"—maybe Gandhi said that. Lighten up, I say: I read the tabs to the tea bags too. Children, a station wagon, a state-of-the-art lawn mower, a placid yellow dog. I am living, in better words, in the last lovely words of Salter's novel, "deep in the life we all agree is so greatly to be desired."

And so it is. But.

There is little, in this life, of leisure, of the sensory catalog of bedrooms in country French hotels, of train travel, beautiful cheese. Little of the expansive, patient feeling that opens Salter's book: "September. It seems these luminous days will never end." For pages then, slowly, we move into open country. "There are hills now, not very high. Poplars. . . . Hay is stacked in the shape of boxes, coops, loaves of bread." We are fleeing through the towns. Such a lovely, quiet beginning, I think, so resolutely held against the crappy counsel to "grab the reader" with the first line. Grab. Hook. Handle.

Salter lulls. He cares for compression, yes, but not momentum. His seduction is slow and painterly; it's like stepping into a painting by Millet. It is morning and the field is suffused, swollen, with a molten light. You can warm your hands at such a painting.

You can slide Salter's book into your pocket and feel somewhat less and more yourself and capable of love. I mean early, febrile love, the shot in the arm, the terrible flux. The incandescent dream.

It's true: I can find fault with the novel now. I can be teacherly, writerly, disgruntled by its soft spots, its occasionally droopy similes. But these are nothing against the happiness it returns me to, to the "voyage that is more like an illness," the fluency, the fecundity of the erotic. I am finding that finding a flaw in the book, a lapse in its strictness and austerity, can be a comfort, can deepen my affection for it, the way Anne-Marie and Dean's love becomes truer and more complex when he discovers the prickly, reddened patch of skin between her shoulders. Her imperfection—she looks common at times, *gauche* is the word; she has lousy teeth—these flaws elicit tenderness, mostly: he has the power to overcome them. Salter calls it "satanic happiness," what these lovers share. It will end abruptly. Their time is over. Abrupted—willfully or not, we can't know.

We can't go far enough with them. We are privy to no more than what the narrator invents; they are his creatures, even as he is at their mercy, fugitive from their lives. "I am the pursuer . . . ," he admits, "I am only the servant of life." These two lovers are the inhabitants.

The narrator of this slender book is tender, reticent, obsessive. He is envious and overcome. What he knows seems often to be contained in the moment, but then a scrap of information will break through: he knows everything. He is capable of imagining anything. He delivers history with the concision of a butcher; it is the grandeur and dilation of the present to which he is so fiercely drawn. "I have not yet gone deep enough. . . . One must go forward all the way, through bitterness, through righteous feelings, advancing upon it like a holy city, sensing the true joy."

I love advancing with Salter, then as now, through his painterly, bittersweet pages. I love the synthesis of the imagined and the actual, and how desire becomes its own end. Duration is all; love and duration; we walk, singing brightly, to the gallows. We are helpless; I am helped by such a book to live.   ✧

Dreaming of Rome

John Ruff

You were in my dream, David,
and we were in Rome—
your first visit to the Babylon

of your German Lutheran forebears,
and as if they had cursed you
for leaving Iowa and the farm

to write your books,
your critiques of visual piety,
your monographs on miracles

ascribed to weeping Madonnas,
David, you'd gone blind.
I would be your Irish Catholic

seeing eye cicerone, to lead you
through that city you'd never
see, past paintings barely lit

by the acetylene flicker of memory.
In our flat you set your compass
by a loose tile in the hallway,

take your soundings room by room—
so many steps from this wall to
that one, bed here, wardrobe

there, so many narrow channels
and no chart, no stars,
no moon.

****

I had gone out to get us coffee,
and the old neighborhood was new
to me again, a maze of lamp-lit
cobblestone streets throbbing
with pitched voices and the whine
of *motorini*. Grates clattering up

announce the opening of shops,
and I float like a cork as if pulled by
the current of Bernini's *Four Rivers*

into the piazza. There it is light
that holds me hostage like a moth,
the sheen of silk scarves

in the glare of cameras flashing,
the fountain's reflection
like lace on the facade,

and someone breathes fire
and someone swallows a sword
and the people all clap and throw

coins in a cup, as you sit
by the window in the kitchen
waiting for coffee.

Just before dawn, before I woke,
we walk a narrow street festooned
with laundry, sheets, and pillowcases

dripping like forgiveness
on our heads. And then there
we are in Campo dei Fiori,

where vendors like gods
bellow vegetables into being—
"Carciofi! Fagioli! Melone! Pomodori!"

a din as in the beginning—pure vowel
and then haggling. "*Troppo, troppo,*"
"Too much," a woman says, as if

it's all "too much"—the sun, the operatic
voices, the redolence of basil
and crates of sparkling fish. But no,

non troppo, it's not too much
for you. You grip my arm as if to say
the time has come to weigh these things

in your outstretched beggar's hand,
to empty your pockets and barter all
you are for what you want—oh,

to want again is what you wanted,
your deepest hunger,
your driest thirst, and now

you'd eat to be hungry and drink
to thirst again. But first you insist
I hand you things—one thing

after another. Thus, slowly, sniffing
the air, you take in Rome
through your fingertips.

While Reading Pico della Mirandola's Oration on Human Dignity

John Ruff

I'm in the philosophy library at the university
feeling chest pains, probably heartburn,
I'm in my midthirties, I'm in perfect health,
and it's a beautiful summer day outside,

but I have the same feeling I always get
when the plane takes that final right turn
onto the runway and I think of my wife,
my two daughters, what a wonderful life

I've had. I look up from my book
because I can no longer concentrate
on Pico della Mirandola's great oration
on human dignity. I'm looking around,

studying the other people studying
in the philosophy library, wondering
who among us has training in CPR.
I notice a man at the circulation desk

who seems out of place, a heavyset man
wearing shorts, a T-shirt, running shoes.
As I listen to him speak to the young man
at the desk, it strikes me, my possibly

ailing heart about to burst quickens
at the thought that he's a football coach,
there for no good reason but to push
helpless bystanders away so he can take me

in his arms like a lover, put his lips to mine
as mine turn blue, and blow like hell. It calms me,
comforts me, even half believing there's someone
in the philosophy library who can save my life.

Black Rock City Journal

Len Goldberg

Day 1 (Monday)

The day is finally here. I can't exactly tell you why my wife and I wanted to attend Burning Man, to spend a week in a desert where you must be not only self-sufficient, but also leave no trace of your visit at week's end. Or why we wanted to be in an environment that's 110 degrees during the day and 40 degrees at night—punctuated by sandstorms. Or why we wanted to be spend months sifting through the must-read survival guide and preparing to camp with forty thousand complete strangers. Perhaps it's middle-age crazy. Perhaps we're trying to re-create our youth. Or perhaps we're looking for something that had so many wonderful promises in the '60s yet were never fulfilled. Whatever it was, I had this powerful feeling that it would be a totally unique and maybe life-altering experience.

For one week a year Black Rock City, two and a half hours north of Reno—and truly in the middle of nowhere—becomes one of the largest cities in Nevada, after which it literally disappears. I heard of this event approximately ten years ago, when maybe five or six thousand people gathered to celebrate life and art, and literally to burn a fifty-foot effigy of the outline of a wooden man; but while intrigued, I thought my wife and I were too old to attend and fit in. It slipped my mind until last summer when, visiting the Haight-Ashbury neighborhood in San Francisco, I spied a small sign in a window and spoke out the words "Oh, wow . . . Burning Man supplies" in wonderment. My wife asked what on earth I was talking about. As I recited my limited knowledge of the event, it was as if we had a life-changing moment. We both began to talk it up the rest of the trip, and when we returned home and looked up what we could on the Internet, we were intrigued enough to make preliminary plans to go. When we first made the decision, people we told were divided into three groups: the ones who had never heard of it and looked at us with this look you'd give a crazy uncle, the ones who had never heard of it and thought it could be interesting, and the final small statistical group who had heard of it and thought it was great to be going.

We leave Reno at 6 A.M., both to get to the playa before it really gets hot and to avoid driving in the dark. I'd be lying if I didn't admit to wondering if attending was a wise decision. On Interstate 80 east of Reno we begin to see other cars, trucks RVs, buses, etc., all filled with people, supplies, bikes, and Burning Man signs or slogans. A wagon train of vehicles gets off the only exit to Gerlach, two hours to the north. Sometimes the road is flat and you can see fellow Burners for miles ahead. There are three towns between the interstate and Burning Man, with nothing in between. Personally, I love the vistas and colors of the Southwest, and this is no different. On the other hand, this land can't be used for anything. Even horseback riding would be difficult, given all the rocks. You travel through Indian reservations and signs that say it's open grazing land so watch for cattle on the road. I'm told if you hit one, you have to pay $500 for a replacement. We were also warned in advance about following speed limits, as this becomes a very lucrative time for the local city halls. The road has almost no shoulders, so you have to pay attention. We pass one recent crash from someone who wasn't paying attention and rolled off the road into a ditch. Ambulances are already approaching from another direction to respond. The town seven miles south of Gerlach—Empire—has one gas station with two pumps, and we see a line of vehicles pulling over for gas. There are also townspeople renting bikes. We fill up at a Shell station in Gerlach (also with two pumps) because of warnings about the four-hour exodus at the end of the event and the massive line of vehicles waiting for gas.

As we leave Gerlach, we once again find ourselves in a vehicle caravan; however, in the distance, eight miles away, we see lots of dust being kicked up...yes, it's the turnoff for Burning Man. There is an orange traffic sign stating CAUTION EVENT AHEAD. The anticipation really becomes unbearable as we approach the turnoff. There are three stops: a check of tickets, a thorough check for stowaways, and finally the greeters welcoming you "home." The first stop is about a mile off the road, and to add to the festival feeling, there are signs every few feet with Burning Man sayings and philosophy, some serious, some witty. It takes about an hour to finally arrive at the greeters, with the cars spread into six entrances, much like a tollbooth with colorful flags flying in the air. The greeters are as friendly as I had hoped and give us a thick booklet of the week's planned events and a map showing where the theme camps are and some locations of the artwork. In the distance we can see Burning Man! We know our theme camp, the Elders, is at the intersection of 4:30 and Intertidal.

Black Rock City covers eight square miles of federal land, and as a result the Burning Man organization has to apply for a permit. The permit process appears rigorous and is not without controversy. This year 47,000 people attend—up from 40,000 the year before and up from 10,000 nine years ago. Black Rock City has the earmarks of a real city: there is a post office that delivers mail throughout the week and will mail a letter for you. There is the FAA-approved airport for one week, with landing fees and tie-downs for 150 airplanes. The past few years even corporate jets have made a landing to deliver Burners. The airport has a "customs" area to greet new and returning Burners. The DPW literally builds the city in less than a month and is responsible for the infrastructure. The Black Rock Rangers are a group of Burners who very seriously "keep the peace," primarily through conflict resolution. They patrol the boundaries, interface with fire protection, and perhaps most importantly maintain good working relations with the federal Bureau of Land Management, the sheriffs of two counties involved in the actual policing of the event, and who knows who else. There is a Department of Mutant Vehicles whose responsibility is to register art cars and make sure their propane connections are safe . . . more on that later. Finally, there is even a newspaper published every couple of days called *Piss Clear,* the *Harvard Lampoon* of Burning Man.

The city looks very futuristic from the air and basically is in the shape of a two-thirds clock from 2:00 to 10:00. There are concentric roads that follow that semicircle. The names change each year, but the names start with the letter *A* and follow the alphabet to the last road in the city. Those roads are bisected by roads named for half-hour intervals of a clock. There are street signs at every intersection. It is the DPW that performs all the surveying work to get these streets down and note where theme camps will be built. Most of the major artwork and Burning Man himself are on the playa.

Yet it's still a desert, and the organization contracts to have water trucks go throughout the city spraying water all week to keep the dust down as well as they can, given that it's a desert with degrees in the 100s during the day, with 47,000 Burners doing their thing. It is not unusual to see a parade of both clothed and naked people following the water truck, both to cool down and to shower.

The city is maybe 30 percent filled by now. (People arrive all throughout the week, so the look of the streets changes daily. In coming early on the first day, we were able to see the city literally grow RVs, campers, domes, tents, buildings with steel scaffolding, buses, and other shelters too many to mention.) And while we easily find 4:30 and Intertidal, we're not exactly sure where the Elders camp is. We get out of the RV and look around. As we're about to get back in, a naked male says, "Hi! Are you looking for the Elders?" As we attempt to keep eye contact, he introduces himself as Joe, the Elder we were corresponding with the past few months. All theme camps have their boundaries marked by the DPW, and Joe tells us where to park the RV. About the same time two other couples pull up and are introduced. Most of the campers live in or around Corvallis, Oregon, and this is the fourth year of the theme camp. We all help them set up their tents and shelters. It is hard to explain how welcome you feel. We receive hugs from the Elders we meet and you feel welcome immediately. It's a very communal feeling but not suffocating at all.

Theme camps are an integral part of the experience, so a brief explanation is necessary. Burning Man has been going on for twenty-one years, and people with the same interests bind together into a theme camp.

There are hundreds of theme camps, some very large and intricate, and others relatively small: the Barbie Death Camp and Wine Bistro, Camp Do Nothing, Camp Kinky Queer, Costco Soulmate Trading Outlet, Flattery Camp, the Human Carcass Wash, and many, many, many more.

While a participant absolutely does not have to join a theme camp, we felt that the experience would be that much more enjoyable if we did. Finding a theme camp, on the other hand, takes some doing, as the camps cover the gamut from nerdy to sexual to arty to partiers to literally anything in between. There is a theme camp for everyone, and if you can't find one that reflects your interests, then you just start your own. The Burning Man mantra is "If you have a suggestion, then just do it."

In our search for a theme camp, we came upon the Elders, and given our station in life, it seemed pretty much on target. Each day between 4:30 and 6:00 they offer Brie, Bach, and Talk in their communal dome. As described to me by Joe in an e-mail, the group consists of people between fifty and seventy-five, some retired, some professionals, some artists, etc. This year they expect about twenty participants, all from the West Coast. Sounds good to me.

We settle in and decide to take a walk to Center Camp. Once again, it was something I read about, but reality is much more. It is literally in the center of the city. It's a place where you can buy coffee, tea, chai, etc., for two dollars. There is a stage set up where there is music, singing, poetry, etc., 24/7. There are wooden bench seats, couches, and pillows throughout the Center Camp tent. Center Camp covers—and I'm guessing—two acres of shade. The center of Center Camp is a space for acrobatics, juggling, yoga, and basically anything a person feels like doing. As we walk to Center Camp, we realize that the city is much larger than we anticipated. You begin to see people in all kinds of dress and non-dress, hats of many kinds, and many women with platform boots, and it just seems natural.

We make our way back to the Elders camp and sit with the others and just chat. Joe mentions that some of the Elders like to be clothes optional and asks if it would bother us, and of course we say no, not at all. Actually, this didn't come as much of a surprise, as some of the message boards on the Internet alluded to that fact. Although my wife and I had a lot of laughs about it beforehand when we realized it, in reality we couldn't care less.

At four they start setting up for Brie, Bach, and Talk. Each camp member contributes thirty dollars for the cheese and wine, which Jim and his wife bought. I have to admit that I am surprised when all kinds of people show up at the dome. Young, old, semi-naked, naked, and clothed. There is a woman our age that lives in India, an artist in his thirties who has his first piece on the playa, a young woman from New York via Russia who is intrigued by the event title, and about fifteen others throughout the hour and a half, including visitors from previous years. Another just graduated from Northwestern and is living in New York to pursue his dream of being a film director. Others were invited by other Elders whom they met during the day. It is not unusual to be walking past a theme camp, when someone stops you to talk and proceeds to invite you to their special event. These invitations, we were to find out, are truly meant and taken seriously by everyone.

After the event we sit with the group and chat for a bit. It's like we've known these people forever. There is Joe and his wife, who are both retired; Donna and Skip, who own an art glass business; Juliette and Bob, a nurse and a software person; Carol and Dan, both retired; two couples from L.A. whose married daughter and son, respectively, talked them into attending the previous year; and Matt, who is here alone because his wife just didn't like the dust and the heat. (I think I saw clothes on Matt only once during the week.)

Bikes are a must, and we rent ours from another Burner in Reno. We decide to ride to the Esplanade, which can best be described as "lake-front" property on the playa … really the first circumference of the semi-circle. This is where some of the bigger theme camps are located. Matt asks if he can join us, and he proceeds to explain what's out in the playa and how not to get lost by looking at city landmarks. As we are riding from 4:30 and Intertidal to the Esplanade—ten blocks—we are constantly amazed at the theme camps, and the art cars.

Without a doubt, one of the most enjoyable and fun things for me during the week is the incredible art cars. There are over a thousand art cars licensed, and I see only a small portion of them. The only thing that makes them similar is that they are used for transportation. There are motorized living-room couches, boats, animals, sci-fi objects, birthday cakes and cupcakes, dance floors, rockets, fish, and rolling jails to capture "unlucky" Burners in animal costumes, to name a few. Many have huge propane tanks that shoot out balls of fire at quick intervals. Fire is a huge component at Burning Man, as is music, and many of the art cars take this to heart.

At night they turn into living art. The cars are festooned with el-wire lights, which look similar to neon but can be bent and molded. The result is a spectacular, disorganized parade, with these vehicles going in all different directions all night long on the playa. Even during the day the art cars are seen all throughout the city and playa. The creativity of many of the designers is mesmerizing, as is the cacophony of noise and colors that prevails all night long. It's hard to perfectly capture with words the vision of art cars belching fire in the distance and the pulsating music that just never ends, with the full moon as a spotlight on the whole scene.

In the space of ten minutes we come upon the Black Rock Roller Rink, a theme camp where you can put on skates and skate to techno music; a mini golf course theme camp; radio stations; and many, many bars and discos. Then this scene out on the playa: dozens and dozens of art cars of all shapes and sizes decorated with el-wire or other multi-colored lights, some "moving" to mimic what the car is supposed to be (like a fish swimming or a spaceship flying). Many of the art cars have propane tanks. Burners sure like fire. We come across a stage on the playa that has fire dancers. This is an art form that, while new to me, is spell-binding. It's actually called fire poi, and they literally dance with fire to techno music and drums. Some dancers are topless. Some have spinners they are holding, with three-foot lengths of chain with a ball of fire attached that they swing in beautiful and dangerous arcs until the fire burns itself out ten minutes later. Others have long, five-pronged fire fans, which have fire at the ends and with which they also dance grace-fully. There are many poi camps along the Esplanade.

We ride over to the other pieces of art on the playa, some of which were specifically made for the night and are as good as anything you'd see in a modern-art gallery. It is almost impossible to describe the sight of the huge playa with thousands of bikes and hundreds of art cars, techno music fading away with one art car and coming on with another. It all is very random and myriad, yet it all fits together like a script.

There is one other event that night that is unusual even for Burning Man, a full eclipse of the moon at two in the morning. During the eclipse we are back at the Elders camp with other Elders, but the constant noise, music, and drumming coming from the playa are out of Hollywood. The best way to put it is that it all seems to fit . . . everything is out of the ordi-nary, yet it feels normal. Yeah, crazy, but that's how we feel all week.

Day 2 (Tuesday)

I get up at 7 A.M. and, with my wife sleeping, decide to ride to Center Camp for a coffee and just to see what's going on. A cello player is on the stage, and it is a wonderful way to start the day. In the middle are the acro-bats and practitioners of tai chi and yoga. There are a couple of hundred people of all ages milling around, some talking in groups, others medi-tating, others with laptops (a theme camp gifted Wi-Fi to Center Camp) and so on. A young woman passes around a jar filled with cookies. There are topless women and naked men just walking around—once again it all seems normal. People are friendly, and if you talk to someone, they answer you. The previous night's adventures are compared.

It still being relatively cool, I ride out to the playa to look at some of the art during the day. But as I look out on the playa, something is miss-ing. Where is the Man? It turns out, the previous night during the eclipse someone shimmied up a guide wire and set the Man on fire. It was a total loss, and they had to take the Man down. We later find out it was a "political act" from a long-term Burner who thinks the city is getting too big and "Disneyfied" and who isn't without his supporters.

It is wonderful to be on the playa at eight in the morning, not a cloud in the sky. You're a kid again, riding your bike from one art piece to another. The one art piece I find profound and poignant is *The Temple of Forgiveness*. This is an ornate temple with simple lines, made out of plywood. It looks Oriental and is three stories tall. What sets this apart from everything else is that the artist, David Best, left Sharpies for people to write their innermost thoughts in private on the plywood. People leave pictures of deceased loved ones, including animals; serious sayings; and observations, etc. All in all, it is a very sobering place for people to come to grieve. On the final night of Burning Man it is burned, and with it, the wishes and thoughts are "released." It's a very somber moment. One of the more poignant sayings I see is "Burn this Cancer"—it is tear-jerking. You see many people just sitting in tears, others holding each other tight, reliving their grief, yet happy to write something that releases the pain a bit. Once again, given that stage with Burners in all types of wild dress, it messes with your mind. Things are not as they seem in the real world.

I make my way back to the Elders, where some of the others are gathered around Skip's truck and shelter. He is in the process of making breakfast for everyone . . . something he ends up doing every day. It is something he enjoys and his "gift" to the camp. Once again, it's done out of desire and not obligation. I have to admit that food just tastes better in the desert with friendly people. Across the street is someone who gives out free cups of coffee each morning. It turns out that this person lives in Hawaii, and grows and roasts Kona coffee. He used to be a software engineer but is now doing something he loves.

We sit at camp for nearly the rest of the day . . . time almost disappears. Although I mention times, it is a complete guess, as time is insignificant. Carol brings out a huge bag of crazy hats and clothes she picked up during the year at yard sales. There are many laughs as people try on the various outlandish outfits to be worn during the week. Once again at four we get ready for Brie, Bach, and Talk, and once again, to my surprise, people of all ages come to partake. One Burner from Moab, Utah, brings some colorful red rocks from the Moab desert that he painted as a gift to the Elders. It is a wonderful hour, talking about life, how different and similar the generations are, etc. Juliette gets so carried away that at the end she gives a toast, basically telling these young people how wonderful they are, they are the future, etc. It is very touching. Juliette and a couple of others are in near tears, and everyone gives a group hug. I'll never see these visitors again, yet it is another memorable experience. We have a potluck supper that night, and some stay, they enjoyed the time with us so much.

After dinner we do what we did the previous night. This time Donna asks if she can ride along with us. We begin to visit the playa art, and about a mile from Center Camp, in the middle of nowhere, what do I come to? A hot dog stand! Complete with all the condiments! Finding a hot dog cart in the middle of the desert is like being in a *New Yorker* cartoon. We also visit the last theme camp at ten on the Esplanade, which turns out to be a group from the Boston area. They are still setting up, but we're invited to their party on Friday. They have three huge domes. One dome has beds and mattresses to relax on, the other dome has acrobats practicing for the Friday party, and a third has some kind of psychiatric purpose . . . I never figured out what that was about. Nearby on the playa is a kissing booth with two guys looking for kisses—no hidden agendas, just two guys having fun. Joe from our camp tells us about a table in the middle of the playa with two chairs and the sign TELL ME YOUR TROUBLES. Well, Joe sits, and before he knows it, some young man is telling him his troubles, crying and so on. They speak for over an hour and both feel good.

We realize the second day that the desert weather isn't as bad as we expected. It is hot, but there is a constant breeze, and if you sit in the shade, it's pretty comfortable. I guess that's what low humidity does to you. Burners are constantly warned to drink a lot of water. In fact, most Web sites suggest two gallons of water a day per person. Unlike in the East, you don't realize you're sweating, as the sweat evaporates immediately, so you can get dehydrated without realizing it. We are also fortunate at night, when we never have to wear a jacket. Next year could be different, but aside from the two dust storms—and another, I understand, during the height of the exodus—the weather isn't too bad.

Day 3 (Wednesday)

The week is going by much faster than I would like. I get up at seven and do what I did the previous day. Center Camp for some coffee, music, and people watching, and then I decide to ride around the city. I did a ton of planning for Burning Man and anticipated a lot. But the one thing that continues to surprise me is the size of the city. It is enormous. The Esplanade "lakefront" alone is almost nine football fields long, and as the city is in the shape of a semicircle, the circumference becomes larger and larger. I come across Hushville, a theme camp for people who want quiet (i.e., no loud music or generators); and Alternate Energy Zone, a theme camp that is run by solar energy and other green devices. There is AntiM's Wayward Art theme camp, where you can "adopt" a piece of art you might like. Kidsville, a theme camp where parents can bring their kids to Burning Man, and so on. You can literally turn the corner and see something you never saw before. Since there is always a wind and many theme camps have colorful flags and banners, the city takes on the look of a medieval fair at times.

That afternoon there is the first of two sandstorms. I was looking forward to just seeing what they were like. Two of the things they warn you to bring are goggles and face masks, and they are godsends. At least here it's not like at the beach, where the sand stings as it hits you in a strong wind. The dust is like charcoal dust, very fine and light. You really don't even feel it. Certainly it gets into everything, and without goggles it must be horrible, but with goggles and a face mask you can handle it. Of course, you can't see twenty feet in front of you, so it's easy to get lost and you can get hit by an idiot driving an art car. But all in all, not a disaster.

That night we look for a theme camp on the Esplanade we heard about called Dance Dance Immolation. You know those games at an arcade where you look at the screen and it tells you where to put your feet to dance? Well, this is the same thing; however, when you dance the wrong step, a giant fireball of propane is aimed at you. It's not as dangerous as it sounds, because they put the volunteer in a fire-resistant suit and helmet. Not dangerous, but oh, so strange. Seeing volunteers trying to dance in a heavy suit, getting bombarded with balls of fire . . . just another night in Black Rock City.

Day 4 (Thursday)

The Elders are invited by Camp Chaos to march at four. We are to wear green and orange. No meaning here . . . just another goofy stunt. We are given armfuls of green beaded necklaces to give out, masks to wear. We proceed down to the Esplanade, gifting beads all the way. People are normally friendly here, but gifting anything really gets you a great smile whether they take it or not. We happen by chance to run into another group who are marching for green for no particular reason, and you'd think we'd met long-lost relatives. We all stop for a group picture. Along the way we stop at a bar gifting cans of cold beer. What a sight, about forty crazies wearing as much green and orange as they can, with masks, drinking beer, talking to the others gathered around the bar. We then all retreat to Camp Chaos for a cocktail hour. Crazy, nothing you'd do in the default world, but seeming normal here. All in all, ton of fun.

On my way to buy ice earlier in the day, I met the Shower Guy. He walks down the street, shouting, "Shower guy." He has a plastic backpack filled with water and a contraption that looks like a shower attached to him—he stands there as you take a quick shower.

I came upon the S'more Whore, whose gift is actually making s'mores.

Farther down the road was a person with a rolling bar gifting cold sake.

And still farther on, a person playing a piano on wheels. With so many things going on, it's easy to forget the two Burners playing a game of golf in the city with an oversize ball and golf clubs, the Burner whose gift is to stand in the street during the hottest part of the day and ask if you want him to pour cold water on you as his gift, and finally, entering Center Camp during the day and walking over a topless woman lying completely still, prone on the floor.

After the march with Camp Chaos we're told that we missed the lightsaber fight right out of *Star Wars*, where some theme camp gave away five thousand light swords for a playa fight at dusk.

There are more bars and discos than you can shake a stick at, as well as many arts-and-crafts theme camps, but you just can't do everything.

Day 5 (Friday)

The day of the annual Critical Tits Parade! This is a bike parade of mostly topless (and some bottomless) women, who ride their bikes from the Man to a "secret" location, that ends with a huge party. Approximately six to eight thousand women participate. All ages and all shapes. The sidelines along the route remind me of the spectators at the Boston Marathon, clapping and yelling encouragement. The line of bikes looks like it goes on for miles.

I attend the after party. A live band and many places to get drinks. One thing was different this year: a half an hour or so after the ride ended, a huge dust storm appeared. It was hard to see anyone, and it seemed like it would never end. I can see how people can get confused and go in the wrong direction and get lost. It lasted for two hours, and I was beginning to wonder when it would end. I finally got fed up, but not being exactly sure what direction to take, I asked if I could join two female Burners who were walking their bikes back to the city. As with everything else during the week, they couldn't have been nicer, and we had a nice chat walking back. As the sky cleared, we were treated to a double rainbow, just another wonderful memory.

Day 6 (Saturday)

Unfortunately, this is to be our last day. Although the event ends at midnight on Monday, we have to leave one day earlier. This is the night they burn the Man.

Once again we are involved in a Burning Man phenomenon. While visiting *The Temple of Forgiveness* prior to the burn, we come across a wedding about to take place. It's not unusual for people to get married at Burning Man. What is unusual is the bride in a white baby-doll negligee, complete with white garters and white high heels. The groom is in a simple South Seas–type of sarong. The bride's family is there, as is a minister who has the power to marry them. The surrounding crowd cheers as they are married. I wish them well. It was actually a lovely experience.

Burning the Man is some event. As mentioned earlier, the original Man was burned on Monday night, and the DPW spent the rest of the week making a replacement. The only difference is this one has a phoenix rising from the ashes on its head. Always looking for the bright side, many people joke that Burning Man is so good this year that he will be burned twice.

Before the actual burn, there is a choreographed one-hour fire dancing show. First there is the procession of the lamplighters, a group of people who each night go through a performance where they light lamps on the poles leading from Center Camp to the Man, and who in the morning take them down. There are hundreds of fire dancers in this performance, with some of the most complex fire dancing I've seen. These are professional fire dancers. Along with the dancers is a large number of drums. It eventually ends and there is quiet. Seconds later fireworks go off. I've been to many fireworks shows, but this goes on for twenty minutes. Finally, with a resulting large fireball, the wood under the Man is exploded. The Man burns for a half hour and then finally falls, to a huge cheer. The tradition is for the crowd to rush toward the Man and party until the embers are cold.

This year there is another burn that night. The Oil Derrick was supposed to be burned the night before, but it was postponed, as they couldn't finish their preparation because of the sandstorm. So while many people rush toward the Man, a much larger number rush to the Oil Derrick to await the burn. We aren't disappointed. Once again music, drums, and fireworks precede the burn. Eventually an enormous fireball envelops the derrick, and the crowd cheers. It's a bittersweet experience because at 7 A.M. tomorrow we leave.

Epilogue

Well, I'm not a virgin anymore, and now I can say each year that the previous year was better. But Burning Man is not without its controversies. Burning Man itself is a for-profit corporation owned by three people, including Larry Harvey, the founder. It was sued last year by another sharcholder who felt that Larry shouldn't be able to sell the logo or license anything about it. We shall see where that leads. Much of the DPW and Black Rock Rangers are entirely volunteers. There is a not-for-profit entity that gives out art grants. Each year there is a theme to the event. This year's was "The Green Man," and as part of the environmental theme the space under the Man was set aside for exhibits, some of which were commercial in nature. Although no logos or handouts were permitted, the idea of allowing commercial exhibits was controversial, as is next year's theme: "The American Dream." Many Burners feel that this does not encompass all the people who attend and is even xenophobic.

In a way, I feel for the "old-timers," who are seeing their baby change each year. Am I the type of Burner that was sought years ago? I may have the attitude down pat, but am I a participant in the eyes and definition of the old-time Burners? When they see people like me attend the event, is that a sign of the Burning Man apocalypse? I don't know these answers, but I do feel bad for the Burners who don't like change and see the event metamorphosing in front of their eyes.

A post–Burning Man episode that summed up the whole event for me: We had to leave Sunday to wash and clean the RV, get rid of trash, etc., in order to make our flight. By late Monday we were all finished, with a whole case of water left over. Not wanting to waste it, we offered it to various individuals, who declined. We had dinner at the hotel we were staying at and went back to the RV for one last attempt to give away the water. Parked next to us was an RV that had obviously been on the playa—even an idiot like me could see playa dust caked on and know that the occupants might be Burners. We saw six people headed toward the RV: two older people in their late sixties or early seventies, a middle-aged couple, and a young couple. I tentatively asked if they had been at Burning Man, and immediately we got a huge smile from all with an affirmative answer. It turned out the older couple was from Lafayette, California, and the younger from the UK. We chatted for a while about the week's experiences, and as we said our good-byes, we asked if they'd like the water. The older woman said she could use it for an earthquake stash. She asked what she could pay for it, and of course we said it was a gift. She said she felt as though they should pay something, and I suggested a hug. The middle-aged man had a T-shirt with an interesting design on the front and the Burning Man logo on the back. My wife mentioned that she liked the shirt. Without a thought, the man took it off and gifted it to her. We will never see these people again, but we belong to the same "family." A wonderful way to end a wonderful week. ✧

The Day They Were Shooting Dogs

Samuel Reifler

The snap of gunshots could be heard from the other side of the highway that ran past the school.

"They're shooting the dogs!" Some of the boys whooped and darted out the double glass doors into the parking lot.

One of the teachers, a gray-haired woman in blue padded overalls, pulled a remote from her pocket. The doors slid shut and locked. "It's nothing, people," she said.

"My Brando is out. They're going to shoot my Brando." A girl in a pink sweater was slapping her hands against the glass.

"If he's out, he deserves to be shot," said a boy.

"I want to go home."

"He's breaking the law," said another child. "Your dog is supposed to be inside the house or tied up."

"I want to call Omni and have Mommy pick me up."

"I'm sorry, Candace, we're in intense learning mode," said the teacher, indicating a large circular LED, which was now pulsing above the television screen.

"Somebody should shoot *you*!" screamed Candace.

"You should be glad that it's only your dog that's going to get shot," said a small, owl-faced child. "It's really your parents who are breaking the law. Your dog doesn't know any better."

"Don't worry," said another boy. "If your dog gets shot, I'll come over and poop on your lawn."

Candace charged the teacher, who raised her arms and let the girl hammer at her chest. She wasn't quick enough to stop another child from reaching into her pocket for the remote.

With a snap the doors unlocked, and most of the class ran out and away across the blacktop.

In the hush that followed, the teachers sat beside a window and chatted softly. "It's *The Village of the Damned*," said one. The others laughed. The gunshots came less frequently. The sound of the yelling children had faded. In an office down the hall the principal was phoning the parents.

A man with tousled hair and heavy-lidded eyes burst into the classroom as the final beep sounded. "Come on, Liberty, we've got to go. They're shooting the dogs."

"I know," said his daughter without looking up from a large computer screen. "Most of the kids went out to watch."

"I believe it," said her father grimly. "We have to go to Mother Kugel's and make sure she keeps Brownie and Schnaapsie in."

"Take it easy, take it easy," said Liberty. "Keep in the right state of mind, remember?"

"Put the screen back in your desk and let's go. When you grow up, you'll understand."

As they drove through town, Liberty watched her father attempt to get into the right state of mind. He took a deep breath, dropped his shoulders, settled his weight evenly on his buttocks, and exhaled slowly. He ran his fingertips over his lips to reduce their tension. His mouth dropped slightly open. He let his thoughts flow above him, as if he were the bed of a stream. In only a minute or two, though, he was hunching his shoulders and drumming his fingers on the steering wheel. With a tragic droop of his mouth, he pulled a joint out of the ashtray.

Through the window of the old Honda pickup Liberty saw that the city was quieter than usual. Even when they passed the hospital, where there was usually a throng in wheelchairs going in and out, she saw no one. When they reached Mother Kugel's neighborhood, a band of hollering children suddenly dashed from one driveway to another and disappeared. They passed a large yellow dog, unleashed, urinating on a rhododendron beside a house, a yellow face watching it through a window. Her father was driving slowly now so he could finish his joint before they arrived at Mother Kugel's.

Mother Kugel's tiny living room was dominated by a curvaceous brown velvet sofa and a pink and green marble coffee table supported by a pair of elaborately carved, bare-breasted mahogany mermaids. Across the room from the sofa were two deep, soft green armchairs, a small plush footstool, two mahogany end tables, and an empty, fan-shaped mahogany magazine stand. On a number of small bookshelves and in narrow cabinets were displayed souvenir plates, pastoral ceramic figurines, and family photographs. A worn, faded Oriental carpet covered the floor.

In a straight chair near the sofa, like a dry, wrinkled nut in a rich fruitcake, sat Mother Kugel, slapping her knees. Liberty had sunk into one of the green armchairs, her father into the other. Brownie, one of Mother Kugel's dogs, lay on the couch, one eye cocked open.

Liberty's father jounced fitfully in his chair. "I should really go look for Schnaapsie," he said.

"Sit awhile, sit awhile, bubby," said Mother Kugel, waving him down as she continued slapping her knees. "Where you going in such a hurry?"

"To find Schnaapsie before he gets shot."

"A shot? He's going to the vet's?"

"No. No. With guns. It's like when they put him in the pound, only they shoot them instead."

Mother Kugel laughed. "Don't worry. Schnaapsie is a tiny little hot dog. They'll miss him for sure."

"They won't miss him. They'll shoot him dead. Kaput."

"So?" Mother Kugel shrugged. "That's why I have two dogs. If one dies, then I already got another one, and he's good training for the next one, by example, since he already knows his way around. Listen, I hear on the radio there are plenty people want to give away their dogs. No trouble getting another dog."

Liberty's father struggled to rise from his chair.

"Sit awhile, sit awhile, bubby. Where you going in such a hurry?"

"I've got to find Schnaapsie so he doesn't get shot."

"Who could have the heart to shoot Schnaapsie? He's just a fat little hot dog."

"There are people out there with guns who are looking for excuses to use them."

"Would you like a cup of tea, or some soda?"

"What about Schnaapsie?"

"Here in this house," said Mother Kugel, "there are three of us: Schnaapsie, Brownie, and me. This one"—she motioned toward Brownie—"he can take care of himself, *kinnahurra*, but Schnaapsie is old and not so smart. There is no way to stop from what happens. It's all up to God. You can never tell. What the future will be, not a single person can tell for sure. You could walk out the door and get hit by a car, God forbid, and your daughter, God forbid a hundred times, could get a cramp swimming, and the people could shoot Schnaapsie, and this one, Brownie, could fall down a hole and break his neck. So. Who would be left? Me. I'd be the only one left. There is no way to tell for sure."

"Listen, Great-Grandma," said Liberty's father, "you have an obligation to watch out for Schnaapsie, and I have an obligation to take care of you. Uhhhh!" He heaved himself into an upright posture.

"Sit awhile, sit awhile. Where you going in such a hurry?"

"Don't you care whether Schnaapsie lives or dies?"

"Sure, sure. But I care about something else much more. That is to have you sit here with me for half an hour. That really is important for me."

Liberty's father sank back into the chair and shook his head. "Why is everyone else so wise and I'm so stupid?"

"You're just mixed up in here, bubby"—Mother Kugel pointed to the center of her chest—"not stupid. You remind me of my father. His father was a pretzel baker in Cernovitz, and my father, naturally in the old country the son put on the father's shoes, so he was a pretzel baker too. When he married my stepmother, she brought with her a little bit of money. It was the custom in the old country that the bride would bring some money to the groom, something she had put aside, maybe, or her parents had put aside for the occasion, maybe a little something left to her by an older person, already dead, in her family. So. Now that my father had some money, he decided that he wanted to go into business for himself, so we moved to another town, I can't remember the name, so let's call it Poughkeepsie; it was about as far from Cernovitz to this new place as it is from here to New York. And there, in the Poughkeepsie that was in the old country, he took a shop and went into business, but as a pastry baker, not a pretzel baker. Why? Who knows? Maybe it was a step up the ladder, as we used to say. But the other pastry bakers in that place, that Poughkeepsie, not this one, the one in the old country, there were already four or three pastry bakers there, they had made a kind of union together, for protection, and they didn't want another pastry baker in that place. So. These four or three pastry bakers, this union of pastry bakers, came to my father and said, 'We have enough pastry bakers in this town. You can't be a pastry baker here.' And my father, who was very stubborn, very gruff, he goes like this: 'Who says?' he says. 'Who says?' he says to these men. They were standing in the shop. 'We are asking you nicely, Herr Schniemann,' they said to my father, 'there is no reason for you to be so gruff.' 'You so-and-sos,' my father said. 'You so-and-sos,' he says to these men, 'you mind your business and let me mind my business.' Then he puffs himself up, like this. 'I am paying the taxes.'

"These pastry bakers were afraid of my brother. He was big and strong, so the pastry bakers were afraid to get rough with my father. They knew that Yakob, that was my brother, Yakob, they knew he could fight them all down. He was big and strong, like this. So. The pastry bakers went away and made a clever plan, a clever plan about how to make my father not to be a pastry baker. They waited outside the *schule* until Yakob came out, and then they were friendly to him, like this, 'How are you, old pal?' they said to him, or whatever a man said to his friends at that time in the old country, and they slapped him on the back, or whatever. 'Come on, Yakob,' they said to him, 'come on, Yakob,' they said to my brother, 'let's go have a schnaaps.' I cannot truthfully say that my brother was a smart person, but beside that, he was a very friendly person, a happy person, he liked to have a good time. So. He went to a bar with these pastry bakers, or maybe it was friends of the pastry bakers, but anyway, he went to a bar and got drunk, and when these men had gotten Yakob good and drunk, they came to my father's shop—I think they had to carry Yakob or help him on his sides because he was so drunk—and Yakob went up to my father, and he was so bad that he had to lean against the wall not to fall down. The pastry bakers stood around to see what was going to happen, and Yakob said to my father, 'Papa, these men are right. We must get out of the pastry business. They will let us go into the pretzel business.'

"Right away my father could see that Yakob was drunk, so he took his fist and made to hit him with it, like this. As soon as my father did this, as soon as he raised his hand against his son, like this, the pastry bakers, they were acting as a kind of union, and when my father made to hit Yakob, like this, it was, what you call it, a signal, and they all came and grabbed my father and began punching him. Yakob just stood there. He was so drunk that he could not leave the wall to lean on. 'Please, Papa, do what they say. Please, Papa, do what they say.' So my father agreed. What could he do? 'All right. I'll be a pretzel baker,' he said. Maybe there were no other pretzel bakers in that place, or maybe just one, maybe there was enough business for a new pretzel baker in that place, or maybe whatever pretzel bakers were there were not as friendly with each other as the pastry bakers were. So. That is how we came to be pretzel bakers in that place, whatever the name of it was, I just say Poughkeepsie in the old country because I can't remember, but it was the same distance from Cernovitz to that place as the distance from New York to this Poughkeepsie, the one we live in now."

Depressed by the dark, overheated room, Liberty was not listening to Mother Kugel, nor was her father. For a while he had pretended to listen, but at the end his attentive expression failed him and, like Liberty, he simply stared, unfocused, into space.

A gunshot broke the silence that followed Mother Kugel's story. A screech of tires was followed by another shot and the sound of children calling to one another. Liberty jumped to the window and pulled aside the heavy drapes, then ran out the front door onto the porch. A brown-spotted white mongrel was wobbling along the sidewalk on the other side of the street, laying down a train of shiny blood. A small group of children, walking backwards, watched it with rapt, silent concentration, while the dog gazed trustingly up into their faces, the tip of its tail flicking back and forth in confusion.

An electric car buzzed down the street, its horn blaring, a bare arm holding a long pistol protruding from a window. The children scattered. The dog glanced backwards, stumbled, and fell as three rapid shots rang out. The car sped away around a corner.

Liberty dashed down the steps and across the street, joining the children, who had regrouped around the dog. She heard her father call her name but paid no attention.

The dog lay on its side, making swimming motions. Liberty counted four holes in it. One was in its jaw. Broken teeth protruded through the rip in its black chops; behind the teeth a scarlet tongue trembled. The second hole was in the dog's shoulder. It was a perfect little circle, the source of a rhythmic geyser of blood that ran down the white fur to pool on the sidewalk. A third hole was in the dog's back. The fur around it looked much like the other reddish brown blots that mottled the dog's coat, except that it was moist. The fourth bullet had torn a rent in the dog's penis. The white sheath hung open like a purse; the bloody glans lay inert on the moist concrete.

Liberty felt her father's hand grip her shoulder. "You answer me when I call you."

"What do you want?" she said.

"We're going home." Her father raised his voice. "And I think you all should let this poor animal die in peace."

"We're not bothering him," said one of the children. "He's already unconscious."

Her father grabbed Liberty's wrist, wrenching her toward the street. "Now," he snarled.

"No. I want to watch! *Salveme!*"

With a yell, the children turned from the dog and swarmed on Liberty's father, some of them pulling him backwards by his belt, others butting his stomach. He let go of Liberty and fell over onto the pavement, curling up to protect himself.

"*Non los muertos,*" said Liberty.

The children laughed, returning to their vigil around the dog. Liberty's father stood up and tucked in his shirt. "I'm going home, Liberty. You can do whatever the hell you want. I don't care if I never set eyes on you again." He crossed the street, threw himself into his car, slammed the door, and started the engine. He turned it off after a few seconds, slumped down in his seat, and began to read a newspaper, which he propped up on the steering wheel.

The dog was no longer swimming. Its blood flowed more slowly.

"Watch his eyes. When they begin to glaze, it means he's starting to die."

"They're glazed now."

"No, they're not. Glazed means they get foggy."

"Glazed means shiny."

"Crystals form on the eyes."

The dog was motionless now, except for an intermittent dilation of its nostrils.

One of the children sighed in satisfaction.

From her father's car came the wail of a shenai. The dog squeaked, as if in response to the sound. Liberty looked at its eyes. They seemed to be made of glass.

On the way home Liberty's father smoked a joint, absorbed in the intricate runs of a bluegrass banjo. When the music was over, he turned to his daughter. "Do you understand what it means for a grown-up to be attacked by children? Can you imagine what it feels like inside?"

"How could I?" said Liberty.

"It is degrading. Humiliating. Emasculating."

"Do you know what it feels like for a child to have a grown-up pull her away from sharing an activity with other children?"

"Of course I do. It's not the same thing."

"It is degrading, humiliating, and emasculating."

"You can't be emasculated," said her father. "It means cutting off the testicles."

"Yech!"

Her father slapped the steering wheel with his hand. "This is so surrealistic. I can't believe it."

"Everything is surrealistic to you."

"Shooting dogs on Worrall Avenue."

"But people are being attacked by dogs, and the police won't do anything."

"This is the What Is. If I had inner peace, I could accept it, I could be happy. Instead I'm involved in the What Was and the What Should Be."

"You make things too complicated," said Liberty.

"But things *are* complicated, and when you say I make things too complicated, they get even more complicated."

"Why?"

"I can't explain. It's too complicated." He laughed.

"Why don't you smoke some more grass, Daddy. Maybe that will help you figure it out."

Liberty's father grinned. "Don't get fresh with me, young lady," he said. He switched on the CD player, and the reverberations of an electric oud filled the van with the sound of swarming bees. ✧

SALAMANDER

*Where discerning readers
encounter
outstanding writers*

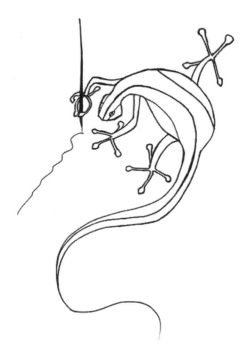

HAPPY ALL THE TIME: Loving Laurie Colwin

Margo Rabb

There are times in life when you need a book that doesn't rend your soul or make you want to crawl under the covers and weep. Yet you don't want fluff, you're loath to have your brain invaded by young ladies dithering over where to find their next man/martini/Manolo, and you're not in the mood to see how long it takes Miss Marple to find the murderer. You want to find a book that's meaningful, smart, funny, and—dare one even hope?—maybe even joyful.

You need Laurie Colwin.

I read my first Laurie Colwin book, the story collection *Passion and Affect*, when I was twenty-one. I immediately fell in love with the Oreo-eating Greenie Frenzel, the misanthropic Misty Berkowitz, the gum-cracking Binnie Chester, and all her characters, but I didn't race out and read her other books right away. I'd spent most of my college years reading classics and was just discovering contemporary fiction; I imagined that there must be a wealth of authors just like Laurie Colwin awaiting me.

I was wrong. As the years passed, I often asked friends, "Can you recommend someone who writes fiction that's smart, literary, and kind of, well ... happy? You know—someone like Laurie Colwin?"

Few could.

I devoured the rest of Laurie Colwin's books. *Happy All the Time*, a novel grown out of two stories from *Passion and Affect*, instantly joined my list of all-time favorite books. Published in 1978, my very-seventies-looking copy (complete with gold embossed heart and clinking champagne glasses) boasts this quote from a *New Yorker* review: "A pleasure ... endless surprises and ultimately boundless joy ... It would be difficult not to enjoy it all!" I can't recall the last time I read a *New Yorker* book review that used the term "boundless joy" and, shock upon shocks, an *exclamation point*. But the reviewer was right: the novel is a celebration. Colwin's characters are misanthropes and misfits, often pessimistic, cynical, sarcastic people who manage, despite themselves, to find a contented life.

The more fiction I wrote myself, the more I realized how difficult this is to carry off. Most "joyful" fiction tends to be unrealistic, clichéd, and so unbelievable that it's depressing. But for Colwin's contented misanthropes, joy takes them by surprise. "I hate other people," states Jane Louise, the protagonist of Colwin's last novel, *A Big Storm Knocked It Over*, even though Jane Louise is floored by the depth of love she feels for her baby daughter. Billy Delielle is similarly taken aback by love for her baby in the story cycle *Another Marvelous Thing*, which contains a line that captured exactly what I felt after my daughter was born: "Billy . . . found the experience of having a baby exactly like being madly in love."

"Both happy and sad people can be cheered up by a nice meal," Colwin writes in *More Home Cooking: A Writer Returns to the Kitchen*, the second of her two collections of food essays. In a gourmet-lit world rife with purple prose Colwin is a rarity: unpretentious, sarcastic, and self-mocking. For today's time-crunched cook she suggests *"la cuisine de la 'slobbe' raffinée,"* or "the cooking of the refined slob," which happily eliminates peeling potatoes and garlic, trussing chickens, and other superfluities. She's not besotted by her own prose, nor is she self-indulgent. In her answer to Proust's madeleine, she explains why she no longer makes beef tea, a favorite food from her childhood: "I am afraid that my childhood will overwhelm me with the first sip or that I will be compelled to sit down at once and write a novel in many volumes."

"My friends are constantly driven crazy by me because I want to know what they had for dinner," she writes in *More Home Cooking*. "I want to know what they had and how they cooked it. I'm not very curious about what people had *out*. I'm interested in what people have *in*, because I'm very interested in people's domestic lives. I used to think I was frittering away my time, but the fact is, what is more interesting than how people live? I personally can't think of anything. Maybe war, or death or something, but not to me."

Laurie Colwin died in 1992 at the age of forty-eight. I can't express what a loss it is that she died so young, that the eleven books she wrote are all we have left. There's no other writer like her, and on many rainy Sunday afternoons she's the only company I want to keep. ✧

Hold Your Horses the Elephants Are Coming

Christopher Higgs

In the first coliseum it was people killing people, animals killing animals, animals killing people, and people eating people.

Remember Juvenal, "Two things only the people anxiously desire— bread and circuses."

Not bread alone.

It was the fifth king of Rome, not of the republic nor the empire, but the kingdom, Tarquinius Priscus, who waged war on a neighboring village, massacred everyone, and in honor of the victory built the Circus Maximus. Later, Pompey held a rhinoceros fight in the arena, the railing broke, and the rhinoceroses proceeded to stomp two dozen children, to the delight of countless onlookers. Shortly thereafter Caesar added a moat to ensure a safer distance for the audience, but then Nero filled it back in—he, of course, rather enjoyed the titillating possibility of collateral damage.

Come the age of Hannibal vs. Roman dictator Fabius Maximus Verrucosus Cunctator, between the era of Tarquinius and Pompey. Picture the badass Romans versus the strategically prodigious Carthaginians. Sunday! Sunday! Sunday! Unfortunately, neither diplomacy nor sword could end their feud. Instead it was a Carthaginian elephant named Jumbo and a little Roman girl named Julia Domna who befriended each other on the battlefield of Cannae and began the first traveling troupe of like-minded entertainers. Together they strolled through the piles of dead bodies, nearly seventy thousand total, and began to lay the framework for a movable circus.

Much in the Saxon fashion, circa the Dark Ages, going from village to village spreading news, singing songs, and telling stories. Gypsies? No. Gleemen? Minstrels? Living the plush and fancy. With muscles and mustaches, animals and love.

Then the Normans invaded and introduced a new kind of entertainer, one who quickly became the talk of every town: the juggler. Fuck face. Job displacer. Who needs a storyteller when a juggler can simulate the movement of the cosmos?

Penniless, in the winter, all the traveling performers nearly froze. One town kicked them out, another put them in jail. Women made do with prostitution. Men buried themselves in garbage heaps for warmth.

Enter the Great Famine, 1315 to 1322, which not only left plates bare and stomachs empty, but decimated the European populace with rampant outbreaks of infanticide and cannibalism and overall malaise. Entertainers of every stripe starved alongside their persecutors.

By 1322, Europe had returned to relative normalcy, until Mongol armies on the Silk Road carried Black Death to them around 1340. Between one third and two thirds of the entire continent went violently into that good night. Yes, death grew more common than Sundays. As might be expected, traveling entertainers ceased to find eager audiences to exploit. Turns out, most folks aren't particularly interested in buying a laugh when their children are covered in lesions and their spouses are coughing up blood.

Over in eastern Europe, Romanian prince of Walachia, Vlad Dracul III, known then and now as the Impaler, held off the expansion of the Ottoman Empire from 1448 to 1476. All the while in his heart he yearned for the return of the circus.

In various incarnations the plague reoccurred until the 1700s, popping up here and there to eliminate entire villages before vanishing again. Eventually people stopped fearing for their lives and learned to take their pandemics without flinching. Traveling bands of showmen started touring again.

But during the reign of Queen Elizabeth I, in sixteenth-century Tudor society, such wandering vagabonds found persecution everywhere. Laws made them fugitives. Rope dancers and bear trainers became synonymous with rogues. Evildoers. Baby killers.

Picture a slick, quick roundup of everyone even remotely jolly. A lineup of smiling bastards who think they're getting a job at the royal court, only to learn their fate: to be scalded with burning sulfur, molten lead, and boiling oil, before having their flesh torn by pincers, and then neatly drawn and quartered.

In Deutschland in the seventeenth century Pickelherring and his confederates started wearing oversized shoes, ratty waistcoats, and bright ruffs around their necks. They spit in the face of melancholia. But then later that century the whiteface pantomimist Jean-Baptiste-Gaspard Deburau sold out to sadness by creating the famous lovesick wag, whose influence infects pathetic buffoons still to this day, most notably in the form of the sad-faced clown. Luckily for those fellows, the age of executing jesters was on the wane.

At that time a shapely Harlequin named Madame Nightingale showed up on the traveling entertainment scene. A real comic valet, a real zany, acrobatic trickster who wore a domino-patterned mask and carried a noisy slapstick with which she spanked her horny victims. One husband after another would flee into the forest, weeping, his bare bottom blistered red as iron fresh from the forge.

Then in 1759, at the age of seventeen, Philip Astley borrowed a horse and joined the Fifteenth Dragoons as a roughrider and horse breaker, slaughtered innocents for the king of Prussia, then returned to England and invented the modern circus. His father was a cabinetmaker.

Charles Hughes, a former horse rider in Astley's circus, opened a competing company in 1782. The ungrateful wanker was not content to play second fiddle. Of course, this was exactly the same time period when free-market fanatic Adam Smith was pushing his Machiavellian theory of capitalism. Hence, the cultural milieu responsible for fostering such a notion as one circus minus competition would never do. But that was really nothing new. Since the inaugural collaboration between the little Roman girl and her Carthaginian elephant, seeds of competition had sprouted rivals everywhere.

What about Antonio Franconi? He killed a man in a duel and fled Italy for France, where he disguised his identity, married three women simultaneously for their money, as well as to satiate his unquenchable sexual desires, and then used the money to found the first Parisian circus in 1793.

It's sick how competition can become so contagious.

The first complete circus program presented in the United States was also in 1793, in a building on the southwest corner of Twelfth and Market in Philadelphia, by a man named John Bill Ricketts. The awestruck crowd vomited in unison. George Washington saw a Ricketts show just after his first term in office ended, fell in love with the spectacle, toyed with the idea of ditching politics, divorcing his wife and joining the circus, then changed his mind, got reelected, and sold Ricketts his presidential horse for a cup of coffee.

Imagine a horse wearing trousers and a top hat, eating a warm dinner at a clean table with a cherry-scented candle burning till the wee hours of the night. This is what became of Washington's horse in Ricketts's circus. And when that horse finally retired to bed, he never forgot to blow the candle out.

Back across the ocean, on November 12, 1859, at the Cirque Napoléon in Paris, Jules Léotard became the first man to perform on the flying trapeze. His mother had just forsaken him. His only friend was locked in an insane asylum, and everyone in the troupe doubted him. After a whiskey he slapped his wife for the first time, before climbing that platform to his destiny.

In 1882 the *New York Times* declared Butler Township, Indiana, the circus capital of the world, under the command of Col. Benjamin E. Wallace and his mind-blowing extravaganza: Wallace and Company's Great World Menagerie, Grand International Mardi Gras, Highway Holiday Hidalgo, and Alliance of Novelties. Sadly, the show itself did not debut until 1884 because a drunk cook forgot to turn off a gas stove, which met unfavorably with a discarded cigarette, combusted like a supernova, and took most of the animals and many of the performers with it.

When it did finally debut, to a crowd of nearly half a million, it opened with a giant woman floating in the sky, eating cupcakes, tethered to the ground like a hot-air balloon. There at the entrance to the midway, for all the crowd to see, her big blue dress ballooned out just enough to expose her white thighs and the menstrual stain on her panties, officially ushering in the era of the big top, and with it the world's greatest entertainers:

The daughter of Patrick Grimlicker, the famous fire-eater, who ate minnows by the handful. Unbeknownst to her, those minnows once swam freely in a very special pond where, before being kidnapped, they fed themselves on microscopic people who lived in microscopic villages on the shore. Forever after, those tiny people lived inside that fire-eater's daughter.

A lion tamer named Picinniny Gossin, who had a glass eye with a sea horse in it. The sea horse was trapped inside, but the lion tamer ate funnel cakes for breakfast and then ran thirteen laps around the giant woman floating in the sky. After an eleven-hour day of work he went back to his trailer to eat dinner alone, with a picture of his dead wife taped to the wall directly across from him. She'd always loved the tiny sea horse in his eye. He told her about his day as if she had not been savagely ripped apart by the organ grinder's monkey and thrown to the seals for fodder.

The bearded ladies, the Sullivan triplets—born to the organ grinder and the ticket taker—who all three happened to fall in love with Barnaby Schuler, the world's greatest whale fighter, simultaneously. Schuler loved none of them; his heart had been torn out ages before. The bearded sisters stopped talking to one another in their jealous pursuit of the suitor who wanted nothing to do with any of them. Eventually they starved to death trying to impress him. One started eating glass instead of cereal, and the others followed unquestioningly.

Hornbeck Fiddler, the greatest living marksman, who, while attempting to arrow an apple atop his daughter's head, missed quite horribly. The audience thought the mistake was part of the show, so they cheered very loudly. Fiddler hanged himself shortly thereafter.

Mons Le Tort, the great French bareback rider, who actually got so many women pregnant that an entire village was formed from his progeny.

Of course, the horses, tigers, leopards, lions, cheetahs, pumas, panthers, giraffes, dogs, goats, zebras, and all other non-human creatures suffered unending cruelty.

Beat those elephants with sugarcane
the giraffes with bamboo.
Lash the hippopotamuses with reeds
then go and salt the wounds
to remind the stupid beasts who is who.

Torture, the ringmaster would say, is just another name for compassion.

Most certainly, the rich frosting on any circus was the clowns. Whiteface clowns like Pipo Sossman or François Fratellini, the oldest of modern clown archetypes, who held the highest status in the clown hierarchy, usually functioned as the straight man and leader of the group. Auguste clowns like Chesty Mortimer or Toto Johnson, who always got a pie in the face, played the Whiteface's sidekick. Mixed in would always be Character clowns like Poodles Hanneford or Bluch Landof, who adopted different personas such as the baker, the policeman, the housewife, or the hobo. Together they would do bits like "The Baseball Gag," "The Boxing Gag," "The Dentist," "The Clown Car," "The Midget Car," and "The Hosing."

At the orgasm of his stellar career Dan Rice was more of a household name than Abraham Lincoln. Referred to as the presidential jester, he was America's most popular clown. Mark Twain paid him homage in *The Adventures of Huckleberry Finn*. Walt Whitman wrote newspaper articles about him. He campaigned for Zachary Taylor by inviting him to join his circus bandwagon—hence the modern idiomatic expression "Jump on the bandwagon." In fact, his likeness was so ubiquitous that it became the model for Uncle Sam, the clown who wants YOU to join the army.

Then came the birth of Ringling Brothers and Barnum & Bailey in 1907. Legend has it this monumental troupe began with a single stilt walker, a pallbearer who went to the cemetery with other stilt walkers to mourn the death of a comrade. Sun setting behind them. Their heads down, crying. Black on all of them, from suit to shoes. Long black dress slacks stretching six feet to the ground. One pair of stilts made entirely of apologies. Another pair contained the greatest mystery in the universe. One pair could've broken at any minute. Another could've grown, if persuaded just right. At the grave site they bickered over final good-byes. A couple of them fell to the ground and shattered like lightbulbs on sidewalks. Some of the pieces fell onto the grave of their fallen brother. The remaining stilt walkers raised their hands and began hopping up and down on their stilts. One by one they toppled to the ground and broke into a billion pieces, until only one was left. The last stilt walker saw he was the only one still standing. He took a giant breath and exhaled with all he could muster, which uprooted many trees; laughter overtook him as he teetered, wobbled, but did not fall. After fifteen years and thirty-eight burials, after living in the shadows of so many other circuses, he remained. His laughter stormed the hillsides and deafened every person in the nearest village. That stilt walker was named John Bailey and his brother-in-law was named Frank Barnum, and their friends from church were named Phil and Terrance Ringling. Together they created "The Greatest Show on Earth."

Beginning in 1919, Merle Evans served as band director for the Ringling Brothers and Barnum & Bailey Circus for a half century. He died at the age of ninety-three, having led the Windjammers to 18,250 performances without ever missing a day.

Besides the smears, rags, serenades, and gallops, the most often-played music in the circus was the march: all except for John Phillip Sousa's "The Stars and Stripes Forever," which was strictly reserved for emergency situations only, used as a warning signal to indicate real trouble.

Signals and superstitions abound in circus life.

Never count the audience. Never whistle in the dressing room. Never sleep inside the big top. Never move a wardrobe trunk once it has been put into place. Never look back during the parade. Never sit on the ring curb facing out.

To a cacophony of drums, cymbals, tubas, trumpets, trombones, and cornets, Dainty Miss Leitzel, the first inductee to the International Circus Hall of Fame, made her dramatic entrance into the ring. When she reached the center, she clutched her famous rope swivel, a metal noose that dangled from the tent top. The spotlight followed her as she rose into the air. High above the arena floor she began to spin like a pinwheel, her face alight with laughter. The audience awed. Then suddenly her rope swivel crystallized and snapped, and she fell helplessly to her death. Born in Breslau, Germany, in 1892, she died in 1931 in Copenhagen, Denmark, two days after her tragic performance on Friday the thirteenth.

Never perform on Friday the thirteenth.

During the presidency of Calvin "KKK" Coolidge, 1923–1929, many crazy inventions popped up: the television, the talking pictures, and the electrically powered vibrator, all of which contributed to the end of the circus's monopoly on the entertainment industry.

Suddenly dwarves spinning plates and sexy human cannonballs equaled diminishing returns. By the 1940s people in the United States were preoccupied with the idea of annihilating the Japanese abroad and rounding them up in detention camps domestically. Few citizens had the urge to go and laugh or cheer at some bumbling brown bears or men with hula hoops, tightrope walkers or somersault throwers. And overseas most of Europe was too busy being taken over by Adolf Hitler to attend the latest big-top extravaganza. Rumor had it, the circus thrived in Switzerland, as they were notoriously neutral, but documents found much later in the twentieth century indicate that no such thing occurred. In fact, quite the opposite. Most of the Swiss actually stopped going to the circus because of the enormous guilt they felt over standing by and watching their neighbors fall to fascism without lifting a sword to help.

For the next few decades the heavy palm of the cold war pressed down on the circus like a bully holding a weakling underwater.

Only five people noticed when the death of the circus finally occurred on March 19, 1978. A few unread newspapers in small towns like Cheyenne, Wyoming, and Great Bend, Kansas, ran brief obituaries, each noting how the death was a long time coming. But overall, no one cared. It was as if the world collectively outgrew the need for it, evolved past it. Like Nietzsche pronouncing the death of God once religion seemed no longer necessary, the same thing happened to the circus, except there was no existential philosopher who decreed it. Instead, a single carrier pigeon traveled from Greenland to Chile with a slip of yellowed paper tied to his ankle that read: "Dear Fellow Circus Performers: It's over. They do not need us or want us anymore." And just like that, the tents evaporated, the animals disappeared, and the performers vanished.

Now nothing physical remains of that ancient enterprise. Children today may hear stories about the circus of yore, but they can never really know the true texture of cotton candy, nor feel the blood-rush of those death-defying acts. All that is left is a whispered echo of the candy butchers' song:

"Popcorn! Peanuts! Hot roasted peanuts! Snow cones! Soda pop! Right this way! Right this way! Step right up! Ladies and Gentlemen, Children of All Ages, the circus is about to begin!" ✧

Kerouac's ON THE ROAD at Fifty

Morris Dickstein

I was seventeen when *On the Road* came out, the perfect age at which to read it, but I was too busy discovering Joseph Conrad and James Joyce, classical music, Joseph Papp's free Shakespeare productions, and *Partisan Review*; Jack Kerouac was a closed book to me. Even after I fell in love with Allen Ginsberg's poetry and began reading the *Evergreen Review*, a vehicle for the Beats, Kerouac's seemingly formless kinetic prose paled in comparison with Ginsberg's mad passion, Dostoyevskian intensity, and zany humor. While writing about Ginsberg in the late 1960s, I finally gave *On the Road* a chance. Soon I assigned it in courses, and with each successive reading I liked it more; what had once seemed shapeless began to look like an eruptive well of energy and flow. The shy Kerouac's portrait of Neal Cassady (as Dean Moriarty) highlighted the charisma, self-possession, physical dexterity, and sexual ease the author himself lacked and longed for. Their cross-country travels, the need to keep moving, tied the book to the whole westward migration in American history, from the pioneers to the new interstate highways. It's a boys' book, one that explodes the domesticity and enforced maturity of the postwar years. Bonding with each other, they take off on the slightest whim, leaving girlfriends, wives, children behind. At a time when the culture demanded responsibility and restraint, the book made the lure of irresponsibility irresistible to young men. It still is, though our values have changed.

Becoming famous, finding himself identified with the book's cool hero, made Kerouac's life a misery. Along with the booze, it destroyed his ability to write. Kerouac himself was anything but a hip icon. He had none of Ginsberg's showmanship, William S. Burroughs's dark humor, or Norman Mailer's ego. His strengths were a phenomenal memory, a jazz-like improvisational fluency, a sense of destiny as an artist, and a fascination with outsize characters like Ginsberg and Cassady who seemed more at home in their own skin. A family man, closely tied to his imperious French-Canadian mother, in his novel he played the conventional Tom Sawyer to Cassady's orphaned Huck Finn, Ishmael to his Captain Ahab, the faithful Nick Carraway to his fabulous Jay Gatsby. The moment was right. Other picaresque works as different as *The Catcher in the Rye*, *The Adventures of Augie March*, and *Invisible Man* had broken through the tight mesh of fictional form as they challenged the Apollonian cultural ideal it represented. The superego was losing its moral authority. The new gods would be energy, spontaneity, self-discovery. Sex beckoned

as the key to a brave new world; madness itself became a form of icono-
clasm, a badge of authenticity. Along with Mailer's *Advertisements for
Myself*, Robert Lowell's *Life Studies*, and Ginsberg's *Howl, On the Road*
was at the center of a cultural revolution. By making the road itself—
sheer movement—the book's real hero, Kerouac gave new life to a fun-
damental American myth that spanned a continent and recalled a lost
frontier. *On the Road* somehow became a great book without bothering
to assume the guise of a well-made novel. ✧

My Older Brother, June Bug

Jason Lee Brown

Roots with the hogs in the field's shallow burrows
and picks through the thick lawns and meadows
with the shrews and crows for those fat white grubs
with the brown heads that feed on the roots of weeds,
and he collects the bait until he finds a fishing pole
to borrow, though he rarely catches anything but a buzz.

Illinois June bugs usually land in July, but my brother
shows up whenever he needs a night or three of sleep,
basement hibernation, he always says, his head hunting
for the musty yellow cushions of the couch to burrow
his face from the rest of the world. He curls up, arms
around knees, underneath his leather coat, a brown shell

that never hardened, even when the slick black belt
blurred like a corner-of-the-eye shadow, the silver buckle
flickering the fluorescent light above our father's head,
my brother purposely acting up, attracting the brunt
of the licks for our blue jeans with mud-stained knees,
live grubs in plastic cups, one dead crappie on a string.

Name I Will Never Forget

Jason Lee Brown

I called him D because I could never remember his name, only that it started with *D*.

You remember everything: D of the green DEKALB corn seed hat; D of the six-sodas-a-day habit; D of the small dip tucked between cheek and gum, spitting black on the pavement; D of the couldn't-sit-still-during-downtime, sweeping dirt that wasn't there; D who took the pressman job just to buy a house with more rooms than children, children who eventually left to live with the ex-wife.

All I have are flashes, small scenes of the Christmas party: An open bar. One pool table. Tequila, SoCo, and vodka celebrated our victories. Too drunk to play, we bellied the bar. More talk. More shots. We laughed when D's face hit the counter. Cameras flashed.

Remember you said D puked in the parking lot, crawled into the van, and you, the designated driver, slammed the door shut. You drove up and down every country road that night listening to D's incoherent directions, couldn't find D's large, empty home. You actually pulled down the driveway once but didn't know it.

You walked D three laps around the van, hoping for one clear thought, a direction other than where it ended. D said it was fun to sit in the ditch and did, arms braced out to the sides, head back, looking at the sky as if asking for something.

You did everything you could before and after headlights flickered through the trees, across the van, into D's eyes. "Police!" D said, and took off sprinting into the woods, as if stone sober, an explosion of energy.

You searched the tree line with a flashlight, screaming "Derrick! Derrick! Derrick!" so many times the word didn't weigh the same. I was in my living room then, half asleep in the recliner, trying to remember his name, when it hit me, as if your voice had found its way out of the trees, the soft night breeze pushing it through my window.

On the table next to me a police scanner beeped. The dispatcher told the officer that a train had hit something on the tracks, better get out there and take a look.

crazyhorse

Jawsmiths,

nightwalkers,

moonbirds:

Unite!

--from the Crazyhorse manifesto, 1960

crazyhorse

READ AND SUBSCRIBE ONLINE
http://crazyhorse.cofc.edu

Excerpt from GINT (an adaptation of Henrik Ibsen's PEER GYNT)

Will Eno

Dramatis Personae

MOTHER

PETER GINT

Act First, Scene First

The GINT home. Lights up on MOTHER, alone, in bed, recovering from a hysterectomy. She moves with some difficulty.

MOTHER: Never have children. Or, I don't know. Have children. You end up talking to yourself, either way.

PETER enters, with a small box. He stands by the bed, looking at MOTHER. Pause.

MOTHER: Liar.

PETER: I didn't even . . . God. I was trying to—

MOTHER: *(Interrupting.)* You're a liar. *(Pause. Looking at the small box that PETER holds. Softening in tone.)* Is that for me?

PETER: What, this? This is just . . . yeah. Yeah, I got this for you. You might not like it.

She opens it. It's a men's tie, yellowish green. She shakes her head almost imperceptibly and tries not to cry.

MOTHER: Thank you, Peter. Very thoughtful, of you. *(Brief pause.)* Let me share something with you, Peter. Just because I had this operation and can't have children anymore, because I don't have the organs for it anymore, doesn't mean I suddenly stopped being a woman, and suddenly stopped needing pretty things in life, or kindness. And suddenly started goddamn wearing ties. *(Brief pause.)* Ah, but we're in luck. It's your color.

PETER: You're hard to shop for. I had this great thing, but it was going to take too long. *(He takes back the tie.)* If you don't want it, I'll give it a try. *(He begins putting it on.)*

MOTHER: How kind.

PETER: Hey, it fits.

MOTHER: Aren't you even going to ask how I am?

PETER: How are you?

MOTHER: Don't you dare ask me how I am. You said that you'd be here. You said that you'd be there by my side in the hospital and help me when I was scared. And be there when I woke up and be there to help me home. And be here at home to help around the house and talk with me and hold my hand. I was almost looking forward to it, Peter, having half my insides taken out, because I thought it would give us a little time together. You promised you'd be here. My only son. What a darling boy. You lied.

PETER: I said I was sorry.

MOTHER: No, in fact, you didn't.

PETER: Well, I am.

MOTHER: No, in fact, you aren't.

PETER: Why don't you ever believe me?

MOTHER: Because you're always lying, Peter. Because you never tell the truth. Because when you start sentences with "I," I don't even think you know who you're talking about. Because maybe I didn't hold you enough when you were little. Because maybe I wasn't born to be a mother. Because how was I supposed to know. And who knows what your father was born for. Certainly not providing. Certainly not chitchat. So I didn't know what to do. And there we were. You scared me, with all those sounds and faces you made. And your father scared you, with all his sounds and faces. So there we were, with our faces and our sounds—a family, scared, together. And now here you are a liar. And here I am a person who gets lied to. Because I don't know why. Because I have no idea why.

PETER: You held me a lot.

MOTHER: I held you all the time. I never let you go. You were so hold-able. So content, we liked to think. Always busy, with your sledding and your night terrors. Bright red shrieker full of mystery. I told you little stories filled with talking animals and strong male characters, while your father piddled our futures away. *(Pause.)* I needed you, Peter. I don't have anyone. We'll see how you like it when the students and interns start sharpening their knives on you. I missed you. Your mother felt very alone.

PETER: I'm sorry, Mom.

MOTHER: I know you are, sweetheart. You're very sorry. You always were. *(Brief pause.)* Where were you?

PETER: I was trying to get home. The weather got so strange. And so I, kind of, I looked sort of skyward to see if I—

MOTHER: *(Interrupting.)* Maybe if I'd let you babble more when you were a baby, or listened more while you babbled, you wouldn't still be babbling now. Into the dark, by the way. Into dead ears, by the way, Peter. Dead from overuse or neglect, or from listening for you in vain for too long. Left, at every stupid awful step, alone. "Mrs. Gint, will someone be coming?" they asked. "My son should be here any minute. I think he's going to surprise me. I'll just wait." And so we all sat and stood there, waiting, staring down an empty echoing shiny hospital hall. Surprise. If you don't tell the truth, Peter, after a while, it's all just goo-goo ga-ga and saliva.

PETER: I was trying to—

MOTHER: *(Interrupting.)* Shhh.

PETER: *(Pause.)* So now I can't even open my mouth?

MOTHER: That's all you can do. Like a little fuzzy baby bird. Making little peeps for its dirty worm.

PETER: *(Pause.)* Goo-goo ga-ga. Peep. *(They share a little laugh.)* I like your dress.

MOTHER: I'm glad you're home, Peter. My little disillusionment.

PETER: Yeah. *(Wanting to tell a story.)* Well, I almost didn't make it.

MOTHER: *(Not wanting to hear it.)* But you did. Can you get me the blanket? I think it's under the bed.

PETER starts looking for the blanket, which isn't under the bed, and continues looking throughout the next few exchanges.

PETER: So, yeah, no, I almost didn't make it. Hey, by the way, I think I might have met someone.

MOTHER: You usually do. Think that.

PETER: No, I did. She's great. She was. Duty called, though, so I had to go. The open road. Responsibility. Anyway, a few days ago, I was starting to think about starting to make my way home. And what do I see, but a—

MOTHER: *(Interrupting. Pointing to a closet.)* Try in there.

He looks in the closet and continues to look around, on and off, through the following.

PETER: What do I see, but a crazy dog. Wild, but familiar; recognizable, but unknowable. Matted brown fur, Dad's eyes. It looked like it had every disease and every cure. All the answers and all the questions and the teeth to make you listen. So I took off after it—howling, a mess of bones and flies, a filthy rag around the scabby neck.

MOTHER: That's my boy.

PETER: This was the dog. I could so easily see the thing out in the rain or snow, shivering on a rusty tangled chain, while a family dined inside, in candlelight, in silence. There it sits, outside, banished—hungry and sick and getting smarter. "Scrawniness is power," it seemed to say. "Disease is knowledge." And here it was, on the loose. I wanted to know its secret. To see how it lived, as itself, free from the comfort of its chain, on the growling edges of civilization. Banishéd.

MOTHER: *(Brief pause. Admiring her own dress.)* The buttons were just lying around.

PETER: *(Brief pause.)* Yeah, so this dog. I started screaming my own name, chasing after it. God. *(He stares off, dreamily.)*

MOTHER: *(Pause. Wanting the end of the story.)* And? *(Brief pause.)* I'm not interested—but, don't leave us hanging. *(Brief pause.)* Did you catch it?

PETER: Yes and no. No, really. We ran through backyards, boy and dog, together, through clothing on clotheslines and wading pools and prayer gardens, through people wading and people praying, over un-landscaped wilderness and frantically manicured corporate properties. I tore my legs to hell. We got more and more lost. Somebody shot at us, I think.

MOTHER: No.

PETER: Yeah. People screamed. I didn't recognize anything. The dog, now limping, now half wearing a pretty blouse from a clothesline we had run through, and me. Man and Nature, Mom. Man and Nature. And more. We moved like angels, like little gods, like new improved angels, through night and day, o'er land and sea, on a journey without maps, through a new theology, Bible-less.

MOTHER: God, what is that smell? Do you smell that? Oh, God, it's terrible.

PETER: *(He sniffs around.)* I don't smell anything. But, so there we were. I saw the world as if I'd just turned a corner onto it. It looked beautiful. It looked possible. My moment. I wanted to begin, right there, to start—

MOTHER: *(Interrupting. Still trying to find the source of the smell.)* Is it your shoes? Did you step in something?

PETER: Oh, God. Yeah, I did. Wow. Sorry. Shit.

MOTHER: God, it's disgusting. Take them outside. Get them out of here. And don't swear.

PETER exits.

MOTHER: *(Pause.)* Love is in the air.

PETER returns with his shoes off.

MOTHER: Light a candle or some matches. *(Brief pause.)* We don't have any candles. I might have put that blanket in one of the broken windows in the little room.

PETER exits momentarily, looking for the blanket. He returns and momentarily forgets what he was talking about.

PETER: Oh, yeah—so, the dog and I, barreling through life. It had been a few days now and the hunger and blood loss were getting us somewhere special. I was seeing stars. I don't know what the dog was seeing. Sticks and bones? Kittens? Stars, too? I don't know. We stopped to breathe and then both lost interest. I didn't know where I was. Or care. Then I looked up, and, there was the house, and, here I was, home.

MOTHER: *(Brief pause.)* Really?

PETER: Really. Mom, I never felt so alive.

MOTHER: No? Not even last year? When the exact same thing happened? And you couldn't get home in time to take me in for my tests? And you told me the exact same goddamn story?

PETER: What do you mean, last . . . No, I felt alive then, too. This was different. This time, at first, I thought the dog—

MOTHER: *(Interrupting.)* Enough. I can't, okay, Peter. No more. You're just a liar. And hardly anything else. Which comes first, do you think, the awful mother, or, the awful son? Enough. *(Brief pause.)* God, I can't get warm.

PETER: Here. *(He puts his jacket over her.)*

MOTHER: I never left you alone. I never let you shiver. Not knowingly. I was reliable, whatever else I wasn't. I was always there when you fell. Purely coincidentally, by the way—I see that look. You have no idea what you took out of me. Why were you born? I ask, to know. Do you have any idea? Because I don't. I certainly don't. *(Pause. She finds a little bag of hard candies in PETER's jacket pocket.)* What are these?

PETER: I thought you used to like those.

MOTHER: *(Brief pause.)* Yes, I did, Pee-Wee. I did used to like these. *(She tries one.)* You're a good boy, Peter. You have your good sides. You're like your father.

PETER: You hated dad.

MOTHER: I *disliked* your father, and *mistrusted* him. And I found him offensive. I never hated him. You be careful or you'll end up just like him.

PETER: Oh, no. I've got bigger plans.

MOTHER: So did he.

PETER: I'm on a journey to discover, to uncover, the authentic self.

MOTHER: Get some milk, while you're out. *(Pause.)* I'm sorry about what I said, Peter. You were born because I needed you. That's the truth. Let me see your legs.

PETER rolls up his torn pants.

PETER: Dueling scars, from my run-in with the world.

MOTHER: Cuts on your legs from running in the woods like an idiot. *(Pointing to a cabinet.)* There's rubbing alcohol in there.

PETER gets the rubbing alcohol. MOTHER prepares to put it on his cuts.

MOTHER: That girl should be doing this. That girl you used to skate with.

PETER: Sarah.

MOTHER: I'm sure she still loves you, you know. My God. With her brains and looks, and your . . . all your wonderful things, your posture—what children you'd have. You could do worse than marrying her. What a sunny future. Can you imagine? We could get new windows.

PETER: Maybe I should. She always got me, somehow. *(He winces, due to the sting of the alcohol being applied, and will do so again throughout the following lines.)* Jesus! Her family is really wealthy. I liked talking to her. I should. Christ! She'd make me happy and calm. I could find myself. We'd be rich. You could live on our property. God, fuck! On the edge of it, maybe. She loved me. I should marry her. I'm sorry for swearing. Owww! Fucking Jesus owww! I will. I'll marry her.

MOTHER: I'm sorry, Peter. It's too late. I don't know why I even brought it up. She's getting married today.

PETER: *(Very calmly, softly.)* Fucking Jesus owww.

MOTHER: Don't swear, Peter. Maybe if you hadn't left, then she might have . . . Oh, I don't know, who knows?

PETER: You know what, I'm going to go to the wedding. I'll just show up. I'll go offer my curses. I'll never forever hold my peace. I'll have her, and with her idiot father's stupid idiot consent. I always respected him. He always liked me. *(Brief pause.)* This just somehow feels right.

MOTHER: No, it doesn't. This doesn't feel right, Peter. This is stupid and wrong. Another punch line for our joke of a family history. Another awkward pause for me to offer, when the neighbors brag about their children. Just forget it, please. I just got out of the hospital. I need you here.

PETER: *(Not listening.)* I'll need to leave, right away. And I'll need you to come with me. Talk me up, a little, with the in-laws. The Gints will rise again! *(He tries to lift MOTHER, several times, in several different ways, but cannot.)* You stay here.

MOTHER: Did you even hear one word I just said?

PETER: Yeah. Definitely. *(Brief pause.)* "Children"? I don't know. You definitely said "children." Listen, I know this seems hectic. I know I seem a little hectic, right now. But I know it's right. This is the moment. I thought it was that dog, but, no. This'll be the moment. When my whole life, everything, changes. I promise. I'm the man of the house, now. I'll take care of you. I will. I'll comfort you, Mother. *(Motioning toward his jacket.)* Could I grab my—great.

PETER takes his jacket back, gently. Starts putting it on.

PETER: Wait, so who's she marrying?

MOTHER: That Moynihan. Come here, dear. Your collar is wrong.

PETER moves toward her bedside.

PETER: Moynihan? I think I'd make a much better person than Moynihan. I don't think that guy's ever even—

MOTHER violently grabs PETER by the collar.

MOTHER: You're killing me. This shitty life is killing me. And you're both humiliating me, while you do it. I can't stand it, anymore, Peter. I'm tired of the cold. I don't like church food. I'm sick of looking homeless. So go ahead, you go and try and get yourself married to that girl. Because, you know what? We need help. We're poor. Did you know that? We're poor people, Peter. In every respect. We don't have money. And we aren't rich in love, and we aren't rich in tradition. People don't care about us, people do not admire this family. Things are much more serious than you know. Did you know that? Things are serious. I have a condition. We have broken windows and medical bills. I'm old. We're in trouble. You're killing me.

She lets PETER go.

PETER: Desperate times. Okay. I understand.

MOTHER: No, you don't. No, you absolutely don't.

PETER: I won't be long, Mom. Don't wiggle. Bye.

MOTHER: Try not to make too much of a fool of yourself, okay? Be careful, Peter.

PETER: I will, Mom.

PETER exits. MOTHER eats another piece of candy.

MOTHER: The little son of a bitch. I have to admit, it still happens. Like it did when I was only six months gone with him. And now here it is, all these years later, and, I still get a little kick out of him. ✧

"I always read *Post Road* with great enthusiasm. In its stealthy, unassuming way, it has become one of the most reliable and ambitious literary magazines in America."

RICK MOODY

THE LAWS OF EVENING, by Mary Yukari Waters

Tod Goldberg

My wife, Wendy, and I remember the summer of 1996 affectionately as the Summer of Nothing. We had no money of our own, neither of us had jobs, and we subsisted on a steady diet of Pop-Tarts, Rice-A-Roni, and Boboli. Our only source of income came from our respective families: My grandfather, seeing how despondent I was about not pursuing my life's dream—to become a midlist novelist—encouraged me to quit my high-paying job pimping temps to companies by offering to give me enough money each month to cover my expenses, provided I actually got off my ass and started writing. Wendy's mother also gave generously, probably because she saw great hope in my ability to become a midlist novelist too, which is surprising, since at the time I wasn't even married to her daughter yet.

To make good on all of this financial investment—which, candidly, we mostly wasted on the above-noted meals and whatever blockbuster bowed at the Sherman Oaks Galleria—and apparent creative promise, I eventually concluded that I should maybe look into taking a couple classes . . . somewhere . . . anywhere . . . since I was clearly not going to make my big splash in our 600-square-foot apartment writing fiction that was either derivative of *The Wonder Years* or derivative of Richard Ford, if Richard Ford spent a lot of time watching *The Wonder Years*. So, as the Summer of Nothing wound down, I ended up at the UCLA Extension Writers' Program in a course taught by a fellow named Tom Filer. Tom had been an actor, novelist, and screenwriter since the 1950s and approached writing exceptionally seriously, quoting from Flaubert and Flannery O'Connor and generally making me feel like my Cal State–Northridge undergraduate education wasn't sufficient credential to enter the august halls of literature, but nevertheless, at the conclusion of the class he invited me to join a private workshop he taught out of his house in Santa Monica Canyon, which was actually a cozy guesthouse behind Peter Graves's sprawling Spanish-style home.

On the first night of the workshop—after getting over the shock of having Peter Graves yell at me for nearly running him down in the road— I sat beside a quiet and reserved woman named Mary. She was a few years older than me—six, I'd learn later—and looked a bit like Parker Posey, if Parker Posey had a little Japanese in her genes. We made idle talk, and I learned that she was a corporate accountant. "What do you do?" she asked.

"Nothing," I said.

"That must be so nice," she said. "I'd like to do nothing."

That evening we workshopped three stories by other members of the group. What I recall is that the three stories were awful, or rather, that with my vast knowledge of human emotions at age twenty-five, the stories seemed awful to me. I recall saying things like "I don't know why you wrote this" and "This had no purpose beyond sentimentality" and suggesting cuts that involved "pretty much everything after the title." Mary, on the other hand, gave nuanced and intellectual notes that made me feel like a silly frat boy who'd just figured out that it was inappropriate to vomit on himself in public. (That I was only two years removed from being that very frat boy didn't help the situation.)

But then a funny thing happened: at the break that first night, Mary and I talked confidentially over brie, fruit, and wine about how frustrated we were reading stories that bored us, like the ones on display that week. It seemed, inconceivably, that Mary actually liked me and respected my opinion. There wasn't any good reason for this, since Mary was the kind of person who typically found me, well, annoying. And to be fair, I was annoying. And so when stories for the following meeting were handed out and I found Mary's on the top of the stack, I felt a little worried. What if it sucked? What if I said all that stupid stuff I tended to say?

That night I got back to our little apartment and told Wendy all about the night. And then, since I didn't have a job and we were out of brown-sugar Pop-Tarts, I stayed up and started reading the stories, starting with Mary's.

Mary's story was called "Since My House Burned Down," and by the end of the first paragraph she had me. Back then, nearly a dozen years in the dust now, the opening paragraph read like this: "They are burning leaves at Toh-Daji Temple. The monks do it constantly this time of year, in late afternoon when there is the least amount of wind. From upstairs, above the pan tiled slate roofs of neighborhood houses, I watch the smoke unravel above branches of red maple. Even from four alleys away it reaches me through the closed glass window: pungent, like incense; reminiscent of some lost memory."

How do I know that's how it read? Because I still have the original manuscript in a box in my garage. Because that night, after reading the story maybe ten times, each time with a growing sense of wonder, I woke Wendy up and told her that I had just read the most remarkable, heartbreaking, and, finally, hopeful short story I'd ever read, that the writer would someday be like Alice Munro, that we needed to find a safe place to keep the original because one day it would be really valuable after she won the Pulitzer or the Nobel or the National Book Award or something else equally earth-shattering.

The Mary in question here was Mary Yukari Waters (though back then she was just Mary Waters), and over the course of the next four years I'd read several more stories that knocked me over—"Aftermath," "Egg-Face," "Shibusa," and "Kami," among others, all of which would eventually end up finding homes in prestigious publications and every conceivable best-of anthology before ending up in her acclaimed collection *The Laws of Evening*—and that would change the way I looked at short fiction. Before Mary, I was strictly married to that school of fiction that used to be called Dirty Realism. I thought good short fiction had to involve a man who was dangerous with his hands, who might be on the wrong side of the law, was most assuredly a drunk, but, by virtue of a shocking bit of violence or a stirring epiphany, found himself and steadied his shifting moral center. (That he usually found himself in some Midwestern town I'd never visit really appealed to me too.) If you'd told me that I would become enamored with elegant tales of women struggling to find traction in post–World War II Japan, I would have laughed in your face.

Yet what I found in Mary's stories then, and what I find in them today when I teach them to my own creative-writing students, or when I reread them in hopes of finding clarity in my own fiction or simply leaving this world behind for a few minutes, is that Mary had such a palpable sense of empathy for her characters even as a beginning writer. None of the stories in *Laws* is rushed. Instead, they feel like the result of erosion; so that each character, each emotion, each shimmering image, is there because it's all that's left, it's all the author could possibly show. It's not about economy in a story by Mary Yukari Waters; it's about passion, each story in the collection pivoting on a subtle realization.

That first night I kept rereading "Since My House Burned Down" so that I could experience the last few paragraphs again, to get to these words of hope and renewal:

> I head down toward a sunny bench overlooking the water. These days walking exhausts me. The river flows past, sunlight glinting on its surface like bright bees swarming over a hive. I can actually hear the bees buzzing, so I take out my hearing aid and put it in my handbag. I sun myself like this for a long time, eyes half shut. I conjure up from memory the surface sounds of the river, its tiny slurps and licks as countless currents tumble over one another. I remember too the soft roar in flood time of the undercurrent as it drags silt and pebbles out to sea.
>
> The music comforts me. I imagine dissolving into the water, being borne along its current. Something slowly unclenches in my chest. I am pared down, I think suddenly, to Masahide's poem. And I sense with a slow-mounting joy how wide this river is, and how very deep, with its waters rolling out towards an even vaster sea; and the quiet surge of my happiness fills my chest to bursting.

At twenty-five, what did I know about growing old? About the chasm of memory? About anything? And still, this story captured me. Today, of course, things are different. I've had a prostate exam. I've lived long enough to compile palpable regret. I've found myself near tears driving across the wide desert highway a few miles from my home, suddenly filled with the realization that all the people I've loved, all the people I've hated, everyone I've ever known, will eventually leave me. That life is transitive. And it's when I feel these things that I inevitably turn to *The Laws of Evening* again, particularly the story "Aftermath."

"What is to be done with such memories?" Mary writes in the middle of the story as her main character deals with unpleasant memories of her dead husband, a man she's tried to romanticize for her young (and increasingly Americanized) son Toshi in the aftermath of World War II.

> They get scattered, left behind. Over the past few years, more pleasant recollections have taken the lead, informing all the rest, like a flock of birds, heading as one body along an altered course of nostalgia.
>
> She has tried hard to remain true to the past. But the weight of her need must have been too great: her need to be comforted, her need to provide a legacy for a small, fatherless boy. Tonight she senses how far beneath the surface her own past has sunk, its outline distorted by deceptively clear waters.

Today when I read these words bound between two covers, it's hard to conceive of them existing in some other form, but I remember reading "Aftermath" in our workshop, remember that the story was longer, that I had issues with ... something. I don't remember what anymore, because by that point I'd stopped keeping secret copies of Mary's work. And when I look at the published version of "Since My House Burned Down," I see that an editor's pen has gone through that wonderful opening paragraph too. Words have been changed, sentences rearranged slightly, and I can't help but wonder why. It seemed perfect in 1996.

The odd thing about being friends with the writers who inspire you the most is that you never really get the chance to tell them how important their words are to you. Of course they see you at their book signings and readings, they probably know that you teach their work, but when you talk to each other, it's rarely about such trivial things as the words that make your life easier, or provide context, or simply enrich you. No, you talk about life and love and gossip and fun, and in the end you hang up the phone and maybe you think you should have told that person, again, how much they've touched you with their words, but inside you're still a twenty-five-year-old without much to say of credence and you think maybe you'll do it some other time.

Except that I'm thirty-six now. Except that I'm happy to say with whatever credence age and time have given me that *The Laws of Evening*, by my friend Mary Yukari Waters, was one of my favorite books long before it was ever published, and that with each year that passes, it grows in importance, its relevance changes, and I find comfort knowing Mary imagined things long before I'd experience them myself. ✧

Body Language

Kim Chinquee

While he telephoned his mother in Greece, his girlfriend, Elle, read an article about the newest panda. He spoke Greek into the phone, like a song. The pandas were in danger. He paced around, between his two pianos, then sat next to Elle, reading on the sofa, where they'd just finished doing their thing with the blinds closed. Now the blinds were open; the mum garden bloomed in the back. He laughed with his mother. He touched Elle's hair. The pandas ate bamboo, and the females ovulated only once each year. The captive males hardly had a sex drive. His mother's name was Iris. Or was it Violet? He touched Elle's neck. It tickled. It was hard to tell when the female panda ovulated. Elle could hear his mother's voice from the phone. She talked fast. Elle had spoken to his mother, though his mother didn't know English. When the female finally ovulated, a team put the male under, making him ejaculate through known methods. They took his sperm. He'd been talking about moving back to Greece. He missed his mom. He had a son from a one-nighter in America, almost five now. Last night he and Elle had gone out to eat at the restaurant where his neighbor was the chef and recommended the bruschetta, the salmon with the kiwi. They ate it all, then came back and got ready to make love, but Elle had forgotten to take her pill and he didn't have any condoms. They did other things. The team was scared and hopeful for the panda, watching, documenting everything. The insemination had been successful. Some words sounded familiar, and Elle could tell by his body language he was happy, or was he sad or nervous? He paced. Was he talking about her? His words didn't sound like words. At first they didn't know if the panda was pregnant. Usually the mother had twins, abandoning one of them to let the other survive. Elle heard the word that meant "goodbye." The panda had had one. The baby lived. They watched it grow. ✧

Balloons and Clowns and Popcorn

Kim Chinquee

It was hot and he got iced, but I was always cold and ordered hot, adding lots of cream and Equal. He told me it would kill me.

We took baths inside his tub, and he scrubbed me with his Zest. His heart turned to putty at the Bang Saloon, where he drank tequila—I had beer and ate up all the peanuts, letting the shells drop. He was allergic to most things, was tall and blond with glasses. He always needed something.

He didn't have a shower, and when I first told him I didn't have one either, he said that was a sign. I told him it meant we were poor, then took another sip of Guinness and slipped a peanut into my mouth and sucked it.

He was drunk our first time fucking. I met him through his friend, a guy who got afraid and wouldn't do me any longer. They met through an ex-girlfriend, crazy like that.

He had a grand piano, which I was bad at playing, and he made his money with computers, sang country music with guitar, had a dog named Quarter, old and lazy, big and black. He had a recording studio in a room that used to be a child's bedroom—you could see the paper on the wall, all balloons and clowns and popcorn. When I stepped into that room and put his headphones on, I listened to his recordings, and imagined him singing to me about longing.

I took him to work every single morning. I didn't have anything till noon. We went out for morning coffee.

Sometimes we were still hung over from the night before. I didn't know what I wanted, but I wanted something.

When I dropped him off at work, I'd say, "Have a splendid day," and he'd lean over and kiss me. He always told me that he loved me, nothing more. I told him I'd be back. I couldn't wait to see him. That was it. It wasn't much. ✧

Mash

Kim Chinquee

The poet said to all the listeners: "I've always wanted to meet her." People sang to him "Happy Birthday" and he read his love poems, dedicating them to her, calling her sweet vegetable names like rosy radish and artichoke candy. He said he'd read her stories. They hadn't met and people listened. He read a fuck-me poem, every line starting with a fuck-me. He was a decent poet, making some want to fuck.

They went for drinks afterwards. The students and the teachers, and the poet leaned over to her. She was a teacher and bought him a drink: the best and straightest whiskey. The place was a dive and she drank 7-Up. She sipped.

He smoked chimney-style, ran a hand over his bald head, raving about supper.

He played pool. Her boyfriend for real was somewhere else. A student bought her a beer and she said thanks and went up to the poet. He said he wanted to kiss her, hitting a stripe, knocking in a solid. She said, "No way," leaning to whisper. She stayed there, close, grabbing his cue for a shot. ✧

NINTH
LETTER

Ninth Letter
An award winning literary/arts journal
Published in the Fall and Spring by the University of Illinois, Urbana-Champaign

FICTION
POETRY
CREATIVE NONFICTION
TRANSLATIONS
ART
AND MORE

AVAILABLE AT BOOKSTORES NATIONWIDE OR AT WWW.NINTHLETTER.COM

OCTOBER SNOW, by Samuel Reifler

Nelly Reifler

When I was a little girl, my father and I would play games with the type-writer. It was an electric typewriter, and its keys had a keen pounce; it was fun to poke them and make words appear. The typewriter would be out in the main room of Dad's house in the woods, perched on a steel stand. Sometimes we'd just visit it alternately throughout the day, each of us typing a word when we happened by. Other times we wrote plays together, going back and forth with lines of dialogue and stage directions. For me, the ele-ments of surprise and chance—the understanding that you must really relinquish control of what you make—came to me with those writing games. My father and I both found the absurdist results hilarious. I was an easily amused little kid, and most of the time Dad was stoned on weed he grew in a clearing off one of his dirt roads.

When we weren't playing typewriter games, watching *Star Trek*, or playing gin rummy, I could be found pedaling around the open space of the house on one of two brightly colored plastic wheely dinosaurs with a book propped on its horns, and Dad would be off in his study working on his real writing.

At twenty-two, eight years before I was born, my father had been chosen as the literary voice of his generation by Richard Yates. *Esquire* magazine had held a contest to find the writers that would define the new decade, and they'd hired Yates to be the judge. My father's story, "Two Semesters at Wagner's Inn," won first prize and was published in Esquire in an issue that also included the odd pairing of Graham Greene and Terry Southern. An anthology of the winners and other notable entries was put out by Bantam in 1962. Dad went on to publish other stories (in *Harper's Bazaar*, *New Directions*, *Denver Quarterly*, and *TriQuarterly*, among others). Everybody's assumption was that he would soon publish a book of his own. But he couldn't find an agent; everyone he approached wanted a novel, and he didn't have one.

Meanwhile, the sixties, the decade he was supposed to represent, began in earnest. He got stoned for the first time with Harry Smith. He met my mother, a dancer and weaver, and together they learned about Eastern philosophy and logged tapes for Alan Lomax. He got her preg-nant on an ocean liner bound for Europe. They got married in Gibraltar. I was born in Poughkeepsie, but after three wild years in rural Dutchess County they moved to Europe, disgusted and frightened by the vibe in the United States. In 1974, back in America and separated from my mother, Dad published a nonfiction book, *I Ching: A New Interpretation for Modern Times* (Bantam).

In spite of the fact that he did not have good luck getting a book of fiction published, my father continued to write with great commitment and diligence. Through the late sixties and the seventies he finished two novellas, *October Snow* and *Zimmer*, and two epic experimental pieces, *The 180 Commerce Street Blues* and *On Saul Apricots*. He also completed a collection of stories and dozens of poems.

My parents were not harsh disciplinarians. That's why it was so puzzling for me when they forbade me to read one particular story of Dad's, "Retrospections of an American Girlhood." This was when I was around ten, and I used to peruse books I saw them reading, like Wilhelm Reich's *Love and Orgasm* and Hannah Arendt's *Eichmann in Jerusalem* (wondering to myself why anyone would choose to read these boring tomes over *The Wonderful Wizard of Oz* or *Prince Caspian*).

Of course, when my parents told me I was not allowed to read my father's story, I was fantastically intrigued. After resisting for a year or so, I finally gave in to temptation. My parents had remained remarkably involved in each other's artistic lives after they separated, and Dad gave Mom copies of most everything he wrote. So one day, alone in the apartment where I lived with my mother, I pulled out the binder in which my father's collection was snapped together with a locking steel arm. And I read the forbidden story.

"Retrospections of an American Girlhood" starts out, seemingly, as a biography of me. The first scene is a familiar one from my childhood: I am there, but with a different name—and so are Dad, Mom, Charlotte (a family friend and one of Dad's exes), Aunt Cynthia, and Uncle Bruce. As usual, they are shooting the shit and arguing about art and culture; the story opens on the day of Picasso's death. After that things start to get odd. In the middle section of the story the daughter and the dad character are visiting a great-grandma character (mine was alive until I was eleven) in Poughkeepsie on a day that the cops are slaughtering stray dogs. By the last scene the father is living alone in the woods, and his daughter has grown up to be one of the hard, alien people of the outside world—so different from her elders that we met in scene one. The father has chosen to take a drug that will bring him enlightenment once, but which he knows will kill him. The daughter comes over, finds him dead, throws his cat in the trash compactor, and calls the state troopers. The final scene gives us the daughter, frozen in her ugly world, greeting a new day after having screwed one of the troopers who came to deal with her father's corpse.

I remember closing the binder and sitting for a long time on my mother's bed, a mattress on the floor covered with an Indian-print spread. I was shocked, dismayed, and above all confused by what felt like a projection of my future, and of our future as father and daughter. I couldn't talk about it with anyone because that would mean admitting I had disobeyed my parents.

Now I understand. I, too, write stories that people call dark, and they often have endings that are—I'm told—unsatisfying or depressing. Most rejection letters I get tell me this. I know, I think, why my father wrote a story like that. Maybe difficult stories are "Fuck you's" to those who say you have to tie tales up in a comfortable way. But even more, a story like this one is a kind of totem: by committing your darkest fears, most gnawing anxieties, and ugliest, most cynical suspicions to words—by naming them and exposing them to light—you are containing them in some way, for the time being gaining the upper hand in a titanic internal struggle.

That sad and timeless story, "Retrospections of an American Girlhood," hasn't been published in its entirety, but the revised middle section can be found elsewhere in this issue of *Post Road*. I also recommend that you read Samuel Reifler's nearly perfect novella, *October Snow*, which was given to the world, finally, in 2004 by Pressed Wafer. ✧

NOON

NOON

A LITERARY ANNUAL

1324 LEXINGTON AVENUE   PMB 298   NEW YORK   NEW YORK   10128

EDITION PRICE $12 DOMESTIC $17 FOREIGN

Die Fledermaus

G. C. Waldrep

"In my country things had not gone on that long yet. The postal workers, for instance, were still at their posts; mail arrived regularly at the châteaux in & around the village where I was living. There were birds— in the aviary, and beyond it, in the open air. Some days the distinction seemed painful, other days elegant. At night, weather permitting, servants scrubbed the carefully set panes until the interruption represented by their unyielding presence seemed hardly worth noting.

"I kept a notebook during those years, full of pensive jottings about the scenery, my hosts, my fellow guests—even the colleagues I had left behind in the capital. It seemed to me important that everything be set down, if not in the sort of script or format a court of law would honor, then at least in accord with the sensual reality of the place. Which is to say, in spite of my relative comfort I was aware of the passage of TIME, as I was of the aviary glass. I even fancied myself a sort of clockmaker, with my pastes & pens.

"The war went badly, of course, for nearly everyone, and I will not deny any of the kindnesses or cruelties subsequently attributed to my name or reputation. It seemed we were all creatures of the moon then, pocked & hung & moved about in strict conformity with forces beyond our immediate control. In such a dramatic economy every dimension was discrete, non-accretive, non-complementary: merest fragment of an image, an act, an alphabet.

"By then the funerary practices of my people had all been well-established. The ribbons were difficult to come by, cut off as we were from the manufacturing centers of the coast. But the trees were yet plentiful, and so were the axes for cutting them. We made the most improbable woodsmen: I realize that now. We were neither timid nor (especially) shy."

Sisyphus in Paradise

G. C. Waldrep

After my car was stolen all I was able to drive was its ghost. I drove the ghost of my car up and down Massachusetts Avenue in the wrong lanes, which is to say in all the wrong directions, but when you are driving a ghost nobody cares. The other cars passed right through me. It was as if in driving the ghost of my car I too became a ghost. I wondered whether the same would be true for passengers, so I asked a friend of mine to get into the ghost of my car and travel with me. He was understandably suspicious but finally consented once I showed him how to work the latch on the ectoplasmic passenger door.

We drove to Newburyport, where we observed the candy shops and the nearly vertical burying grounds used by the theosophists and the Portuguese. We drove to the state line of New Hampshire, which on the day we visited was just a little stone pyramid in the middle of a grassy field. We drove to the coast, where enormous castles constructed from sandwiches were toppling slowly into the surf.

We drove to the Quabbin Reservoir, tailed the entire time by the Newburyport theosophists. Somewhere near Petersham we shook them and were thus able to have a bite to eat in peace in the playground of the abandoned seminary.

The reservoir itself was creepy, so we simply circled for several days in its vicinity, clockwise and then counterclockwise, as if we were a small hurricane that had lost both its electromagnetism and its way. When the theosophists got too close we hurled jeweled barometers at them.

We took a few photos, though later, when we had them developed, they all turned out to be overexposed.

The problem with ghosts is that eventually they tire of the living. They long for their own kind, whatever kind that may turn out to be. I had thought maybe the ghost of my car was different, but in the end it decided it had heard enough about Augustinian metallurgy and my second cousin's sexual torment and that venerable and highly stylized school of traditional Japanese floral arrangement whose name I can't remember now but which my friend and I talked about quite a bit that spring. All of which eventually came to bore the ghost of my car, the way salt bores an army of imaginary mice, the way shipping lanes bore anatomically incorrect postage stamps and dolls bore fire hydrants. The way politicians bore Heaven. Ghosts, like John Berryman, have no inner resources, a deficiency that can kill a living poet but not a phantom automobile. Automobile ghosts are tough. Automobile ghosts leave replicas of themselves in the toothpick drawers of hypoglycemic industrialists. Automobile ghosts win at Scrabble without cheating. Automobile ghosts go clamming in Long Island Sound and then fire up the grill for a weekend of thick steaks and cold beer even when the temperatures are so low neither the schools nor the proctologists bother to open. Automobile ghosts can do just about anything, but in the end they leave us, just like automobiles do, fading into heaps of clothespins and shaving equipment and otherwise unidentifiable patches of lathered glass.

" I trumpet *Post Road* not out of kindness but out of the purely selfish pleasure I take in a frisky, alert, indepedent magazine whose words and images spring off the page and sometimes turn a somersault or two before they stick their landings in my brain. I also admire the magazine's artistic promiscuity in embracing whatever's good wherever it comes from however it works and whomever it's by. "

WALTER KIRN

THE DOG OF THE MARRIAGE, by Amy Hempel

Perrin Ireland

For years I buried an awkward secret deep in a pile of shame—the first time I read Amy Hempel's work, I didn't get it.

Her name was legend, but as I raced through a book of her stories (for racing, alas, was my too-frequent approach to reading), it seemed to me that there was no there there. I was accustomed to large, noisy, grab-you-by-the-throat, high-voltage drama, the kind of thing that can get your attention if you're not paying much.

A few months later I reread her most famous story—"In the Cemetery Where Al Jolson Is Buried"—more slowly this time. When I finished, I was paralyzed, breathless, destined to remember always where I was at that moment.

As a result of extensive research, consisting of a chat with a clerk in a bookstore in Harvard Square, I believe this phenomenon—getting it later rather than sooner—is not uncommon. The young clerk clucked with approval when I bought Hempel's *The Collected Stories*, and spoke in reverential tones of "In the Cemetery Where Al Jolson Is Buried." I asked him if he'd liked it the first time he read it. No, he said, not until the second or third time. His professors had persisted in assigning it.

There's the matter of taste, of course, and Amy Hempel's work may not be yours. But if you've had this initial reaction to her work, or to her literary relatives, like Mary Robison or Christine Schutt, perhaps you'll give them another shot, and Hempel's newest collection, *The Dog of the Marriage* (currently available in the new paperback of the *Collected* stories), is a good place to start. As is the first line of the first story, entitled "Beach Town": "The house next door was rented for the summer to a couple who swore at missed croquet shots."

The apparent ease with which so much information—emotional and factual—is packed into one sentence, with its deliciously skewed angle of vision . . .

Later, on the day the narrator hears the voice of a woman who is not the man's wife, the narrator "watch[es] the woman do something memorable to him with her mouth."

How gratifying to read prose where all dots are not connected, where the reader is permitted to participate; every sentence in this story is interesting, unpredictable. Poetry, but not poetry. Although its power is in its indirection, and loving attention is paid to metaphor.

In the last paragraph of the three-page story the narrator addresses the husband and wife's relationship again:

The weekend the couple next door had moved in—their rental began on Memorial Day—I heard them place a bet on the moon. She said waxing, he said waning. Days later the moon nearly full in the night sky, I listened for the woman to tell her husband she had won, knowing they had not named the terms of the bet, and that the woman next door would collect nothing.

(Not the least of the pleasures of the paragraph is the rhythm established by the addition of the longer sentence to the shorter ones.)

To paraphrase Jim Shepard when speaking of Amy Hempel—who else portrays despair so offhandedly (and, frequently, so hilariously), rendering it all the more potent as a result of its obliqueness? Almost Japanese in their aesthetic, Hempel's beautiful sentences, as is frequently said, can break your heart. She's been called a miniaturist, a writer's writer, a master of compression, a precisionist. She has the ability, as William Kennedy said, to "leave out all the right things." The work is elegant, pointillist, and quiet, often with astonishingly acute observations—astonishing in their honesty, as well as in their originality.

As with all collections, you'll like some stories better than others, and if you're a writer, you might partake of the sensation so many of us have, that we may as well give up, that there's no hope of keeping up. Early on, writers like Hempel and Raymond Carver—although there are differences in their styles—were called minimalists (a pejorative?), but their influence has so permeated the culture that their linguistic rigor, the lack of sentimentality and judgment, might just as easily be called good writing.

Disclosure: I was once a student of Amy Hempel's. I scratched and clawed to get into her class after I read "In the Cemetery Where Al Jolson Is Buried"—the second time. And the remarkable freedom her work extends to other writers is one of its greatest gifts, the permission to break some rules of conventional narrative. A comment I saw from a reader on the Internet (my apologies to the unknown and hence uncredited author) reflects her/his reaction after reading *The Dog of the Marriage*: "Wow. Can you do that?"

Yes. You can. ✧

Slow Freeze

Laurah Norton Raines

It was the same all summer long. We sat in our apartment because we couldn't afford to go out. We didn't like to do the same things anyhow. You liked pot and video games, and I liked punk-rock shows. You wouldn't take me to see bands because you said the music was too loud. Really, you were afraid you'd get beaten up. So we stayed home.

Every evening you sat out on the deck with a case of PBR; the screen door yawned open so that Johnny Cash drifted out into the atmosphere. You were always cooking something, and it gave you an excuse to drink with impunity. Sometimes you barbecued chicken, mostly breasts because I was dieting. On other nights you charred eggplant; the skins split and seeped as I passed you tumblers of iced tea and whiskey. You smoked so many cigarettes, leaving the filters scattered like rat droppings over the stained concrete. Heat settled into everything.

After dinner, we watched horror movies with the volume turned down, playing records over them until everything muddled into one howling death. It wasn't like we needed dialogue—we'd seen them before. In June and July, I didn't bother shaving my legs. I saw *Texas Chainsaw Massacre* seven times, but I couldn't remember the weight of your body.

In August you got fired. You told me laid off, but I saw the termination papers crumpled up on your dashboard. You had been late too many times. Where were you? We always left our apartment at the same time, you in chef pants printed with chili peppers, me with students' papers and borrowed grown-up clothes. I held my face still when you told me, because of your temper. Our walls were pockmarked with holes. You sulked off anyway, to the bedroom, with your video games and the beer. I didn't know how I would pay the bills, if I would have to call my parents and beg for money. My father didn't like you but was too far away to do anything about it. I was still in grad school; my tiny paycheck barely covered your essentials: marijuana, beer, cable.

I stood in the doorway, watching you watching the TV. Your blond hair had grown so thin. I had gotten fat. When I looked in the cheap mirror mounted on the bedroom door, I saw my body warped. I didn't mention the job again.

In the two weeks after you were fired, you cooked out every single night. You did your best with the tiny porch, with fans—but our furniture began to smell of ash. You made dozens of hamburgers, which sat on plastic plates in the refrigerator until I threw them out. I started paying for groceries with my credit card.

Late August. I came home from the store, still in my work clothes, thinking about whether my students could see my slip when I wrote on the blackboard. They had laughed, but I wasn't sure why. I was a pretend person in a long-sleeved blouse that covered my tattoos, arms laddered with grocery bags full of food I didn't eat. I found you in the bedroom, talking on the cell phone you hadn't consulted me about buying, and when I said hello, you ignored me. You turned your back and put your hand over the mouthpiece. Twenty minutes later I had changed into my Social Distortion T-shirt and tried playing with the dog; she just wanted to sleep. You came out and went out onto the porch to start the grill.

"Who was on the phone?"

"No one."

"Then what? What were you talking about?"

You tell me, "Nothing. You don't have enough to do, that's why you ask me all these stupid questions. You need to do something. Why don't you write anymore?"

I opened my mouth but the words stayed in. You were right. I marked up my students' stories with red pen, wrote questions in the margins: "Where's the epiphany?" "Is there a defining moment?" "What does this character want?" I wanted answers from them. I required exactness. But I didn't write myself. I had tried; I had stared down blank Word documents, typed a sentence, backspaced. Nothing. So I went back to criticizing my students' use of adjectives, of time, of narrative collage. You wouldn't have read my stories anyway.

You grilled the hamburgers, and I fixed salad, cut up onions, toasted buns. We turned on *The Prophecy*, that movie about angels that kill one another and everything else. I pushed ketchup into pools of mustard until my plate was a mess. You reached for your beer, and I noticed you'd shaved off your sideburns. I was the only girlfriend you'd ever had that liked them.

I stacked the dinner dishes, carried them away, dropped them into the sink, and the crashing and the clanking was like a gunshot. I jumped despite myself.

In the unholy fluorescence, among the ruin of peppers and onions and everything, our kitchen was a massacre. The tile looked dirty even after I mopped. Your new cell phone was abandoned on our counter, a sleek and shining beast among the rubble. I didn't know what to do, so I hovered, uninvited, between the kitchen and living room.

I could see you on the couch. You'd put in another movie. I watched closely, but your eyes showed nothing. How many beers had you had? How many had I? I picked up the phone.

My father answered distractedly, and I knew he'd been working in his basement office, probably on his new book. He was successful. He'd paid for my college, my MFA. He had hopes.

"Hello? Hello?" He asked it over and over, like a person without spare time is apt to.

"Can you come and get me?" I said to him when he asked again. "Can you just come get me?"

If you heard me, you showed no sign. The heat rolled over us in waves. On TV, someone died. ✧

from Arrowsmith

Fifty-Two
MELISSA GREEN

Ric's Progress
DONALD HALL

The Kingdom of His Will
CATHERINE PARNELL

Return to the Sea
ETNAIRIS RIVERA
TRANSLATED BY ERICA MENA

Beyond Alchemy
DANIEL BERRIGAN, S.J.

Arrow Breaking Apart
JASON SHINDER

and more...

arrowsmithpress.org

Monster

Rebekah Frumkin

Most of the time the panther slept. Its breaths were resonant and shallow in the apartment. Perhaps it was sick; Danny couldn't tell. His mother and father never heard it. When he looked up from his breakfast and cocked his head one way, they told him to go back to eating. He awakened his father in the middle of the night to tell him about it. "There is an animal in our house," he said. His father rolled over onto his side and said, "Danny, honey, I don't know if there's a new bully at school, but you need to tell him to stop picking on you." It was almost dawn. Danny was alarmed by his father's apathy. He couldn't believe such a tall, smart man would be willing to risk his family's lives just to get some sleep. "Who will be here to pour milk on my breakfast tomorrow?" Danny asked. "There is nothing in our house but us," his father said.

When Danny came home from school, he gave himself the job of trying to find the panther. He started in the kitchen, the north star of his compass, and waited for the breathing. It was a raspy breathing, like a grandfather's. Sometimes it spoke. These days were particularly frightening, and Danny always thanked the afternoon sun for being out. When the panther spoke, it said, "Kill me for the fun of it."

Or it said, "I'm very tired."

Or it said, "I'm under your chair right now."

It said all these things in the raspy grandfather's voice. It sounded like it smoked the Havana cigars Danny's father used to favor. Danny listened to it and wondered what it wanted. He knew from the start that he wouldn't be heard if he spoke back. He sat at the kitchen table like a pilot in his cockpit. If the breathing got louder, his neck started to tingle and he knew the panther was right behind him. He could feel the wetness of the animal's nostrils, the heavy abandon of its paws. He thought he'd go deaf from listening so much.

One day at school Mrs. Welles was smiling broadly as her class took their seats. She told them something that didn't matter to them, something about talking to the principal and the other second-grade teacher for a long time.

"We will do a pen pal project," she said, the first thing they listened to.

Marcus, whom everybody hated, raised his hand. "Do we have to write to them first?"

"Let me explain," Mrs. Welles said. "Our pen pals live in Tangier, which is a city in Morocco. They go to the Darul Arqam School. We have been chosen to write to them because we are a magnet school, and all of you are excellent writers. They have sent us the first batch of letters. We will write letters back and forth for the next nine months. In May we'll get to meet our pen pals. They will fly to America and then spend three weeks here as part of an exchange program. We have been given the job of introducing them to our country before they come."

Emma, the girl who sat next to Danny, jabbed him in the ribs. "They can't speak English," she whispered.

At the end of the day Mrs. Welles gave them the first batch of letters. Danny opened his. The letter was written in blue pen, in cursive, and had a picture of a dove drawn at the top.

Dear Pen Pal,
I am named Djamel Abd al-Hakiim. My last name means "servant of the wise." We are learning to speak the American langage.

Danny turned the letter over. There was nothing else. The bell rang and he stayed in his seat. Emma sat down next to him and looked at him, her eyes wide. She kissed him on the cheek.

"Stop it," he said.

"Mine's named Aisha," she whispered, ignoring him. "She has a pet monkey."

"No, she doesn't."

Emma produced a letter. Aisha had written six paragraphs. At the bottom she'd pasted a picture of a scrawny, hairy thing.

"It's her pet," Emma said.

At home Danny put the letter from Djamel up on the refrigerator. Then he opened the door and got out a carton of milk. There was a sudden loudness, the noise of glasses rattling. The kitchen became a threatening mauve. Danny held his breath and looked into the living room. His father was reading the paper; he had set a tray out in front of him with a variety of glass bottles, some orange and some red.

"What're you drinking?" his father asked.

A sudden warmth flooded Danny's body, leaving his fingers tingling. "I'm having cookies," he said. He realized he hadn't really answered the question. "I just poured milk."

"I'm having a mixture of things," his father said. "Your mother won't be home for a while."

Danny almost corrected him, but he knew better. His father was not to be corrected. If Danny's mother wouldn't be home for a while, then Danny's mother would be staying out until midnight. As if by fault of a weak foundation, a smile cracked across his father's face.

"Danny, sit down here. Come sit down next to me."

Danny did.

"How was your day at school?"

"It was all right."

They sat in silence. Danny's father reached down and planted his hand on Danny's head. He began to pet Danny with heavy strokes. This lasted until Danny's hair became a disorganized nest, and his father looked down at him and grinned.

"You'll come back tomorrow and tell me how school went?"

Danny nodded. He stood up and went back into the kitchen. His father had begun humming a melody that would have been operatic had he opened his mouth to sing. Outside, a truck coming from the East Loop buckled loudly beneath its cargo. Danny became aware of the dull throb of radio voices in the living room, a noise that had been going on since he got home. He positioned three cookies on a plate and looked out the window at the sky. The sun was painfully bright, probably afraid to give up summer. He wanted to tell his father about this, or at least see if he had noticed it, and he leaned into the living room to announce his discovery apropos the sun. His father was not sitting in the chair. The panther had taken his place. It wore his father's robe and socks and held his father's glass of colors.

"You're here." It was all Danny could think to say.

The panther smiled, showing two rows of fragile, conical teeth. "I'm usually here." This was the first time it had responded to anything Danny said.

"You took my father's spot."

"I did."

"Did you eat him?"

It laughed at this. Danny couldn't recall having said anything funny.

"Did you eat him?"

"Of course not. How inelegant would that be? I've merely thrown him out the window."

Danny felt something catch in his throat. The panther set the glass of colors down and gestured to the window. Danny walked forward and pulled up the blinds. There was something on the pavement that looked like the remains of a baby bird. It had the wings and beak of a pigeon and the eyes and thin-lipped mouth of Danny's father.

Danny looked at the panther. "Is he dead?"

"Yes," it said.

He looked back out the window. A small pool of blood had formed around the bird. The blood was the deepest sort of crimson Danny had ever seen.

"I'll tell the police about you," he said.

The panther laughed again. It crossed its legs, and the floor shifted with the terrifying weight of a real man.

Danny knew he had to tell his mother, but she wasn't home anymore to be told. She was usually teaching at the university. When she was home, she wanted to go straight to the kitchen to work on Danny's tux. She had decided a month ago that Danny needed a fancy outfit and had gone out and bought him a "crisp white shirt and a roll of the finest black silk," the latter of which she intended to make into a jacket. She had not given any thought to the pants. There was no reason for Danny to want or need formalwear, but he liked standing on the table while his mother pulled at the hem of his jacket, which sat on him Tarzan-like without a row of buttons.

While Danny's mother worked, Danny's father stood in the doorway or sat in a chair with his hands on his knees. The wife and son were two free agents independent of his influence. He could comment on the jacket, on how nice the fabric was, he could ask if anyone wanted dinner, but he never got a response. Ignored thusly, he left the room and started making noise elsewhere in the apartment. He was always back in the kitchen doorway ten or fifteen minutes later. He was a failure. The place had a magnetic pull on him.

Danny's mother told Danny to smile and said he looked like a Nobel laureate. She wrapped her hands around his waist to take a measurement of his hips. From above she looked older than she was. Danny could see pieces of silver in her hair. She was beautiful, but in a hidden way. She wore a strong prescription for farsightedness. She was always having to adjust her eyes to see Danny. When he was far away, she put her glasses on her head to see him. When he was close, she had to wear the glasses and squint at him through them. Her eyes were huge, and white halos of light ringed her eyebrows when she looked up at him from below. The glasses ruined her face. Danny would gladly guide her by the hand if she ever chose to give them up.

It was because his mother had such difficulty seeing that he didn't want to tell her about the panther. But it was necessary, it was important; if he didn't tell her, she'd die. While she worked on his tux jacket, while his father leaned in the doorway, Danny decided he couldn't postpone it any longer.

"There's no such thing as a creature living in our house," his mother said. "I'd know, honey."

"I'd be the first to know," his father said.

Danny looked over at his father. He was forlorn, bearlike.

"But it's hard to recognize because it acts like a person," Danny said.

"Are you having these dreams again?" His mother smiled a little. "When I was little, I used to dream that I lived in a house of water. Everything in the house was liquid, and all of my toys were this really bright aquamarine. I couldn't touch anything without my hand going right through, but everyone else could."

"Could what?" his father asked.

"Could touch things," she said without looking at him. "I was completely powerless. I felt like a ghost."

Danny could feel the cold pressure of a pin against his side. There was a sharpness, and he winced. He placed two fingers under the jacket and then put them in his mouth. His mother had accidentally drawn his blood.

"I'm so sorry," she said.

He shook his head. He could feel tears forming in his eyes. His father turned around and went into the living room. The dusk made a specter of his huge frame.

"Danny, you have to put pressure on it," his mother said. She pressed her hand deep into his side. Danny thought he could feel his bones shifting.

"Don't prick me again," he said. She nodded.

**

Dear Djamel,

I go to a school called the Lab School Lower School. It is ~~is~~ in Chicago wich is a city in Illinois. I am in the second grade. I like to play chess with my dad and meet new frends. My teacher says you are from Morocco, and that you are very smart. Plese tell me about what you have to eat there.

Yours,

Daniel J. Fein II

**

On a very rainy morning Mrs. Welles announced to the class that she was pregnant. She said jokingly that many of the preschool students had been asking her why she was looking fatter lately.

"I didn't think you could tell yet, but I guess you all could. I'm carrying a baby."

She smiled a haphazard smile that made Danny nervous.

"Can we feel it kicking yet?" a girl asked.

Mrs. Welles frowned. "It's just a shrimp now. We don't know if it's a boy or a girl."

"It looks like a shrimp?" Emma asked.

"Sort of, Emma. Do you all know that you start from a single cell that divides over and over again into many cells? A zygote?"

Marcus wanted to know how big a single cell was. A skinny girl in the front row reached across her desk to touch Mrs. Welles's stomach. The girl reeled back in delight.

"It's hard!" she said. "Hard like a rock!"

Danny walked home by himself in the rain. When he opened the door, the panther was standing on its haunches in the kitchen, reading Djamel's letter. Danny held his breath. Maybe catching the panther while it was distracted would make it go away.

"Were you busy at school?" it asked.

"I only answer questions like that when my dad asks them," Danny said.

The panther nodded and opened the freezer, staring at something pink.

"What are you doing?"

"Nothing," it said. It still hadn't turned around. "The refrigerator is pregnant too."

Danny set his backpack down. The panther turned, making obvious the gruesome curvature of its spine. It was a hunchback today with a C-shaped neck.

"Pregnant with what?"

The panther said nothing. Danny stood on a chair and looked into the freezer. An infant was frozen in a block of ice, its spine bony like a crustacean's. It was breathing somehow, and it blinked every so often. A blue cord connected it at the belly to the ice machine.

"This refrigerator is pregnant," the panther said again. Danny didn't know why, but this made him cry. Tears froze on his cheeks and stung his skin. The panther reached a paw into the freezer to touch the frozen child.

Breathless, Danny stood at his mother's bedside.

"You can't keep ignoring it!" he said. "The panther put a baby in the fridge."

"What?" his mother asked. She kept her eyes closed when she spoke to him. "It's nighttime, Danny."

"There's a baby in the fridge. I saw it just now."

"You were dreaming," Danny's mother said.

"The panther was reading my pen pal letter."

Danny's mother opened her eyes. She put her glasses on and stood up. She walked without bending her knee joints, half her body still asleep. She was pushing Danny into his room. He lay down in bed and she sat next to him.

"Will you go look in the kitchen?" he asked.

"Yes. As soon as you fall asleep, I'll check to see if it put a baby in the fridge."

Danny closed his eyes. He didn't want her to go, and he fidgeted every time the mattress threatened to leaven with her departure. He knew that she'd leave eventually, though, no matter how much he fidgeted. He knew he'd have to think of Mrs. Welles, and he'd have to imagine her stomach soft and sagging without a child in it. He would get in trouble for stealing her baby.

Danny was falling asleep. This was hard to postpone. Sleep was a demanding audience that insisted he stage dreams every night. His mother left the mattress slowly. He could feel himself rise. He grabbed the back of her shirt. She had to know by now that he was awake. She didn't. She stood up and went from the room without looking back. He saw a crescent of light blink on in the kitchen, and he watched her shadow. She was getting something from the cabinet. The light blinked off, and she hadn't checked the freezer. Danny pulled the covers up around his neck. She was too scared. She knew the truth.

Danny counted four weeks before Djamel sent him anything back. When he did send something, it wasn't a letter. The only thing in the envelope was a picture of two children with skin the color of bark, a boy and a girl. The boy looked to be about Danny's age, with large eyes and a tall column of black hair. The girl was small, maybe four or five. Both of them were bare chested and wet as if from a recent bath. The girl pointed to a hole in her mouth where she'd lost a tooth. Blood covered her lower lip. The boy looked at her as though she were a stranger, but he held her by the shoulders. There was a nervous excitement in the girl's face. Her cheeks were blotched from crying.

Danny put the picture in his backpack. He spent recess inside while the other children ran beneath the sky, which was a swollen dome of gray. He wrote three drafts of a letter and finally decided on one he liked:

> Djamel,
> There is a monster that lives in my house. It is a panther. My parent's don't think it is real. It has gigantic paws and oringe eyes. I'm very frihtened of it, since it wants to kill everything. I dream about it a lot.
> Yours,
> Daniel J. Fein II

When he was done, he watched Mrs. Welles through the window. She had begun to wear long dresses with pleats just below the bust. Her stomach was a small hill, upon which she rested both hands. Danny wondered if she had to stuff the bulge with cotton to keep it so large. He wondered how the baby had gotten in there in the first place, and imagined Mrs. Welles and a faceless man who was Mrs. Welles's husband standing naked in a room with a lot of sunshine, holding a wet infant between them. They rocked it to sleep and they rocked it awake and they never left the spot where they stood.

Danny's mother stopped being home enough to work on the tuxedo jacket, and Danny began to worry. He worried while watching cartoons, and his father mixed drinks of colors and said nothing. They never spoke. They let the TV speak. Every sound effect, joke, and indignant whistle contributed to their afternoon lingua franca. Sometimes Danny's father would attempt eloquence by trying to speak with his eyes and mouth. He would look at Danny as if to say, *We are damned, and there is nothing we can do about it.* When Danny's mother finally came home at eight or nine or ten, the silence was broken. A new and frightening foreign tongue was introduced. She spoke loudly about overeager students keeping her until all hours, talking about semiotics. She smelled like earth and dry flesh. When she was done taking off her coat and boots, she went down the hall to the master bedroom and called Danny's father, who rose from the couch majestically. They spoke together for a while, and the speaking became sharp; eventually they were yelling. This happened for several nights. Danny thought of Mrs. Welles's infant on these nights. He thought of what the noise in his house might sound like from inside the womb. He could only imagine the *thrum, thrum, thrum* of a woman's heartbeat. He held his chest and felt the pulse beneath his hands, drumlike, explosive.

"When will the baby be born?" he asked Mrs. Welles during class.

She had never heard him ask about the baby before. His question came as a surprise. "In four months. In the summertime, when you don't have school anymore."

Danny watched her touch the mound. She invited him to feel the child move. He didn't want to.

"I only want to see it when it's out of you," he said. "When it's alive."

"What do you mean, Danny?"

Some giggles could be heard from the back. One boy was practicing his whistling.

"I want to make sure it isn't dead inside of you. You know, from all the noise."

Nothing happened for a long time, and then Danny felt himself being pulled by the collar somewhere. Mrs. Welles was taking him to the principal. This sudden rift in their intimacy stunned him, and he felt betrayed.

"You are never to speak like that to me again," she said. Her face was dark. Her words sounded like barking. "Do you hear me, Mr. Fein?"

"I was just thinking about all the noise."

She stood up and left him at the office door. He thought he could see her crying.

When he came home from school that day, the baby was back in the freezer. It had grown since he'd last seen it. It had human features now: a smooth spine, toes, and fingers.

Djamel's second letter was shorter than his first:

Dear Daniel,
There was a lot of rain this week so that we never had playtime. During prayer today, I wished for your health.
Djamel Abd al-Hakiim

Djamel had drawn a picture of the boy he thought Danny was. The boy had blond hair and a large pair of glasses. His smile was an orange gash halfway across his face. A catlike black mass lurked behind him. Danny looked at the picture for a long time. Then he took a piece of paper from inside his desk and wrote "Dear Djamel" at the top. He erased it. He wrote the rest of the letter without thinking.

I bet there is a monster that follows you too.
Yours,
Daniel J. Fein II

Emma was looking at him. She smiled. It was easy to tell from her smile how she'd looked as a toddler.

"You're pale," she said.

"I know."

"You sad, Danny?"

Danny didn't say anything.

"You'll be all right," she said. He could smell something like lilacs on her breath. "It'll be all right."

Ren knocked on Danny's door one afternoon when neither of Danny's parents were home. He had the loose joints and lazy, haggard face of a teenager. He had white hair, which he wore long under a ski cap, and a white goatee. He smiled when Danny answered, and Danny saw that he was missing both his front teeth.

"Does Professor Fein live here?" he asked. His eyes were glassy. "She gave me this address."

Danny watched him.

"Hey, little big man?"

"Professor Fein isn't home for another hour."

The teenager stood for a while, processing what he'd heard. When he was done, he offered his hand to shake.

"I'm Ren Wrolstad," he said.

Danny shook. He didn't introduce himself.

"Can I come in, Lieutenant?"

"Yes."

Ren stood in the kitchen and then looked in the living room. He wasn't satisfied with appreciating a room when he was actually in it; he always had to eavesdrop on the creaks and rattles of another room from afar. He did this in the living room, then the hallway, then in Danny's room. When he got to the master bedroom, however, he stopped pining for different rooms. He went to Professor Fein's vanity and began playing with her jewelry boxes. He tried several different perfumes on his neck until he sniffed with satisfaction—*That's the one*—and set the bottle down.

"Eau de lilac," Ren said. "So your mother smells good, right?"

Danny nodded. All he could see of Ren were his eyes, which glimmered a little when they caught the light from the window. Trucks drove by, casting obtuse, moving shadows on the opposite wall. One of these became the panther's uneven silhouette. It was sitting in a corner at the back of the room. It batted a paw against the wall and moved its mouth without speaking. It had metal teeth tonight, the top row golden and the bottom row bronze.

Danny almost screamed, but not because he was scared. He was angry now. The creature had appeared with a stranger in the house, the perfect time to make Danny look crazy. "There's a monster behind you," he whispered.

"Oh yeah? What kind?"

"A panther. A panther that lives in my house." It was an embarrassed confession.

Ren sat down carefully. He was so close that Danny could feel their foreheads touching.

"Don't turn around," Danny said.

"Is it real?"

"Yes."

"You want me to fight it?"

"Yes."

The air became thick, unbreathable, and time slowed as Ren turned around to fight the panther. This would be the end. Danny knew it would be the end because he was good at judging the beginning and end of things. He felt the finality, he felt Ren's strength, he felt the fibers of his own muscles stretch and ache with nervousness. There was a crashing noise, and a geometric beam of light was cast across the room. Danny's father was in the doorway, arms folded. He was home early from work. He looked at Danny and then Ren.

"Are you him?" Danny's father asked Ren.

Ren said, "*Jesus.*"

Danny's father grabbed Ren's collar and pulled him from the floor so fast his neck almost snapped. Then he took him to the kitchen. When Danny came out of the bedroom, Ren's face was a mosaic of purple and red, and his breaths were short and tortured.

***

Dear Daniel,

You are afrayed, afrayed. I know it because you write to me like that. Remember: Only the bravest and wisest amonge us gets rewarded.

Djamel Abd al-Hakiim

***

Danny's mother started to be home every day, right when Danny got home. Danny stopped making snacks for himself and let his mother toast the bread, wash the apples, put the dishes in the dishwasher. He stood on the kitchen table and ate a peanut butter sandwich while his mother made adjustments to his tuxedo jacket. She pinned a felt rose to his lapel. Danny watched birds out the kitchen window. He counted four, ten, twelve pigeons, all of them flying straight up. He wondered how free they'd be, whether they'd meet the edge of the sky and burst into heaven, or singe their feathers and fall while trying to pass through the clouds.

He didn't write to Djamel for months. Djamel didn't write back. Mrs. Welles made the class sit in a circle and discuss what they had learned about Morocco: The flag is red with a green star. The motto is "God, Country, King." They eat mint, olives, and couscous for dinner. When you are a Muslim, you must follow the five pillars of Islam. You have to go to a mosque. The parents in the poor towns kill baby lambs right in front of the children. If they have to learn English, we should learn Arabic. Casablanca is a big city.

Mrs. Welles nodded. "Someone share something else they've learned. Someone who hasn't spoken."

Danny looked up at Mrs. Welles. He could barely see her face over her stomach.

"Mr. Fein?"

"My pen pal has nothing to tell me."

The whole class looked at him. Emma broke her posture to crawl to him, but Mrs. Welles wouldn't let her go.

"Why is that?"

Danny was silent.

Mrs. Welles scrutinized him and then leaned back in her chair. She rubbed her stomach. There was an oppressive silence that the class seemed unable to bear. She called on another student who hadn't spoken.

That night Danny felt something warm and heavy on his shoulder.

"Are you asleep yet?" it asked.

"What?"

There was a claw at his back, then one at his side.

"Don't prick me," he said.

"Wake up!" The panther's scream was furious. "Wake up!"

Danny turned over. The creature was lying in his bed, stretched long from post to post. He tried to get out, but it grabbed his shoulders.

"Don't leave or I'll get lonely."

"You're going to kill me," Danny said. "You've gotten sick of me."

The panther said nothing. It didn't even smile.

"I thought you were gone last time. What did you do?"

A cacophony of grinding metal ensued as it opened its mouth, which was mechanized tonight. Danny could see a steel tongue and jaws.

"What am I going to do?" it asked. Sparks flew in its mouth.

"No. What did you do?"

It pointed a claw at Danny's eye. He would be losing his sight. The panther was going to blind him. The claw stabbed his left eye, then his right. He blinked. He could see only the explosion of his vision, a webbed haze of red, then white, finally black. His head felt swollen. He kicked his feet against the covers. He could hear the creature breathing; he felt its tongue against his cheek, licking what tears or blood he could still muster from his damaged eyes. He tried to punch the creature, but his hands passed through it as through water.

Then there was someone's hand on his forehead, the heavy meter of adult breathing.

"Danny, honey," his father said. "Danny, you were yelling."

Danny pressed his fists against his eyes. His father would not like to see this. "I'm blind," he said.

"You're what?"

"I'm blind. The panther blinded me. It came when I was sleeping and stuck its claws in my eyes."

Danny started to cry the sort of climactic cry that invokes colors and shapes and skinny lines of neon. Danny's father pulled his son's hands from his face and pried his eyes open. He turned on a light. He waited for the pupils to get smaller. They did.

"You're not blind," he said. "Don't cry." He kissed Danny on the forehead and laid his head in the space between his son's chin and bent elbow. He waited until the wails became hiccups. Expressionless, Danny watched his father's face move as he spoke.

"Danny?" he said. His mouth was out of sync with his words. "You can see. You can see me."

Mrs. Welles's stomach had become so large and hard that it threatened to rip her skin apart. She never stood up from her chair to help the class with fractions or diagramming sentences. One afternoon she left for a doctor's appointment. She didn't come back for two weeks. The substitute was a short, thin man named Mr. Song. He wrote his name on the chalkboard and then told the class that Mrs. Welles was having problems with her baby. Someone asked him what kind of problems, and he said big ones. Bad ones. He'd have to accompany the class to the airport to meet the children from the Darul Arqam School.

Danny saw it when he opened the freezer to take out a Popsicle. The oppressive cold, the metal railings of the fridge like the edges of an examination table, the child's stomach girded with its umbilical cord. No breathing, no crying. A faceless, senseless blob of infant. A smear of jaundice covering its eyes. The block of ice latticed with white cracks.

On the day he would meet Djamel, Danny's mother sent him to school in the tuxedo jacket. Mr. Song gave each student a piece of construction paper on which to write the name of his or her pen pal. Danny wrote "Djamel" in black marker. They took their papers with them to the bus, everyone laughing and throwing things at one another. Emma came up behind Danny and held his hand.

"Aren't you excited?"

"Yeah."

She giggled. She made him sit in a seat with her and grabbed his chin so he wouldn't look out the window. She had stretch pants and ribboned hair and a runny nose. She licked her upper lip. She had lost a tooth, most likely in the middle of the night, when she wouldn't feel pain.

"Aisha says she's going to bring me a flower necklace. She wrote me a letter about how I'm her sister."

The bus lurched, and they drove.

"She wants to meet you, too. I told her about you."

Danny nodded.

"She thinks you're like a brother."

Emma laid her head on his shoulder, and he looked out the window. He could feel her breathing, and for a moment he believed he could synchronize their breaths.

They waited at the end of the airport for international flights, in front of a door labeled RABAT. There was a vulcanized hiss, and a henlike matron appeared from inside the terminal, dressed in a pantsuit and scarf. A line of children followed her. It looked as if she had taken pains to Americanize them: they wore shorts and Velcro sandals, with shirts that advertised movie stars and beverages. They all looked tired and confused. Danny's class began to scream the names of their pen pals, holding the signs over their heads. Emma found Aisha and hugged her, whispered into her ear over her shoulder. The boys matched up with other boys, high-fived, offered each other metal cars and bottle caps. The girls stood across from each other at arm's length and compared bracelets and told each other secrets. Mr. Song shook hands with the matron and apologized that Mrs. Welles had to miss the occasion. Danny searched among the faces, all of them older looking than his, all of them thin lipped, and tried to see Djamel. He kept his sign behind his back.

The matron was dragging a stunned boy by the hand. His movements were mechanical, puppetlike, and he appeared to be dancing next to her as she moved with him. She stood him in front of Danny and announced that he was Djamel Abd al-Hakiim. Danny looked at him. He had a sunken face and very thick skin. He wore dark glasses. He was a withered version of the boy in the picture. The matron told them they'd get along fine. She said Djamel was very tired because he had been fasting for three days. She didn't say why.

"I'll leave you two boys alone." She smiled and left.

Djamel took off his glasses and looked directly into the sun.

"It's setting," Danny said. "It's almost nighttime here."

Djamel blinked and looked at Danny. "A monster chases you, Daniel?"

Danny said nothing.

"A monster is chasing you. I thought about it on the plane. A monster is chasing you, and it is trying to kill you."

Danny sighed. "Yes."

Djamel put his hand on Danny's shoulder. He hung his head and arched his back.

"You are afraid," he said.

Danny nodded.

"Your heart beats fast? When you are dreaming?"

"Yes."

Somewhere far off, the other children had begun to sing a song in Arabic. Their voices were a symphony of colors: reds, purples, oranges, greens.

"Do you dream of heaven?"

"Once, maybe."

"You will look into my eyes?"

The boy raised his head and stared at Danny. His eyes were clouded, his pupils drowned. He looked to be asleep.

"You see it?"

Danny searched. He didn't know what he was looking for. He could feel Djamel's hand trembling as it gripped his shoulder. "See it?"

And Danny saw it at last, swathed in steam and smoke and dust. He imagined windows, staircases, the sounds of parents' voices. He could hear himself crying as a newborn. He imagined sky—cold, gray expanses of it—clouds weighty but soft. Then Djamel coughed and fell, and Danny caught him. He barely weighed anything at all.

"You've seen it?"

Danny nodded. Noises began to come back: the sounds of feet moving, whispers and screams, engines throttling. In the distance a plane took off from the runway, its nose pointed triumphantly toward the sky. ✧

Breathless, My Venom Spent, I Lay Down My Weapons

Sarah Murphy

So many winters, dear reader, forging through the snow,
ice-rimed and chiming with cold. So many nights, keeled
in ether, steeped in sleet. Shattered, shackled, craggy,
and daft, I fought, and fought again, with bows and arrows,

with stones. My eyes sewn and swollen, sealed in frost.
My hands wind-torn and slivered. And my bones worn
and whittled, loathed and hollow, frail as moss. I salted
my wounds and walked, I laced my veins with razors,

traced my pulse with knives. Steel-eyed and dreaming
of coal. Reader, I would have done anything to find
the past, that ravaged mass of asters. I had the map,
the lantern, the flag. I wrapped my feet in rags.

The snow was a chant, a hammer, a rain of needles and bees.
Staving off terror, I lay in wait. I carved my path in the dark.
I was beyond reason, reader, my heart snared and bitten, baring
its teeth. My heart, rabid, blistered, heavy with salt. Then,

in the seventh season, I woke in the fevered darkness, spine
on fire, eyes filled with smoke. The past was standing over me,
sloe-eyed stranger in a heavy cloak. He came, as ever,
silent as stars, or singing. He came offering me his city,

its streets unfolding like the sea, its towers, its turrets, its spires
bathed in light. Its ginger and lilies, its rising sun. He smelled
like crushed mint, like cinnamon. His hair was the color of fire.
Reader, I admit I listened, bone-numb and shivering. And reader,

his skin! It glowed like molten glass, like melted honey, like a bolt
of gold. I admit I considered it. But, reader, so many mornings
down on my knees and pleading, my hands filled with ash. Nights
frozen in the slope of silence, its ice. So reader, I married him

to the knife, to the dagger, to the lance. I cast him down the ladder.
To the garden, mauled and fallen. To the loam, to the toads! At last,
the bride unbridled, the queen of ether, little sister death. And then,
breathless, my venom spent, I lay down my weapons and wept.

Horoscope

Sarah Murphy

I'm hoarse from roaring, my sword
gorged with gore. In short, I abhor
you, need I say more? I've scorched
the borders, I've torched the door,

the boats, the scrolls, the stormy shores.
What's my reward? Horror, the horror,
the hordes on all fours. I was born for
glory, then ignored. More and more,

a morsel of remorse. The war is over,
the corpses cold, my orders aborted,
fortune told. Lord of fire, hoarding
coal. Gorgeous forger, stolen gold:

I swore you sold my soul for a song. But
what if I forced it? What if I'm wrong?

More Real Than Reality: The Frozen Art of Alistair MacLeod

Jon Clinch

In "Winter Dog," the centerpiece of Alistair MacLeod's mighty and mightily humane short story collection, *Island*, a boy and his fractious dog lose themselves on an ice sheet and find upon it a frozen seal, lodged in the ice, staring straight ahead toward land. "Even now in memory it seems more real than reality," says the narrator, the boy himself now grown to manhood, "as if it were transformed by frozen art into something more arresting than life itself."

All you need to know about Alistair MacLeod's work, and about why his stories affect me more deeply than most anyone else's, is present in that image and that observation. The simplicity of the language; the understated implication of constant peril in a hard physical world; the shocking contrast between the living and the dead; the notion of the sea as the source of all things mysterious and extraordinary; the framing of a remote story within a very present one; and above all the sure belief that by means of art the past can be captured and understood and perhaps even brought to life once again.

Consider the smallest detail, his choice of that word *arresting*. MacLeod desires everywhere to *stop* things. To stop our heedless and hurried forward progress. To stop the slow decay of forgetting. He wants us to pause and to wait and to look, and he wants us by looking to understand and above all to remember. In many ways his goal is the impossible one shared by certain characters in Mark Helprin's *Winter's Tale*: "to stop time and bring back the dead." Except that MacLeod actually manages the trick.

Exactly how, I cannot say.

I *can* say that he returns time and again to certain subjects and motifs. The passage of time. The conflicting desires of the young and the old. The loss of rural tradition. The secret knowledge and habits of small groups of people set apart.

His stories—and *Island* collects every one of them, a lifetime of reflection and attempted resurrection assembled into a single volume—his stories are set among the stubborn and hardworking and isolated people of Cape Breton. They follow young men leaving the coast to pursue the attractions of the city, and old men returning to the coast in search of histories and families long abandoned. They show us the perils and pleasures of lives lived in boats on the sea and in tunnels beneath the earth. And they share with us the ineffable private and public joys of music, "the lubricant of the poor all over the world."

Above all, they give us the sense of truth. MacLeod's narrators are often old men, or at least mature men of some experience and gravity, drawn by the events of a present moment to look back upon some particular scene from their youth. This framing device, which MacLeod returns to again and again, is grounding and disorienting at the same time. The narrator of "Winter Dog," for example, is prompted to tell the story of his troublesome dog and the danger on the ice and the eventual unstoppable death of that strange misfit creature by the sight of his own children, risen early on Christmas morning, out playing in the snow. "It is almost as if they have danced out of the world of folklore like happy elves," he says. "I am tempted to check the recently vacated beds to confirm what perhaps I think I know."

And even in that small image we sense another circling back to the past, another frame within a frame, another conflation of the things of this world with the things of some other. Such is MacLeod's gift, and such in turn is his gift to us. ✧

(Unexpurgated) Tour Journal

Wesley Stace, John Wesley Harding, and George Fisher (of Henley)

Monday, August 20, 2007
George Fisher vs. MySpace: The Pre-Bumbershoot Blog

Bumbershoot is my favourite festival in America and I'm doing triple duty this year: panel on Sunday, a gig (under the name John Wesley Harding) that night, and then reading from my new novel *by George* on the Monday.

A little background: the George of the title, or one of the two, is a ventriloquist dummy, who (which?) narrates half of the novel. George is not just based on, but is, a "real" dummy who (which!) belonged to my grandfather. And the actual George will be accompanying me on tour. You can see him here: www.myspace.com/bygeorgefisher.

The best thing that happened in pre-publicity was that MySpace featured the first chapter, narrated by George (as though it were his own blog), for a week on their books front-page.

This had the immediate effect of sending a few thousand people a day to George's site, rather than the usual two or three. And these new visitors were, I think, rather more typical of MySpace than George's usual select clientele. And they left lots of comments under the blog, and these are worth appreciating in full.

There was a lot of very polite "I liked it" etc. The first question was "When does the book come out?" to which came the reply: "It's already out!!! Yay," which I thought a little odd, because it simply wasn't true.

Anyway, there was the occasional off-the-wall classic—and I'm respelling some of these for the public good—("Wretched nubile flesh corrugating the souls of mankind"), the casual ("Yeah I'm sexy"), and the blasé ("i got dis buuk like lazt wkk"); a few pointed remarks ("this is fucked up you should not publicize these kinds a things"); a little literary criticism ("in the beginning it is usual, nothing special, but then you used details that make the story more interesting"), and even a mini-debate about my use of a quotation from *David Copperfield*—the first chapter of *DC* is called "I Am Born," so my chapter, because George is a dummy, is called "I Am Built" and uses the same first line to, one would hope, comic effect. This did not escape keen eyes: "your beginning sounds a lot like david copperfield." It even provoked an accusation: "a word for word copy! plagerism?"

Then someone said: "I just finished reading the book it was sweet so many twists and the Epilogue!" which was great to hear, but weird because it seemed unlikely that this commenter would have an advance copy and, besides, *by George* doesn't have an epilogue. And somebody replied: "i cant believe this is the last book i love them but i hate how so many people die as we're speaking my friend is finishin up the book right now we are takin a break so I can write this letter ok got to finish up the last chapter!" (Followed by 25 exclamation marks.) Others agreed: "lmfao, I've read the hole book, got it the very first night finished it two days later, it the best one i think."

And that's when the penny finally dropped: these people who had finished the book, hadn't finished my book. They'd finished A book. But it wasn't just any book, they'd finished THE Book—*Harry Potter*.

But nobody had mentioned *Harry Potter*, or made any reference to it, on the entire page. And though *George* does have similarities to *Harry Potter*—part of it is set in a prep school, though the magic is all sleight of hand rather than spells and a "load of all warlocks"—it was then that I realized that people just saw the phrase "the book" and, as once they may have assumed it was, say, the Bible, so they now assume it is by J. K. Rowling. And this led to the horrible realization that, if they see any publicity for any book anywhere, they just assume it's for *Harry Potter*. Which in a way is fair enough, I suppose.

And when, beneath a blog written from the point of view of a ventriloquist dummy, that very first person had kindly asked: "i can't wait to hear more, george....??when does the novel come out??" the first person who answered: "its already out!!! Yay!" had already Pottered out.

Because, after all—and, though this isn't news—look round you at any person, parents and their children alike, next to you on the train, in the airport, sitting at Starbucks: you have never ever seen so many copies of any book simultaneously read. Who would assume that anybody was asking about any other novel?

Wednesday, September 05, 2007
A Guest Blog: George Fisher on His Recent Performances

Goodness, I've just worked harder than I have in fifty-odd years!

It's awfully tiring. To start with, my box, which is not only my digs but my mode of transportation, has been changed. I admit the old Romando one was heavy; too heavy in fact. But I'm worried about this new one—it's a piece of carry-on, in which I am bent double, then wrapped in a green towel that smells rather of dog. Simply isn't sturdy enough! (No calamities as yet, though, so perhaps I shouldn't worry. Touch wood.)

Our first engagement was at a bookshop, which surely must be the biggest one in the world, called Barnes and Noble. (They had over a *thousand* books in there.) First surprise: we were in America! Not only that, but the Big Apple itself! I remember all the jokes from the war, but America seems very civil in 2007. My first impression: lots of well-behaved citizens, with simply incredible teeth, drinking from paper cups—there must be a porcelain shortage. This Noble place was where we did our first performance. It went well.

My new ventriloquist is, dare I say it, not terribly good: in fact, he can barely do it at all. But I'll say this for him: people laugh. I don't know WHY they laugh precisely, because they're not hearing any of my real zingers like "I'll have a beacon and eggs" or "Why am I feeling poorly? Because I haven't got any money!" But people seem to like it nonetheless. (And they look at me a little nervously. It used to be QUITE the opposite!) It's a new modern "humor" and perhaps I'm a little behind the times. I'll catch up, have no fear. Oh, perhaps it's just normal humour, but the "u" is missing. We need to put that "u" back in "humor."

Anyway, first he read from my memoirs. (I've had a bit of a sore throat.) And then we did our little routine. And then there was a HECKLER! What the devil! At first, it was a bit awkward—we were taken aback and didn't have the necessary comebacks—but then I realised what I should have known all the time: it was Cecil, at the hands of the humanly female Carla Rhodes. He's somehow also pitched up in New York City at the same time, and apparently went out of his way to come to Noble's just to heckle me! It all harks back to a rather unsavory incident on Brighton's West Pier in 1939, which involved Cecil, me and a purloined stick of Brighton Rock, which resulted in some rather unpleasant daubing. At the reading, we made a rather unhappy peace and he shut up so I could continue. There'll be more to this story, I'm sure. (I expunged him from my memoirs entirely—on the basis that any publicity is good publicity—and that may also be the root of the trouble.)

Then it was back in the box, a lot of bumping around, and I'm suddenly in some kind of speakeasy or gin palace, and everyone's congratulating me, feting me, on my book (at last!) and patting me on the head, and drinking and talking, and stealing free copies from a pile by the door. It was quite the liveliest place I've ever been in. A few people had a little fiddle with me. I don't normally like to be passed like a parcel, but there is a time and a place for everything, and this was it. Call me anything you like, but don't call me churlish. (Note: I had asked Cecil not to come, and he respected this wish. Carla, however, handled me rather nicely. Far be it from me to make Cecil jealous . . . but she could do better than him.)

Note to self: "Now is the winter of our discount tents!" I wonder if I can work that in somewhere.

Then a long sleep before my palace was unzipped and I was placed on a piano, with a microphone in front of me. It was another public or saloon bar, filled with people, all with funny accents like from *Gone with the Wind*. Harking back to my previous stage experience, I recall the smell of greasepaint, the whoosh of the satin runners, the moths in the footlights: but that era is long gone. Now it's all plain black stages with tape stuck all over them and big microphones—and the worst thing is: NOBODY is wearing evening dress! They all look like they're going to calisthenics class! It's quite casual, and perhaps all a little too . . . "unbuttoned." I think that's the word. But I don't say anything. (With regards to my partner, sartorial standards are quite high, I'm delighted to say.) And we did our "routine"—which he's stolen from Morecambe and Wise, I happen to know—and answered a few questions from these sweet drawling darlings. If this is America, I like it. I am coming to view it as the land of opportunity, where a boy might be a boy. The trouble with the setup of our show at the moment—because he's not very good, you see—is that we're just getting going when it's all over again and I'm back in the box. And this new "Ventriloquial Mime" thing he's trying to shoehorn into the act is, frankly, ridiculous. But, again, I don't say anything. I keeps my peace, like the wise old owl, and the equally wise Scotsman (of yore).

Our next appearance was more like it—a stage, a theatre, footlights (VERY bright), but no curtain—what's wrong with a curtain? I found myself plunked on one of four chairs. And I sat there as the audience trooped in. And they took pictures of me! That was delightful. And I was just wondering how long this was all going to go on, feeling a bit of a lemon, unable to explain myself, when the show began: and on walked my vocal partner, and two attractive women, one of whom read and then started doing clown animals—she could make a dachshund very well, but her giraffe looked exactly the same as her elephant. When one of the balloon animals untied itself and reverted to being a long pink balloon again, she described it, quite frankly, in anatomical terms. (I'll hark back to the word "unbuttoned" if that helps. . . .) And I tell you this: my eyes nearly popped out! I have NEVER heard such language from a female before, let alone on a stage, and I thought that she would probably be escorted from the theatre, and ducked or some such. But everyone simply laughed, as though it was acceptable! And I'll admit: it was funny. Her name was Monica Drake. I found her reading stimulating and I shall make it my business to have her novel, *Clown Girl*, read to me (though I think it will require substantial expurgation, and perhaps the substitution of a few words). The audience also asked questions, and the accent was entirely different. Someone asked a trick question and I sensed the malign hand of Cecil. But no: it was just someone being funny. Audiences are much bolder these days. They used to do exactly what you told them.

One other thing—a major criticism of my previous partner was that he used to let my box (which, let's face it, is my home) become a kind of receptacle for all the ephemera he gathered on our tour during the war. And my new partner is doing exactly the same! Already I am sharing my living quarters with a board book for babies—which actually looks quite good: it's called *Baby, Make Me a Drink!* and it has simple visual cocktail recipes that anyone could understand; a book of essays by someone called Nick Hornby; a book of short stories by Jana Martin; a magazine called *Swivel*; and a small silver record thing that has a collection of "dummy"-themed songs to be played at the readings: "Puppet on a String," "I'm

Your Puppet," and so on. There is also the Ventril-o stamp, some receipts, a copy of my memoirs, a packet of matches and a rather inquisitive ant. And they're all clanking around me the whole time. And I just don't see why they have to be. It's lazy. It's asking for trouble. And it's a little disrespectful. But I don't say anything. At least, I haven't yet.

When it's all going so swimmingly, it seems a shame to be folded in half and wrapped in a dog blanket. But the great news is that my memoirs seem to be making their way around the world. I hear they're going to be translated into Bahasa Indonesian, which is incredible—though it made me sad. I had a pal out there once.

It's been a quiet last few years; since that war, I suppose. But now we're back in the saddle (not literally) and on the road (also not literally). I'm going to enjoy every single moment.

—George Fisher (of Henley)

Monday, October 08, 2007
Trains, Trains and Locomotives

I'm on the 3.51 from London to Oxford, where I am reading to/being grilled by the Blackwell's Book Club. I'm not exactly sure.

It's all part of the UK launch of *by George*, which keeps me here for a week. A trip to the UK is always a pleasure for me, but a dodgy computer has made this one a little more fraught than usual. The laptop had a major freak-out on arrival and had to spend "three to five" days in the Apple Store on Regent Street. To Apple's credit, this turned into no more than 24 hours. However, despite passing all the necessary tests (with its new RAM and Logic Board), it still seems to be doing some mighty strange things. I'm unconvinced. But I shan't go on about it. However, know this—no computer, no blog.

My book party was on Tuesday—a lovely evening featuring friends (some unglimpsed since teen age), family (some unglimpsed since June), and various writers and publishing people (some unglimpsed entirely). And then the next night was a similar do for Nick Hornby's new teen novel, *Slam*. And there's nothing much better than hanging out with old friends with free booze and few speeches. Interviews have been plentiful. The least interesting opened with this exchange: "How long have you lived in America?" "About seventeen years." "Do you regret it?" At this, I looked a little dumbfounded and said: "What an odd way of putting that. I'm still living there. Why do you put it that way?" The interviewer answered: "Because I can't imagine living anywhere but England." I guess I can.

The UK trip, amidst reviews, a little light shopping, and some surprisingly balmy October walks, has had some surprises. For example, keen readers of this diary will know that I glimpsed Martin Freeman (a man who I'm sure doesn't like to be known as "Tim from *The Office*") on Tokyo Station a few weeks ago. There he was, on the same train, later trundling his trolley next to me. I didn't say anything. However, on Monday, when I was standing outside a pub in Soho waiting for my friend, feeling rather useless, like my computer—perhaps it had jet lag too—Martin Freeman again passed by, pushing a baby in a stroller. At that moment, I felt it was time to say something. Partly this was because I was actually looking at Chris Morris at the time—a comedy hero who just happened to be standing there, in grey fatigues, chatting to someone in the rain. So when I saw Martin Freeman, he felt like an old friend. And I mentioned, apropos of nothing, that I'd just seen him on Tokyo Station, and we had a chat, and that was that. Very nice. Imagine my surprise, then, when the next day, in the Apple Store (that's still on Regent Street), I turned around to find Martin Freeman standing next to me, waiting his machine's turn. That was odd, as we remarked. Doubtless, I'll see him in New York sometime in the near future.

We won't need to make a plan. He'll just be there.

This one's for the cognoscenti: my taxi driver on the way to Paddington was Tony. If I tell you he's Tony from the *Up* series, it may mean something. I was excited. I congratulated him. And if you haven't seen the *Up* series, and it means nothing, then do: one of the most important film events of the last 49 years—I won't go into it, but Tony is one of the participants. And every seven years, as he talks about his life, his job, his family, they film him. And here he is, picking me up in my cab. Well, he's a London cabdriver, so perhaps that isn't surprising (and I do believe that Nick Hornby has had the same experience). But he seemed awfully pleased when I asked him if he was he—which he obviously was. He handed me his card: "Taxie Tony." (You can look him up at www.TonyWalker49up.com.) And then he asked me if I could help him get on *I'm a Celebrity! Get Me out of Here!* I was left in the odd position of encouraging him to continue with the *Up* series, but he seems to want more, or different. He has an agent, though—so perhaps they can sort it out. I know way too much about him for him to be my cabdriver: he's trying to be an actor; he was once a jockey; he's just bought a place in Spain; he once said a very memorable thing about the most important three things in life being the three F's: "Friends, Family, and I'll leave the other one to your imagination" or something like that. Normally, all you know about your cabdriver is that they support QPR. I also had lunch at Pizza Express, sitting next to Gemma Redgrave. But after Martin Freeman and Taxie Tony, this was merely a celebrity sighting. London is a very small pond.

My computer hasn't crashed for a long time.

Last time I wrote that, it crashed immediately and I lost most of this blog—there is nothing less pleasant than writing something all over again—and the sentence "My computer hasn't crashed for a long time" was left floating on the frozen screen, taunting me. And I knew I'd have to turn everything off, and thus destroy it all, to get the computer back on. Is that a mended computer? I think not! However, there are only five minutes left on the battery, so we are coming to the end whether I like it or not. We pass through Reading Station as I wait for my battery to die. I stopped here many times when my father lived here. And then again in 1984, when I taught at a local school. I remember returning very late from a John Hiatt concert at the Half Moon, Putney. I really liked John Hiatt then. That gig was important to me. Now—and this may be more a reflection on me than John Hiatt—I wouldn't cross the road to see him play the greatest show of his career. Three minutes on the battery and counting. What to do? Oh I know: If anyone wants to knows about my first kiss, the moment is here. Look at: www.thefanzine.com.

Of books? I am shortly returning to the USA, where I shall ship immediately to San Francisco, for a reading at Booksmith (Thursday) and then a Literary Death Match as part of Litquake (see the message board). You know how literature isn't a competition? Well, this actually is. So, support me. (My battery has suddenly revivified for no good reason and is showing thirteen minutes. Do I trust this?)

The answer was NO.

OK. It's the next day. Well, what had happened to my computer, which was clearly not right, was that the newly inserted RAM had come loose. This was easily solved, but it meant yet another trip to the Apple Store, which I may as well give as my permanent address next time I come to London.

Anyway, now things seem to be right.

I am now on the 4.15 from London to Hastings, for a little breather. I've taken this train about a million times. But I don't think I ever computed as I listened to *The Best of the Wombles*. (You don't remember the Wombles, sir? Then I put it to you that you are not British.)

One thing I have noticed about being a writer is that you have to do an awful lot of writing. I don't just mean the novel: obviously you have to write that—it's the minimum requirement, for a novelist at least. I mean all the other stuff. You have to explain why you wrote it for keen readers of the paperback, and how you wrote it for keen readers of a journal. And there are various publications, mostly Web, but in this case also the *New York Post*, who like you to do your interview by e-mail, which is far more tiring than just having a thirty-minute chat on the phone. If I were a reviewer—a path a lot of novelists take, a path I won't (probably, can't) take—I'd be writing even more. But it seems to me that I already couldn't write more than I already do, that my computer and I would explode. Particularly because, as my keenest readers know, I type with two fingers (not "at society": you know, actually with two fingers) and occasionally a thumb on the space bar. It's not ideal, but it's always been fine for me. People laugh when they realise the cackhandedness of my approach. There may be a link to my guitar-playing. Perhaps I only have two fingers that are good for anything. Certainly, the little finger on my right hand is broken, and I have to ram it into the pick-guard to keep it out of the way of the rest of my dazzling two-fingerwork. I broke it while driving my motorbike in 1984. A van came round a corner very fast, down a country lane, and drove me off the road. When I got where I was going, my step-mother told me to put it under the tap. (Water famously mends splintered and fractured bones.) And look at it now, perfectly cocked at a perma-nently 35 degree angle. But, like that Roald Dahl story, you just don't really need your little finger so much. Nice that we were given them, however unnecessary. Of course, I can name every station on this line by heart. We have just passed through Tonbridge. The girl opposite me has studiously avoided lifting her bag from the seat next to her so nobody can sit down next to her without actually specifically asking her to move the huge blue bag: she has a rather stern face and a skin complaint, so it's possible they don't want to get involved. We are just about to pass through Tunbridge Wells (no relation to Tonbridge), where my father was born. He's now exchanged England for Italy—Bagni di Lucca, which is (ultimately) more charming and far more beautiful than Tunbridge Wells.

My iPod is on the craziest shuffle: the Wombles, followed by Schubert's 5th, Jobim, "New York Mining Disaster" by the Bee Gees, "When Sin Stops" by Waylon Jennings, Boney M's "Rasputin" ("Russia's favourite love machine/There was a cat that really was gone . . ."), the Amazing Blondel and a track from the new Joni Mitchell album that has a really strange rhythm I neither would nor could have played. I wonder how I can have such good and bad taste in music at the same time. I often wonder that. I am well aware that I like music that is actually not good. I don't mean technically. It's just not great music. You wouldn't like it. Take the Amazing Blondel for example. I am listening to their album *Bad Dreams*, which I recently digitized in part of an ongoing project to get my vinyl onto CD—a move, by the way, that normally beats the official CD release by minus one year—anyway . . . *Bad Dreams* is not good. I'd go so far as to say that it is a bad record, far removed from the grandeur of their earlier classics, far after they should have probably called it a day. And yet, I really like it. And it's not even because I listened to it as a child. Oh no. I had to go out and actively seek this mediocre record at a little independent record store I know called eBay. Because I like Blondel and thus I don't like the idea that there might be a record floating around that has as much as one good second on it that would flesh out the Blondel story and make it even more Amazing. But if there is that second on *Bad Dreams*, they have planted it quite deep within the record in quite a cunning way. But I'll keep looking.

In days of old, when knights were bold, the train stopped at Tunbridge Wells for five minutes, during which you could get a newspaper or smoke a cigarette, have a cup of sugary tea or something equally old-fashioned. Now we speed through to Frant as though Tunbridge Wells barely exists.

I guess there's quite a lot to say.

Now added to the music is the version I did of the English national anthem ("God Save the King"), recorded for the *Song of America* compilation. I hope you like it. Janet Reno said about it, and I'm not even joking: "Somebody's got a sense of humor. . . . A perfect way to present the colonies opposed to the king. And the music that followed was just such a perfect juxtaposition to the song itself." Discuss.

And now my UK tour is done. See you in San Francisco on Thursday (at Booksmith—there I am also going to play the guitar) and on Friday (where I am in competition). . . .

Monday, October 15, 2007

The Literary Death Match: A Full Report

Picture this: a literary festival. Three or four hundred, let's just say "hundreds," of people packed into the Swedish American Hall on Market Street in the Castro. They are paying $15 a head to see four writers read for 8-10 minutes each. That's it. Just imagine that. Oh sure, *Opium Magazine* have gussied up the basic idea, turned it into a Literary Death Match, but basically that's what's happening. That the hall should be sold out, with a large line of people turned away: outrageous. It's a tribute to Elizabeth and Todd of *Opium*.

And Litquake.

How did they gussy? Four writers read against each other in pairs. This produces two finalists, who then compete in an extra-literary competition. There are three judges who evaluate on three criteria—literary merit, presentation and intangibles—and last night, they were an equal part of the show. Anyway, I was one of the four competitors, along with Evany Thomas, Daniel Handler and Gary Kamiya.

In the first round, I was pitted against Evany. A coin was tossed to see who would go first, but she had already asked me to let her go first, so this much, at least, was fixed. And she read an astonishingly funny piece, with which I couldn't compete, about scattering her grandmother's ashes. In fact, she didn't even read it, she recited it. I was worried, because the crowd was large, and wanted a laugh, and I, with the first chapter of my novel, was clearly going to offer them the least laughs of the evening. But I had a secret weapon: George. And when I was up, I placed him front and central, told the audience to "look at him, but listen to me," and read the first chapter as dramatically as I could. It was going well. Then:

In the middle of the reading—and this was jaw-droppingly

unexpected—a woman stood up from her chair and started to heckle me. In particular she was annoyed that I was "reading, not TELLING!"—a point she made freely and forcefully over and over (until she was wrestled to the ground and eliminated). It turned out that she was (a) startlingly drunk on the free gin with which all were plied and (b) under the mistaken impression that the Literary Death Match was an extension of Monday night's "Storytelling Without a Script" event. Initially, people may have thought she was part of the routine, and I even thought she might be a plant, perhaps the stooge of an overly competitive writer out to throw me off by any means possible. (Daniel??) The weird thing is: when I am singing, I have no problem with heckles, or requests, or conversations—it's all part of the show. But I had lost myself in my reading, entered a kind of Dickensian other-consciousness, and when this racket began: I was surprised. All kinds of things went through my head: I thought I'd pretend that it was me throwing my voice; I think I said "Mum! Please be quiet!" or something along those lines; I feared that a beer was about to be thrown—this had famously happened the year before when one of the judges harshly described a writer's work as having "no literary merit"—a dickish thing to say at a good-humoured event— for which he received a free drink (facially). All these thoughts rattled through my mind, and probably out of my mouth, and then I went back to my text. Unbelievably, the next line was: "Nothing ever distracted him from his work." Which brought my house down. Godot moves in mysterious and welcome ways. I believe the offender was ejected.

Anyway, my rival Evany's performance was superb, as was that of the judges: Oscar Villalon of the *Chronicle* had become a father five days previously, and he expressed himself only via American football speak. The only thing I can now remember is that he said of Daniel Handler's gay-themed piece: "What I love about this guy is he loves his teammates, on the field, in the locker room. He's a real team player." Villalon gave four brilliant monologues, all in the name of judging "intangibles." I can only think (he says modestly) that I triumphed because of a sympathy vote due to the heckler, but it could also have been that I bribed the judges. I can't remember which. Anyway: I was through to the final.

Daniel Handler vs. Gary Kamiya was a tough call, but Daniel just swung it—the judges were going to flip for it, but were discouraged, and finally chose Handler because either (a) the whole thing was fixed (and more of this later) or (b) Gary's superb piece of his memories of North Beach ran about half again too long. And thus the final brought me head, or arse to arse (for that is how we stood), with Daniel Handler, of the Lemony Snicket and Magnetic Fields parish.

But were we to make up limericks, or write to the literary death? No such luck: we were to play basketball against each other—one small squashy ball, and one high small hoop each. The first to five: I lost, very enjoyably. I took a quick lead. But at some point (apparently) we were told to move nearer the hoop, since the oche—look it up, Americans! —was set too far back. But this news didn't reach me, and I earnestly kept throwing from my original position, a fact of which everyone was later pleased to inform me. I have this mental image of me standing six feet from my hoop and Handler reaching up and, without breaking sweat, dropping the ball into his, an insanely evil grin on his face. But that's probably not what happened. Anxiety dreams only happen when you're asleep.

I tried to make off with his crown at the end, but he chased me round the hall—and he was a worthy winner: most importantly, his story ("Briefly" from *Adverbs*) was about as good as it gets: very sad, very funny, very very funny. Not to mention the fact that he had never previously won an award for anything athletic—and so I, who have a cabinet full of bronze medals, cannot begrudge him. That aside, I come to bury Daniel Handler not to praise him: he cheated. That's the real headline here.

My trip to San Francisco was fleeting, so I don't know about the rest of Litquake, but the Literary Death Match was the most fun I've had at a reading in a long while, and probably George's sole best event. And if the rest of Litquake was that good, then I salute it and long to take part next year. San Franciscans are very lucky.

In news of my life, my family is still evacuated to Rhode Island, during the redecoration of our house, and so I am on a plane, somewhere over Colorado, returning to the pocket-sized T. F. Green Airport in Providence, Rhode Island, earnestly trying not to watch or hear, or even catch sight of, any of the Robin Williams vehicle *Licensed to Wed*. My next trip—and when you shall hear from me (unless something pops in the next couple of weeks)—is to Memphis, after which an insane piece of routing follows: the next day, New Haven for a gig, and then the next day in Austin for the Texas Book Festival, and (this newly in) a gig at the Cactus Café—I'll be onstage at 10.30 p.m. on Saturday, November 3rd. And check out the interesting PEN event with Sufjan Stevens and Rick Moody later on in November, at Southpaw in Brooklyn, just seconds from my front door.

It's not often I get to take part in a competition, let alone such a good-humoured one.

Viva Literary Death! Viva *Opium*!

Monday, November 05, 2007
Pull the String! Broken Strings and Other Things

It's one of those Sundays when last Thursday seems so long ago that I can't even remember when it was or what happened.

In fact, it all started in Oxford, MS, after a flight to Memphis.

Trip-wise, it was the beginning of a new era, a new world. Due to the birthday gift of an iPhone, I traveled for probably the first time ever without my trusty laptop, as (I suppose) will be the rule on short trips from now on. Weird. I'm still working out how the iPhone does things—but it's the working out what it doesn't do that's more interesting. Such questions inspired a phone call to Apple itself, the gist of which was:

ACT ONE

Consumer: I wanted you to tell me how to delete e-mail in bulk.

Support: Can't be done.

Consumer: Oh OK. Also, to drag music files over onto the iPhone, like I do on my iPod.

Support: Can't be done.

(INTERVAL)

ACT TWO

Consumer: OK. And how do you buy a video direct from the iTunes store to the iPhone?

Support: Can't be done.

Consumer: One last thing. I'd like to customize the front screen so I'm not, for example, forever looking at a little icon that says "Stocks" beneath it.

Support: Can't be done.

(CURTAIN)

Compared to much of the support one gets, this was precise, clear and helpful, so I shouldn't complain. And yet . . . And yet . . . How odd that the invention of the year seems to have taken one step forward and two back. Having said that, I get to watch *Peep Show* and have lots of pictures of my daughter to flash at people, so I'm delighted. It really is the best thing in the world.

I performed on *Thacker Mountain Radio*, a great show for readers and singers, at Square Books in Oxford's delightful, almost New Orleansian main square. Ventriloquism on the radio was once very popular, so I had a go. Unfortunately, there was a ventriloquial calamity. Just before we were due onstage, the string attached to the lever that pulls George's mouth up and down broke. I retied it, but the moment we hit the stage, with the very first pull, it snapped again. And that was that. George was mute.

Thinking hard (and let's face it—I'm used to broken strings), I realized that the only thing to do, since the string was un-retieable, was simply to "pull the string!" (as Bela Lugosi says in the masterpiece *Ed Wood*). And so I did. George probably didn't feel too dignified, but it worked. Square Books gifted me a T-shirt for Tilda, my little girl, and the T-shirt came tied with string. It is that Square Books string that now attaches George's mouth to the lever in his stomach. Thank you, Square Books.

We then ate fine Southern food, almost unimaginably Southern food: deep-fried peanuts in their shells—like soft-shell crabs, you just eat the shells as well: no mess! —hot tamale pie, pickle fritters. You think I'm making at least one of those up, but I'm not. I tell you—it's all going on down there in Oxford. Faulkner knew it. And now you do too. I'd also like to thank Jack Pendarvis for being my honorary heckler on this night of nights.

The next day was a nightmare of travel. The flight to Memphis was two hours late, leaving me stuck in Charlotte, trying to get to New York, whither all flights were cancelled. Finally, after some frantic ringing of promoters and managers, broaching the possibility that this could be my first gig cancellation in many many years of punctual business, I was bundled on a plane for Hartford. This got me much closer to New Haven, and with an hour to spare before showtime, but without guitar, clothes, etc. These appeared in the company of my brilliant wife, and the show went on, featuring a wicked long version of "Annachie Gordon," and a lengthy disquisition on creationevidence.org, which I caught on the Bible Network on TV (and which needs no publicity from me, though I am told that the organization has its home base in Waco, TX, more than which I need not say). This was a long day, and not one you look back and laugh at.

Bed at 1 a.m., and up at 5 a.m. to get the morning Jet Blue flight to Austin to the Texas Book Festival. Military planning and precision meant that this flight coincided with (a) Jet Blue's special "Setanta Saturdays" promotion and (b) Arsenal vs. Manchester Utd. How I pulled this one off, I'll never know. And very exciting it was too.

The Texas Book Festival was a lot of fun, more so than last time. The first panel, at the Continental Club Gallery, was a fiction vs. nonfiction smackdown. George Saunders was among the members of the nonfiction team, but even so, the fiction side won hands down. Of course, there wasn't actually a result: I'm simply claiming victory for fiction. Of course it was a tongue-in-cheek argument to begin with. Keen researcher that I am, and equally anxious not to appear a fool, I looked up the definitions of fiction and nonfiction on the Internet, starting at an educational site for children, where nonfiction was defined as something that is "true" and fiction as something that is "not true." But that's a terrible definition to put in an enquiring mind. In the best possible case, nonfiction purports to be about something real, whereas fiction doesn't, but the lines are so blurry, and you'll end up with funny vision and a twitchy eyelid, like when you've spent too long looking at one of those Magic Eye pictures. Anyway, Amanda Eyre Ward (who wrote my favourite book of a few years ago, *How to Be Lost*), Maxine Swann, and Eric Martin were on my side, and though we were up against tough competition, and as stated above, we won. It was a little like the Literary Death Match, without the grand surroundings and the basketball—in fact, the Continental Club was getting a little bit like the Black Hole of Calcutta, until a few people realized that it was just a bunch of writers yakking and made room for some fresh air.

This ran until about 9.45, when I hot-stepped it to the Cactus Café for my gig. A rather mellow and very enjoyable evening—lots of new songs, or so it seemed to me. And a few requests, one from a woman who knew none of my songs, but simply wanted to make a request, asked someone for a title and shouted it out. Needless to say, and not knowing this at the time, this was the request that got played.

Hey—clocks back! An hour's extra sleep. I like it. But I didn't bother to put mine back, because if I did, I'd only have to put it forward again when I got off the plane in New York that night. The next morning's panel was good too: interesting writers saying interesting things to an audience who seemed with it and were full of good questions. And then a brunch somewhere by a pool in the beautiful hills outside Austin on 2222.

Thanks to Bill for that.

And there you have it. My trip from Brooklyn to Memphis to Oxford to Memphis to Charlotte to Hartford to Brooklyn to Austin to Brooklyn. I then arrived back at JFK to be picked up by a chauffeur who took me, with great confidence, to a street with roughly the same name as mine in a totally different part of Brooklyn. I suppose I should have been paying more attention, but I wasn't.

I was watching a video on my iPhone.

And next weekend, Portland—scene of the crime of my latest album, which was finished, mastered and wrapped last night. I'll be in Oregon by Friday, for a gig at Mississippi Studios that night, and then a reading on Saturday, not to mention an appearance on the fantastic radio show *Live Wire!* from the Aladdin Theater. For those of you in Portland, you know how great that show is, and you are probably going. For those of you elsewhere, you won't be going. So there's not really much point in advertising it either way.

Thanks for listening, reading, watching, laughing.

Thursday, November 08, 2007
(A Lot of) The Writer's Lot

One thing I have noticed about being a writer is that you have to do a lot of writing. By which I mean, more than you thought.

My novels are quite long enough, and require so much work that, though I can write songs on the side, I haven't yet managed to write a single short story, memoir-andum (about how my new novel relates to my personal life—presumably for the *New Yorker*) or lengthy op-ed about the war on terrorism (for example). I am genetically indisposed to writing reviews—somewhat surprisingly for someone with as many opinions as I have, so I must either be too embarrassed or simply too much of a gentleman—which is another accepted way to keep your writerly name out there.

My only extra-curricular writing has been this blog, which I suppose doesn't really add up to a whole hill of beans, though there's always a chance that at a particularly low point of my stellar writing career, I may allow them to be collated, edited and published under the name *Diaries, Vol. 3: The Early Twenty-First Century.*

But what has struck me is how much writing I have had to do in the promotion of *by George*: How I Wrote the Book, Why I Wrote It, What My Favourite Children's Book Is, What I'm Currently Reading, Whether I Prefer the Bible or Shakespeare. It all adds up to a lot of writing, most of it enjoyable—it's always flattering to be asked to do those little lifestyle-type interviews for British papers. I seem to remember that with *Misfortune* I was asked about the book a lot, but this time I seem to be answering questions about everything but. Come to think of it, this probably means that I have worked my way up, or sideways, to the lifestyle portion of newspapers. But it also means that there is a lot of the Internet, and apparently it's not quite full yet, and it has apparently fallen on me, and anybody who can use a computer, to fill it, as I am doing right now. And have been doing over the last couple of months or so. Fact: all these questionnaires are in the United Kingdom, whereas all the e-mail interviews are in America.

An unwelcome addition to the workload is the e-mail interview, out of which I perennially try to wriggle. You can understand how it's easier for the interviewer, but I'd far rather get an interview out of the way in half an hour on the phone. And despite all the guff they give you about how you can't be misquoted if you write it all down, the bottom line is: if you're like me, it's going to take hours, and you'll worry about it disproportionately. I'd rather be misquoted. (Or quoted quite correctly but *claim* I was misquoted. Even BETTER!)

Anyway, since I'm quite proud of the sheer amount of work I've done, I thought I'd make a list. That way I know it exists, that it was all worth it.

P.S.—There is a new song up on the MySpace jukebox. "Wrong Turn," the last of my two collaborations with Tuatara. It replaces "Orpheus Must Die."

In no particular order:

1. The Page 69 Test Applied to *by George*—in which I describe page 69 and how it relates to the book as a whole: page69test.blogspot.com/2007/08/by-george.html

2. My Top Ten Ventriloquism Books for the *Guardian*. I absolutely take the blame for this one: I suggested it. Getting it up to ten was quite hard, though: books.guardian.co.uk/top10s/top10/0,,2193183,00.html

3. Easily the most annoying. I was asked by an English magazine, called (ominously) *Bad Idea*, to write a little piece for them on "something embarrassing." I can't quite remember the exact brief. And so I rewrote the Japanese Food Skirmish incident detailed in a previous blog (www.johnwesleyharding.com/phpBB2/viewtopic.php?t=573&sid=75565 02b92be98b99ba80613ab1572b4) and called it "Lost in Transaction." This was rejected as inappropriate and I was asked to produce something else, by the next day, which offer I (and I think understandably) declined. The rejected piece lives on below (Exhibit A).

4. Easily the weirdest. I was interviewed for Japanese *Esquire*. They were to take a series of photos, and asked if I'd mind wearing a Cartier wristwatch in return for $500. I said yes, as any sane person would have done. But there is no free lunch, and, sometime after the interview, I received an e-mail asking me if I'd answer three questions about my experience of wearing the Cartier wristwatch for a later edition of *Esquire*. Not wanting to be disagreeable, I said I would. It was then that I realised I had some-how been inveigled, in the nicest possible way, into writing ad copy (something I have never done before) for Cartier, and hadn't even come out of it with a free $45,000 watch. And I have to say: it was a nice piece of bling. Anyway, the three questions, which will never be seen anywhere else in English are here (Exhibit B).

5. The *Financial Times* asked me to contribute to their series "Once upon a Time," where writers name their favourite children's book: www.ft.com/cms/s/0/odf1bbf0-8429-11dc-a0a6-0000779fd2ac.html

6. I was asked by the *Fanzine* to answer some questions about my first kiss, which was later edited together to look like a written conversation— and I was delighted to see my first kiss illustrated: www.thefanzine.com/sections.php?s=columns&id=170&a=articles

7. The *Irish Times* asked me what I was currently reading. The answer, and for probably most of this year—it's really a very long book—is Clive James's *Cultural Amnesia*. I can't find the piece online, or maybe it's yet to appear. It appears here (Exhibit C).

8. The *Observer*'s "Just a Minute" questionnaire—yet to appear. Included some tricky questions, as I recall.

9. For Little, Brown's Web site, and presumably for the back of the forth-coming paperback where they print book group notes, "Res Ipsa Loquitur: Why I Wrote *by George*": www.hachettebookgroupusa.com/authorslounge/articles/2007/august/article25427.html

10. A long interview (with illustrations) for Powells.com, which I remember doing mostly in a hotel in Osaka: www.powells.com/ink/stace.html
This was an interesting format: they gave you twenty questions and

you chose the six you liked most—or something like that. They also asked me to write my six favourite books in a category of my choice. I chose football, and, since I don't think it's online yet, I call it Exhibit D.

11. Jonathan Ames, who is a wonderful writer (and I unreservedly recommend *Wake Up, Sir!*), interviewed me for the *New York Post*:
www.nypost.com/seven/09022007/entertainment/dummy_up_a_tale_of__two_george.htm?page=0
We did this (see above) by e-mail. I append the entire unedited version as Exhibit E.

12. There was a lengthy e-mail interview with Scott Butki for Blogcritics.org:
www.boston.com/ae/books/blogcritics/2007/10/wesley_stace_ak.html

13. And *Verb* magazine asked me "What's on Your Desk?" And I told them here: www.readingwriters.com/VERB-Aug07-p3.htm

Tuesday, November 20, 2007
The Trophy Shelf

Portlanders can't imagine moving anywhere else. They love Portland. As do I. Half of Seattle has recently decanted there. It's an arty town with a sleazy underbelly, like John Waters's Baltimore of the '60s. But the underbelly is barely hidden—it's right there on the surface along Burnside, just near Powell's. Which, by the way, is a bookstore. As we landed, the man to my right was telling me all about it, like I wasn't a human being, like I'd never heard of books.

After my nightmare travel day from Oxford to New Haven, I'd had my fill of the close shave, so I flew in a night early, which happily coincided with my friend Jim Brunberg's surprise 40th birthday party. This ended up with a live version of "Don't Fear the Reaper," on which I seem to have sung. A very well-planned surprise it must have been too, for he had no idea.

The next day, I took a trip to the little-known bookstore Powell's, where I found some books. (Like the Peter Cook sketch about the miner: "Look! I've found some coal!" "My goodness! That's the very thing we're looking for!"). So I did manage to locate some books there: one for Abbey, three for Tilda and two for me, durable editions of *The Rock Pool* by Cyril Connolly and Aldous Huxley's *Point Counter Point*. (I have become old, literature taste-wise.) I can't stop reading Huxley at the moment. I get off at *Brave New World*, for I have no patience with visions of the future, ironic utopias, 1984 (or the Eurythmics album of the same name), etc. But I hadn't read the novels written before he became a prophet and subsequently a psychedelicatessen, and these I recommend: *Crome Yellow*, *Point Counter Point* and *Antic Hay*—like Evelyn Waugh but with greater purpose. And now I'll have to stop reading him, because I appear to have run out of pre-*Brave New World* novels. Tilda, on the other hand, bene-fitted from Powell's to the extent of Richard Scarry's *The Rooster Struts* and *The Christmas Mice*, not to mention *I Spy Christmas*. You may have noticed a theme emerging and I can only say that I hope she isn't reading this or, come Christmas morning in Hastings, the surprise will be ruined.

Monica Drake, with whom I read at Bumbershoot, then appeared dressed as a clown, surrounded by rubber chickens in the window of some large Macy's-type store in the middle of downtown Portland, reading from her excellent novel *Clown Girl*, her words broadcast into the street by PA. And it was raining. But still people sat, in luxuriously upholstered red vinyl chairs, as she read. I think this may have been the kickoff event of Wordstock, Portland's book festival, or festival of the book and/or word, my prime reason for being Northwesterly this weekend.

But first, there was the small matter of a gig at Mississippi Studios, my favourite Portland venue, owned by none other than Jim of the previous night's surprise birthday party, who, still fearing the reaper, hadn't got up until 5 p.m., and was in only marginal shape to perform his support set. However, he rose to the occasion and we even did some songs together, the most interesting (or weirdest) of which was "Sweetheart Like You" by Bob Dylan, which Jim suggested. It's rather tragic, since I never really play Dylan songs unless at the suggestion of others, that when the oppor-tunity does arise, I appear to be word perfect on every song in the oeuvre. It's wasted knowledge. Our parents knew reams of Keats and Shelley, Longfellow and Poe—but we know lots of song lyrics. Great song lyrics. But still. We also know lots of bad song lyrics. The other day, I saw a bloke perform a spoken-word version of "Beat It" by Michael Jackson (or was it "Billie Jean"?) with every single "ooh!" and "yeah!" inserted, in the correct place, between the lines. It was a masterpiece of performance and con-cept. It is not entirely relevant here.

Anyway, the gig occurred, I enjoyed myself, the piano was in tune, Jim didn't die and I played these songs, apparently:

Mississippi Studios
Portland, OR
11/09/07

Come Gather Round
Protest Protest Protest
Goth Girl
Congratulations (on Your Hallucinations)
Things Snowball
Your Mind's Playing Tricks on You
The Bull
It Stays

Two Sleepy People
Save a Little Room for Me
Top of the Bottom (w. Jim Brunberg)
Paradise
Someday Soon
Annachie Gordon
Monkey and His Cat
The Devil in Me
Daylight Ghosts
Browning Road (w. Jim Brunberg)
Sweetheart Like You (w. Jim Brunberg)

How these things come together in such a good-looking and reason-able shape, I have no idea. They take on a life of their own, that's for sure. I see that it started off a little protesty, and was then somewhat amusing, before it got serious. I seem to remember that the requests were "Paradise," "The Devil in Me" and "Save a Little Room for Me." Requests shape a show. And having a newly finished but unreleased album also shapes things a little: six new songs, I notice. And I say: thanks to the peo-ple of Portland for not complaining.

The next day Wordstock took over. This started with a reading in the Convention Center. (I had already taken the bus to the Expo Center, by mistake. And I never take busses, so there's a lesson there. Mind you, a helpful fellow traveller had told me confidently that this was the right bus for the Convention Center; the same one who later tapped me on the shoulder and said that I was going in the wrong direction.) The reading before me was Peter Sagal of NPR: the authors had a bird's-eye view of the cavernous Powell's stage from the hospitality suite. The turnout for his reading was simply enormous, and I thought, if I have even a tenth of that audience, it'll be a lot of people. But in fact a tenth didn't seem like that many people at all, particularly in a place the size of Shea Stadium. We have to face the fact that an NPR profile and an extremely funny (I've read it!) nonfiction book is worth a lot more than a novel. Nonfiction—the merits of which, as opposed to those of fiction, we debated so light-heartedly in Austin last weekend—might well have lost that particular argument, but today she reigns triumphant. All you can really say about a novel, publicity-wise, is that it is the *first* novel—which is way more interesting than a second to tenth novel—or that it relates to the author's life in a particular way—i.e., make it as much like a nonfiction book as possible. I didn't hear Peter Sagal's reading, but I did hear him on *Live Wire!* that night and he was absolutely the highlight of the show. As we signed books afterwards, he asked me "if I dated." I demurred, being married, etc, but it turned out that he was asking whether I put the date beneath my signature in the fronts of books. (Answer: yes, if the recipient is in front of me.)

A rather lazy afternoon included a necessary trip to buy some briefs. (I should add that this iPhone has totally screwed up my packing. No laptop anymore, which also means no laptop bag—not that I keep my briefs in my laptop bag—but somehow this has made the whole packing experience exponentially trickier.) It seemed like a good shop to buy underwear but it was in fact *too* good a place to buy underwear. The selection—41 designers from around the world—was simply too wide. I was asked if I'd like any advise, and finally I gave in. The salient point here is that I learned a whole new concept, an apparently vital one in the world of cutting-edge undergarments: the Trophy Shelf. I'm not going into it here—though in the briefs shop, I was shown a cross-section diagram of the shelf, its workings, its contents, its qualities. Impressed, and somewhat cowed, I did not leave with a shelf. I did however buy underwear by Aussie Bum (and when you're modelling Aussie Bum, you might as well shelf it too . . .), Frank Dandy (of Sweden, I was excitedly told), and Papi: this last pair is the sine qua non of modern smalls—but enough about my underwear. What do *you* think of my underwear?

That night was *Live Wire!*—in which I played two songs ("The Bull" and "Top of the Bottom"), was interviewed by my wonderful ex–*Live Wire!* comrade Marc Acito (who was costumed as an NPR presenter, complete with bow tie), did a little ventriloquism and played banjo (including an actual solo) in a version of a Folksmen song (from *A Mighty Wind*), and performed in honour of Harry Shearer, who was there to talk books. They worked me like a dog. And I liked it. Aside from the wonderfulness of the Aladdin Theater, and the astonishing standard of the show's comedy writing, I can't imagine that much more entertainment could have been packed into a single evening (and this, despite me). Again my non-existent hat goes off to *Live Wire!* which is, I believe, the best night out in Portland. It should broadcast farther and wider.

And then, as if planned just for me, it did come to pass that the Minus Five, otherwise known as John Wesley Harding's Negative Quintet, were playing a show at the Towne Lounge. Not only that, but the Tripwires were supporting, which meant that half of my best friends from Seattle were in town. This meant a very late night, which included, I seem to remember, George surprising Scott (and how!) with a ventriloquial duet on "Twilight Distillery," not to mention me popping on and off stage regularly to ornament their songs with my late-night vocal stylings. The show got better and better—you know how this happens—and climaxed with Scott handing over to the Tripwires for "She's a Mod" and then an astonishing guest appearance by Rock Star Heaven's very own Michael Maker. It was all just too good to be true. Quite a night. And thank you, Portland.

I even got home to Brooklyn two hours earlier the next day, for some complicated aeronautical reasons. In this instance, I harnessed the power of the airlines to my advantage. Yes.

Then home for a week before a KGB reading this Sunday, with Daniel Wallace. This was a lite version of the spectacular in North Carolina (see the poster! watch their lips move!) the Saturday after next. And then a dinner for about 25 people, at which one member did that thing at the end where they say, on arrival of the bill, "I only had a beer and a pasta dish, I don't want the bill divided equally by 25." I said I couldn't really negotiate for him, but he could take it to everyone if he liked, to which he responded: "If I'd have known, I would have drunk and eaten a whole lot more." I understand that money is an issue, but who goes out to dinner with 5 drunkards and expects them all to do mathletics (?) with a bill at midnight.

Wow. It's all happening here, as you can tell. This is big news.

We are now back in our house, after the redecoration, and things are roughly back to normal, despite the fact that my new shelves aren't up, so I can't move into (or in) my study for boxes of books. Yesterday called, in order, the dishwasher guy ("No juice going into the back"), the electrician ("It doesn't have its own circuit breaker, this could take some time") and the locksmith ("All your door handles now work, that will be $1705.00 . . . Oh, and I forgot the tax"). Today I have to pick up the dry cleaning, drop off CDs of the mixes of the record with my lawyer, and return a broken hard drive (I had a huge music disaster at the weekend, while *backing up* the contents of my iTunes). So, it's just another normal day at the office.

One last thing: the new record. You keep asking and rightly so. Thanks for asking. The record (title TBA) is now done, mixed, mastered and nearly ready to go. If there was a label putting it out as of now, like, today, then it probably wouldn't have a release date until April or so anyway. As it is, there are other things to consider, one being that the backing band is the Minus Five (essentially, as you know, Peter, Scott and Bill from R.E.M.), and that R.E.M. are going on tour for many a month next year after their new record comes out. Of all records I have ever made, this new one would be the least great to tour without a band, particularly the band who made the record. Of course, that's what will probably turn out happening, but obviously I, and any record company who cared to put the record out, would want to let that occur if possible—so it needs some careful planning. And all this has to fit around the various tour plans for *by George* or, as it's known in France as of now, *Les Garcons*, which I like to loosely translate as *Waiters*. So, all this adds up to: I don't know when the album is coming out. Perhaps I'll release it digitally to you first. The record business being as it is, we artistes now have to think more carefully than ever about whether it's worth being on a record label at all. Laziness normally wins that argument, but there are many good reasons to do most of the work yourself. So we'll run it up the flagpole and see who salutes. I'm certainly saluting as I hoist—it's a noble follow-up to *The*

Confessions and *Adam's Apple*: the end of a trilogy, I think. I didn't think I'd get to make such a lush, ambitious record, but (thanks to the confluence of many elements and, in no small measure, to the kindness of strangers) it's made and ready to go. So now it's over to the people who have to decide whether they can make money off it. And who knows? Perhaps they can't! Or perhaps they can! They certainly won't have spent any money on the making of the music, which was entirely paid for by Plangent Visions (my longtime music publishers) and myself. Thank you, thank you, thank you.

On with my day—a rainy walk with dog and baby in the park. That's actually better than it sounds. In fact, it's great.

Epilogue
Bad Luck in Paris

I am now in Paris, where, in perfect Parisian style, I woke up and went for a wander, sliding ungracefully on a large slime of dog shit, before browsing some beautiful clothing stores (with newly clean shoes). In other words, a typical Parisian morning. Later, I was told that stepping in dog shit is considered good luck, but just when I had clutched this slim superstitious straw, I was informed that this was only if the left foot was implicated: *Zut alors!*

I then ate lunch at Le Procope, "Le Rendez-Vous des Arts et des Lettres" and the oldest literary café in the world, where Franklin wrote some well-known American document, Voltaire and Rousseau argued about the price of milk (and where it should go in the encyclopedia), and Verlaine ate *tête* (but not *langue*) *de veau* ("as cooked in 1686" and I wonder if the menu said that then? Oh, probably). At Le Procope (which I will insist on going to again tomorrow, because the whiting was off, and who doesn't want whiting?) I drank a murky green cocktail of Pernod and absinthe: a good thing to do before an interview with *Elle* and an appearance on France 24 TV? Apparently yes! This arrived at our table accompanied by an extremely flamboyant glass fountain that very slowly dribbled iced water onto the lump of sugar before it decomposed into my glass. It was lovely, the perfect prelude to my marrowbone, and my green bean salad.

Let me cast my mind back to Friday night in North Carolina. But first I'll put that Grand Entertainment in perspective.

Perhaps the most valuable thing I have learned during the promotion of *by George* is that readings are not really that effective. Let me explain.

Some of course are great—Charles Dickens's were probably quite good. And he enjoyed doing them so much that he almost killed himself performing. I'm afraid I mean contemporary readings in bookstores. People don't seem to be very interested in them. Perhaps they were interested in them, but have grown bored as they've grown more common. Or perhaps it's only me and everybody else's readings are simply incredible. What I really mean is: if a writer has the chance to turn their bookstore reading into anything BUT a bookstore reading, then he or she should. It's the wise thing to do.

For example, in San Francisco, I read at Booksmith, one of my favourite bookstores. I was delighted to be invited. It was fine. People came. I read. I even played the guitar. They bought books. It was a good example of a very enjoyable reading. Unlike the last book, there is no music I can (or want to) tie in with *by George*, so despite the presence of the lad George himself, there isn't much going on apart from the reading and the signing bit.

The next night—and of course it's an unfair comparison, but it demonstrates my point—I read at the Literary Death Match, as described in an earlier installment. Here I felt (apart from when I was playing basketball) like Charles Dickens himself: I projected to a packed house from a podium under great lighting. I could be dramatic, play it for laughs, generally turn it on. The stage was made for it. It was marvellous— and people were paying, whereas the previous night was free. (And having just played on Friday to 300 people paying a minimum of $35 a head, I have finally, belatedly, come to the conclusion that people think free entertainment worthless.)

All the best events during this promotional period have been the extra-curricular activities: at Bumbershoot, the panel with Monica Drake; in Portland, the *Live Wire!* radio show; the *Thacker Mountain Radio* show in Oxford, MS; the gig and reading at Decatur; the astonishing fiction vs. nonfiction panel in Austin—basically anything that wasn't a straight reading. That's when I have felt that I am really getting the book across to people. And don't think I'm negative about the readings—quite the reverse, I love doing them and would happily come to your individual homes and delight each of you with a bedtime story. I like to read. But the public seems to agree with me—the extra-curricular events are more fun.

And on Friday we had a truly magnificent evening in North Carolina and I commemorate it thus as not only one of the highlights of the last year, but also (in an odd way, perhaps next to the Seattle *Songs of Misfortune* show a couple of years ago) one of the most ambitious shows I've been part of. I knew I was excited about it because I had two "forget-ting my lines" dreams during the previous week. What was it? Well, I met Daniel Wallace at the Festival America in Paris (coincidentally) last year, and we hatched a plan to do New York and Chapel Hill readings for our new novels, given the way they dovetail in theme. We decided on a variety show, as a benefit, at the Barn in Fearrington, NC, attached to McIntyre's bookshop and we billed the show as a cast of thousands, on the basis that I'm two people on my own, and that made three already. The idea was: a reading each, a few songs (perhaps some duets—Daniel is fingerpickin good on the banjo), a little ventriloquism, some magic if possible.

The evening, "A Feast of the Five Senses"—why not "A Feast FOR the Five Senses"? I don't know, and I came up with the title—turned out beyond out wildest dreams. We had more or less a day's rehearsal, cooked up a running order, got an MC from the local radio station WUNC (one of the beneficiaries) and a fabulous prestidigitator called Geoff Lloyd who performed close-up magic at people's tables. And we wung it.

Here's what they got, apart from food and up-close magic:

ACT ONE

Intro by Frank Stasio, MC

Intro by DW and WS—duet of "Tom of the Bottom" on guitar and banjo

Reading: DW (from *Mr. Sebastian and His Negro Assistant*)

Music: JWH ("Darwin," "Congratulations (on Your Hallucinations)," "The Bull")

Chat: Frank and WS talk about ventriloquism

Reading: WS ("The Birth of George" from *by George*)

Magic Trick—a grand illusion performed by DW, involving a disappearing red handkerchief and an astounded audience, to be explained by DW and WS at the end of Act Two

ACT TWO

Intro by DW and WS, in which DW is mistaken for many other writers, including David Foster Wallace, Wallace Stevens, Wallis Simpson, etc.

Reading: DW (from *Mr. Sebastian and His Negro Assistant*)

Ventriloquist Routine: DW and WS (a much extended version of the bit I've been doing at readings, with DW in the role of Ernie Wise)

Music: JWH ("Hamlet")

Chat: Frank and DW talk about sideshows, magic and carnies

Reading: WS ("Androcles and the Lion" from *by George*)

Music: WS and DW (duets of "Sussex Ghost Story," "It Stays," "Browning Road")

Magic Trick—in which DW and WS explain the trick to the music of *Chariots of Fire*

ENCORE: Ukulele Lady—DW on guitar and WS on the ukulele

(CURTAIN)

The Barn was a spacious, er, barn, with sparse sound equipment and no one to work it, soon filled with 300 people and waiters buzzing round pouring wine and serving canapés, which accounted for a few of the five sense right there. Daniel and I put pretty much everything we could into this performance—if I'd known how to tap-dance I would certainly have lived out the Gene Kelly fantasy (that I don't actually have) at some point. It was a magical night, and a great pleasure to see so many music fans there. (I know I haven't overentertained you in North Carolina recently, so I really appreciate your coming out to the Barn, even with that slightly expensive benefit ticket price, particularly because you didn't know quite what you were going to get. And let's face it: I didn't know what you were going to get until that morning. But you certainly got it.)

Yet, all this grand variety show really was, rather like the Literary Death Match, was a reading with a twist. And this one made about $10,000—if you can believe that—for WUNC public radio and Chatham Young Writers. So everybody felt good about everything. And I got a chance to wear my black suit with the flouncy Vivienne Westwood shirt, which you have only previously seen if you were at my wedding.

Love and thanks also to Laura, Daniel and his lovely daughters, Nick, Geoff "Spirits of Diablos" Lloyd with the magic fingers, and Jamie from the Barn. We should definitely do this again and I think we shall.

Tomorrow is a big day of action and interview, featuring two business meals—one with booksellers, the other with journalists. So tonight finds me back in my hotel quite early, ordering room service, half watching Nantes drawing nil–nil with Montpellier on my television—I will literally watch ANY football on TV—and wondering when my jet lag will allow me to sleep.

Paris is full of potential Christmas presents.

Avoid the dog shit and you're absolutely fine. ✧

Submit to LOST.
        Find yourself.

www.lostmag.com

My First Real Home

Diane Williams

In there, there was this man who developed a habit of sharpening knives. You know he had a house and a yard, so he had a lawn mower and several axes and he had a hedge shears and, of course, he had kitchen knives and scissors, and he and his wife lived in comfort.

Within a relatively short time he had spent half of his fortune on sharpening equipment and they were gracing his basement on every available table and bench and he added special stands for the equipment.

He would end up with knives or shears that were so sharp they just had to come near something and it would cut itself. It's the kind of sharpening that goes beyond comprehension. You just lean the knife against a piece of paper.

Tommy used to use him. Ernie'd do his chain saws.

So, I take my knives under my arm and I drive off to Ernie's and he and I became friends and we'd talk about everything.

"I don't sharpen things right away. You leave it—and see that white box over there?" he'd said. That was his office. It was a little white box attached to the house with a lid you could open and inside there were a couple of ballpoint pens. There was a glass jar with change. There were tags with rubber bands and there was an order form that you filled out in case he wasn't there.

He wasn't there the first time I came back, at least I didn't see him.

I went up to the box and those knives were transformed.

As I was closing the lid, he came up through the basement door that was right there and we started to chat and he has to show me something in the garden, so he takes me to where he has his plantings. It's as if the dirt was all sorted and arranged, and then, when I said he had cut his lawn so nice, he was shining like a plug bayonet.

All the little straws and grass were pointing in one direction.

"I don't mow like my neighbor," he said.

Oh, and then he also had a nice touch—for every packet he had completed there was a Band-Aid included. Just a man after my own heart. He died.

I was sad because whenever I got there I was very happy. ✧

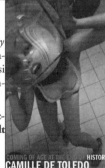

Rara Avis: How to Tell a True Bird Story

Jackson Connor

Part I: Rara Avis

I have seen hawks dive and rise with field rodents. I have seen white-faced hornets snatch houseflies out of the air. I have seen robins pull worms from the ground, woodpeckers force insects from bark, herons stand for hours on one leg. I have never seen a bald eagle hunt, though I have seen them scavenge for food. On the river. In the fields where I grew up.

One time I mistook a bald eagle for a black bear. Until you have seen an eagle close enough to judge its size relative to your own, you simply haven't seen one. I had dumped some leftover pork and sauerkraut from a Crock-Pot onto the river when it was frozen. I had hoped to see crows there the next day. I spent two winters in our family cabin there on the Allegheny, and when you spend four or five days each week without hearing a human voice, seeing a face, you learn to treasure any company.

Each morning after I'd kindled the woodstove and set the coffeepot going, I'd look out at the world. On mornings after a heavy snowfall with little wind, the trees across the river look like ghosts of themselves—a layer of white outlining the tops of each gray twig and fallen tree. This particular winter, 2002–3, the river was frozen for three solid months.

Ice erases color and texture from land, motion from water, smell from the air. Time, on mornings like these, reverts to an older way of passing without springs or gears, levers or shadows, and the ice is blinding. The eagle's head blended itself out of sight, became a part of the morning that had nothing to do with the bird. Watching its shoulders work as it shifted from side to side, I was immediately sure it was the third bear I had ever seen in the wild. It was enormous and eating all of my sauerkraut. I wanted a camera or my family so I could preserve the moment in something other than myself. I realized my mistake after a few seconds, and rather than marveling at the strength and grace of a black bear, I stood in subtle admiration of this great bird.

As soon as it flew off, I called my dad. I told him of the pork and sauerkraut and my plans to attract crows. I told him of the sheer enormity of such a bird and how it didn't offer any criticism about my meal. I was, needless to say, flattered. Dad said, "I don't know if I've ever told you this, and I can't remember who told me, but when an eagle swoops down to catch a fish, if its wings go into the water, it will drown."

There is the old story about the two turkey vultures sitting on a telephone wire watching an old man feed the pigeons. One bird is intent on his lot in life, waiting. He is desperately hungry, but patient. Turkey vultures are pacifists by nature, or they are simply too lazy to hunt. This bird, though, has grown to enjoy the texture of rigor mortis. The other vulture turns to the first and says, "Fuck this, I'm gonna go kill something."

You can tell a turkey vulture from other large birds by its wings—they have fingers, or so it seems. My dad taught me that as I was becoming aware of the world around me. He taught me everything I've ever known about our local birds.

He said, "When a bald eagle hunts, it drops from a great height, slicker than shit, and it grabs the fish from the river by its talons. It don't matter how tough they are or how big, they just can't swim. That's all there is to it."

Their talons can crush a human femur. From a hundred yards an eagle can see the fleas you think you don't have. They can cover twenty square miles in a single hunt. Though bald eagles are perhaps the fiercest hunters in the air, they often resort to scavenging. Don't let them catch you dead. They'll pick you clean.

I have a picture of two bald eagles flying above an island on the Allegheny River as the river approaches Pittsburgh from the north. The head of one is pure white, and its body dwarfs its brown-headed offspring. They are facing each other ten, fifteen feet off the ground, and each has its legs and talons pointed toward the other, their wings fighting against both gravity and forward motion. The young one has its mouth open. On a rock on the island between the two birds, though it is not in the picture, a carp is baking in the sun.

The bald eagles are father and son. If you could possibly know the familial history, the event could be humiliating in its implications—a lesson you hadn't meant to see. In our language the father, teaching the son to scavenge and defend his food, might say, "No, no, not like that. Like this. Watch me." You might even want to put in a good word for the young one, how maybe he's cut out for something else—true, he's not much of a scavenger, but so handsome and so resourceful, and he's always protective of his little sister.

The background of the photograph, the hillside across the river, is poorly done. Too much green. If one of my kids had colored it that way, I might have said, "It sure is pretty, but don't you think there are more colors in nature than that?" Every year it amazes me when the leaves fall and I see how many camps, sheds, cars, boulders, are on that side of the river. The bald eagles stand out like shadows of themselves against the dense hillside.

The birds rose into the air and battled three times. Some feathers fell. No serious damage. After the third fight the mature bald eagle flew upriver; the youth landed and devoured the carp, then flew upriver. I can't help but think the older bird flew off and told his buddies, "You should have seen my boy today, by God, he's something."

* * *

Some people believe the title of Greatest Ecological Recovery in the History of the World belongs to Pittsburgh, whose skyline during the early twentieth century could not be seen for the coal smoke and steel dust in the atmosphere. Others say the title belongs to the city of Lake Erie, which used to catch fire from time to time. Seeing those places now, you would not guess their pasts. They are not going to draw in tourists the way other great cities do, but if you stumble across them on your way from here to there, they can haunt you with their industrial beauty and natural strength.

The Valley That Changed the World, where Oil Creek runs between Oil City and Titusville, Pennsylvania, is another recovery candidate. In Titusville in the autumn of 1859, Edwin Drake built the first commercially successful oil derrick in the world. Over the next ten years his idea to replace whale oil with petroleum became an industry, and today's Western Pennsylvania was born. Between the 1870s and the 1930s the valley was barren of foliage, and the oil ran so haphazardly that it could be scooped off the surface of the water and sold. Truly, the landscape consisted of mud and was packed with greenwood houses, derricks, bars, mule carcasses, dying horses, skinny dogs, rich prostitutes, thousand-dollars-per-roll dice games, long knives, short pistols, leaky barrels, missing fingers, rust, smoke, and fleas. In the 1960s the OC&T Conservation Society decided to clean it up. Now, again, in most places the foliage is too thick to see the forest through, and except for the tourist train that runs through there and some rotting, crumbling derricks and disused oil barrels, it is hard to tell such destruction ever occurred. Nature, slightly encouraged, can undo the work industry breaks backs to perform.

Bald eagles have achieved a similar recovery. They were, of course, hunted nearly to extinction, as were all species we had enough bullets for and whose fur or feathers were thought pretty. In the 1980s you could see them from time to time. In the '90s sightings were common. Now, though they are far from being removed from most endangered-species lists, some people have stopped staring in awe when one flies by.

A family of bald eagles lives a few miles upriver from our camp, fifteen miles downriver from where Oil Creek flows into the Allegheny. We have grown to know them well, my family, and we can tell the difference between the adult male, the adult female, and the immature bald eagles by their flights and tendencies. We miss them when they are not around. When I was young, it made my day to see one—now, though many other things make my day, I always stop to watch as one flies by.

My dad called me in Utah recently to tell me this story: The adult female perched in a tree at the camp. She was less than thirty yards from my parents and did not budge when they approached with cameras.

When they came to stand beneath her, she opened her mouth from time to time. Mom fetched a hot dog, and Dad found a long stick—they thought she was sick and that perhaps a little snack might help her on her way. She sidled away anytime the hot dog came near, further proof that these birds are wiser than we.

My parents built a fire and watched the river. They called the game warden and the fish commission who confirmed our suspicions immediately—they don't know nothing. Dad called his buddies and asked them if they knew anything about such bird behavior. Dad's buddies did not, but several hurried to Mom and Dad's side to stand by the fire, drink beer, and watch the bird not fly away. Night fell. People drifted off. In the morning the bird was gone.

She has been seen since then, apparently well. No theories have been formed. At least none that aren't obvious—sickness, pregnancy, injury— though I prefer to think she was entirely well and simply observing us in ways we could never observe her. For a long time Dad had it in mind that she'd gotten her feathers wet and was drying them out before she flew off.

Part II: He Gets His Feathers Wet

Now, I tell you these stories so I can tell you this:

I don't know if any of it's true. I've never seen an eagle's feather up close, or, more accurately, I wouldn't know an eagle's feather from a hummingbird's foot, so if I have ever seen an eagle's feather, I am, at this point, not aware of it. I have, though, seen the bald eagles by the camp often enough to know them from turkey vultures, at the very least.

Though I am two thousand miles away, Dad keeps me up-to-date on our lives and the world around us back home. Last November, for instance, he shot the biggest buck of his life—an eight pointer, ten-inch brow tines, the base of the rack more than an inch thick, twenty-inch spread. He called me well after midnight eastern time to tell me this— "But," he said, "I don't want to say too much. I'll just wait till Christmas so I can lie to you face-to-face."

Dad called me this morning (Sunday, mid-September 2004) to tell me an anecdote. "I don't know if I ever told you this before," he told me, "and I don't remember whether I read it or heard it or made it up, but did you know that if an eagle gets its feathers wet, it will drown?" Dad was at the camp this weekend. He had looked out at the island in the middle of the river, and there were three great blue herons on three legs looking for fish. The fog was sitting high in the hollow. The adult male bald eagle was flying overhead. He wasn't too interested in anything, so he flew off upriver. Dad continued, "The eagle wasn't too interested in anything, so he flew off upriver. Now, I went inside and made myself a cup of coffee and came back out on the porch a few minutes later. The herons were gone, but I did see what looked like a lone Canada goose flopping around out by the island. About thirty feet above the island and about twenty feet on the other side of the river. It turned out to be that same bald eagle fighting like hell to get out of the water."

I put myself there on the porch beside him. The river doesn't go past my knees on our side of the island. Across the island it gets as deep as I can imagine this river getting, and I'm very afraid of the river. I'm a strong guy, a fair swimmer, and sometimes accidentally courageous. I would do just about anything to save an eagle, but the Allegheny, for all of its apparent docility, has holes, vortexes, drains that are covered with silt and sticks, but it can suck a full-grown cow under and never give it back. Currents run caverns through otherwise solid limestone boulders the size of man-made wonders. Strainers are trees that have become traps, collecting smaller sticks and logs and rocks and air-breathing animals. During any given year I have never heard of fewer than five people drowning in the twenty-mile stretch of river that runs past my family's house, past the camp, through our towns.

The river, after all, has been here longer than these foothills of this mountain range shrinking around it. The Appalachians, the oldest mountain range on Earth, were built up around the creeks, streams, and rivers that run through Pennsylvania. Ice ages drove glaciers through moraines that would carve these mountains down, but the waterways showed the ice the paths of least resistance. If there are places in the earth where a quiet evil resides—and maybe there are, anything's possible—those places might well be in the heart of these hills. I, for one, do not take my chances with such things, so I decided quickly that, had I been on the porch that day, I would have watched that beautiful bastard drown before I would have let him drag me to the bottom.

Dad said, "I couldn't quite believe it, and before I really had a grip, I had several plans running through my head, such as throw on a life vest and save the day. But that bird would have kicked my ass all over the river, then flown off with my fucking floaty. Well, as it turns out, the eagle did make it to the island, and he walked around for five, ten minutes, looking anything but majestic. I don't know if you've ever seen an eagle walk on land, but they just aren't put together right for it, plus he was just about pooped. Anyway, after a bit he took off again and flew upriver."

Part III: My Uncle Dewey Gets Involved

"Now, I told you this story," Dad told me, "so I can tell you this:

"I just got off the phone a little bit ago with your uncle Dewey, and I told him that story about the bald eagle. After I got done, you know how he is, he said, 'Wow, that's neat, man. Jeez, I wish I could have seen that.' And he said, 'You know, I can't help wondering about what it's going to be like when I tell that story next year. I wonder what will be different about it. I know it's not going to be too much longer, I'll be telling that same story, saying stuff like, "Now, I can't remember whether or not old Jack was with me, but I seen this eagle this one time. . . ." A few years further down the road I'll be telling that story, and the nurse will pat me on top of my head and say, "Yes, that's a very interesting story, Mr. Stewart. Now, will you please get your hand out from underneath my dress?"'"

If I say I don't believe that a story's truth lies in how much of it happened versus how much is made up, I have to qualify myself, I have to cite philosophers and fools from contemporary culture, clear back to cave dwellers, if I can find any. But I'll make it short this time.

I believe in Zeus and Hephaestus and Prometheus and the stories told about them. Those gods in their time probably held a power similar to that of my own God in my own time, and though I don't talk about him often, he is very important to me.

I don't believe in pyramids. I'm talking the big ones in Egypt. I've never seen the Pyramids, nor has anyone I know. I've seen almost as many pictures of pyramids as I've seen pictures of Capt. Jean-Luc Picard of the USS *Enterprise*, and I believe Patrick Stewart is a real person, though for reasons I can't explain, I am hesitant to commit myself to the characters he plays so well.

I do believe that a thin current runs through the sea of stories we create, which somehow joins us all together, even if against our will.

My buddy Joe and I were acting in *Antigone*. After a rehearsal we were talking about cars or racing or good buddies or backwards hats or any number of things that would make me think of Dad and Uncle Dewey. Joe and I had not been friends for long, though we now have a lifelong friendship, and he had never heard me mention Dewey.

I said, "One time my dad and my uncle Dewey were at a red light back home. They were sitting in Dewey's old Ford Galaxy. The car wasn't much to look at, and that was the best thing you could say about it. A couple of young guys Dad and Dewey's age pulled up beside them in a Mustang they'd obviously done some work on. They revved the engine a couple times. Well, Dewey puffed up a little bit, turned his hat around backwards, and got ready to run them. The light turned green, Dewey slammed his foot on the gas, the driver's seat snapped off its hinges and flew damn near into the trunk, and Dad reached over and grabbed the wheel while Dewey kept his foot hard on the gas.

"The Mustang, at this point, was just a set of taillights, but by the time they'd duct-taped the seat back into place, Dad and Dewey had told each other the story enough times that somehow they'd won this race."

When I told that story, Joe laughed, but not for the same reason I had when my dad first told it to me. Joe had been expecting a joke. The story, though I find it extremely humorous, has no punch line. After he stopped laughing, Joe said, "You really have an uncle named Dewey?"

"Of course I do. Haven't I ever told you the story about when my uncle Dewey was in an elementary school play? He had one line. When he heard a report from a cannon, he was to rise and announce, 'Hark, I hear a cannon fire.' He rehearsed it to third-grade perfection. The actual cannon was the gym teacher shooting a starter's pistol, but the gym teacher attended only the performance, not the rehearsals. Opening day came. Dewey's family was there to watch him. He wore a purple getup that, as far as he knew, was what a herald of the time might wear. The play went well through the first two acts, and he was finally onstage. He stood steadfast. He breathed deep. The line was familiar to him. The gym teacher fired off the starter's pistol, and my uncle Dewey jumped up and yelled, 'What the fuck was that?'"

Part IV: The True Story

It wasn't the female bald eagle in the tree that day. It was a turkey vulture. Up close they, too, are enormous, intimidating—if put on the defensive, they could kill you as quickly as a gunshot. They are more likely to simply vomit toward you, though—a greenish gray recipe of near bile and near feces is the turkey vulture's natural defense. Against whom? I don't know, but I've smelled the fresh vomit from fifteen feet and sworn never again to approach such a creature. Aesthetically, also, they are generally repulsive to humans, whereas eagles insist on strength, grace, and beauty. Rome would never have searched the edges of the known world for five golden turkey vultures.

The rest of the story is true. I'm certain.

One year in elementary school we were talking about a story we had read, and we were trying to learn not what the moral of that particular story was, but what the idea of a moral is. The walls were pastel cinder blocks. There was one blackboard in the front of the room. I was probably trying to figure out how the clocks knew whether to spin faster or slower in accordance with how much fun I was having. It was raining, so it probably wasn't February. It might have been September or June—the other six school months in Pennsylvania are equally likely.

The teacher asked for a personal story with a moral. The teacher called on Maryanne Winger, who was as bright as her dress was pink and the school day was long, and, at the risk of misrepresenting her, this is what she said: "One time I went out to the barn and put twelve eggs aside and told my parents we were going to have twelve baby chickens, but then only seven of them hatched and I was sad, but at least I had seven new chickens." (Maryanne graduated valedictorian our senior year.)

And the teacher said, "Very good, Mary. Now, what is the moral of that story?"

Maryanne Winger said, "The moral is 'Don't count your chickens before they hatch.'"

That was how I learned what a moral to a story is. The teacher asked for another example, and Mark Mulhauser raised his hand. The teacher called on him. Obviously. Though Mark played kickball like an angry god, he was an angel when at his desk. Mark and Maryanne were cousins, of course, but I don't think that matters much to this story. Mark said, "One time I went out to the barn to get some eggs for breakfast, and I put the eggs in a basket and I was walking back in and my big brother knocked the basket out of my hand and all the eggs broke." (Mark was MVP of our basketball league, and he and his brother have since reconciled about this particular incident.)

Again the teacher said, "Very good, Mark. Now, what is the moral of that story?"

Mark Mulhauser said, "'Don't put all your eggs in one basket.'"

The teacher must have been, at this point, so ecstatic from the two super answers of two such sweet, sweet students that she didn't even think twice about asking for a third response. Her reasons notwithstanding, she called on me, and I lowered my hand to tell my story.

"This one," I said, "takes place in 'Nam.

"My uncle Dewey was a fighter pilot in the Vietnam War, and he flew a number of top secret missions behind enemy lines. In the middle of a routine surveillance flight on New Year's Eve 1968, he was shot down by some technology we didn't even know the enemy had. As he was parachuting, he realized that all he had was an M60, a machete, and a quart of bourbon, so he figured he might as well make good use of his supplies. He drank the bottle on the way down. As luck would have it, he landed directly in the middle of one hundred Vietcong.

"Dewey tossed his chute aside and opened fire. He killed sixty of the commie bastards with his gun before he ran out of ammo. He drew his machete and disposed of another thirty. When the knife was finally knocked out of his hand by a grenade blast, he killed the last ten using the various forms of martial arts he had picked up over the years. When the final Vietcong fell, he spit and began the tedious process of carving his initials into each of their chests, before he called in a chopper and secured an LZ."

I leaned back in my seat as the rest of the class nearly fell out of theirs in anticipation and anxiety. The teacher, who in retrospect must have been teetering between begging an answer and sending me to the principal's office, said, perhaps out of habit, preparation, or sheer stupidity, "Very good, Jackson. Now, what is the moral of that story?"

I leaned forward again in my desk, made eye contact with as many of the students as could bear it. I said, "Don't fuck with my uncle Dewey when he's been drinking."

I can't help it. Neither Maryanne nor Mark has ever been to a farm, for all I know, but for some reason everybody I meet away from home—whether it be in San Francisco or on the Galway canal—thinks I grew up in a pasture, when truly I was bred more for the mill. Think *Deer Hunter*, not *Little House on the Prairie*. But the rest of it is true, if my memory serves any purpose.

Facts about birds of Western Pennsylvania:

Fact one: A group of crows is called a murder.

Fact two: If I'm pressed, and I don't feel like figuring it out, anything bigger than a sparrow is a red-tailed hawk, and anything smaller than a redtail is a sparrow.

Fact three: A group of starlings is called an exaltation.

Fact four: Any bird that I scrutinize and still cannot name is a pink-breasted nutsucker.

Fact five: A group of geese is called a flock, a gaggle, or a skein, depending on whether the birds are in the air, on the water, or on the ground.

Fact six: I don't know whether or not eagles' feathers are hollow. ✧

"Post Road has the goods. I not only fall on them and read them like hot news when they come in the door, I keep them lined up on my shelf like little books, because that's what they are."

JONATHAN LETHEM

What They Don't Tell You About Breast-Feeding

Liz Scheid

A lactation nurse will cup your breast,
arching her thumb & forefinger like an open mouth
or a perfect U.
As in, you will want to be anywhere but there
inside that sterile room, where she squeezes your breast,
squishing it into your newborn's mouth,
who somehow goes on sleeping
but latches on to your breast to suck,
or suckle, as she likes to say.
All those tiny bumps are milk ducts,
which may become infected,
which really hurts
like a sudden surge of needles are tearing through.
But you don't quit, you allow this:
suck sleep suck sleep
this is what your mother did, what her mother did.
Meanwhile, your breasts are lopsided and swollen with milk,
your nipples are red & erect.
Your husband will say,
My god, you smell & taste like milk,
as he peels pieces of it from beneath your breasts.

By the way, milk leaks from your breasts,
staining your sheets like shots of semen.
Many months pass like this:
your baby attached to your breast,
the donut beneath your butt,
Regis on TV,
the ubiquitous smell of milk.
Sitting without her there feels bare, naked,
like sitting in the bathtub after the water has drained.
Suddenly the surge of milk is needed like the release of water
stuck inside your ears;
with your head slightly tilted all you feel is warmth.

What I'm Not Telling You

Liz Scheid

Who need be afraid of the merge?

—*Walt Whitman*

a graphic description of,

A head sliding through a woman's vagina, so open it held the night, light seeping through, tiny fingers waving, everybody waving. As if this wasn't you and you are watching this unfold, a memory that isn't yours. As if this is beautiful: a mother's spine arched, her hands clenching thighs, knees upright—holding the air, legs spread like a moth's wings. Perhaps we're missing her face: purple like a plum, eyes sworn into slivers, her mouth so open she could be grinning.

collected fragments from Live Science,

As it turns out, imagination is just as believable as reality. To remember if something was imagined when we recall it & store it as memory is to remember all the white space around it: the voices around the image, the open hand, the commotion, the smell of wet grass, the person stand-ing in front of you, snapping his fingers, saying, "Imagine this." Only then can we separate between what really happened and what was imagined. As if we could hold these two things in separate hands, weighing us down, our bodies swaying downwards.

what I can tell you,

From the couch, I can see my sister's truck backing out of the driveway. I watch it pass by, a still frame in my head: a blue truck, red hair in the window, moving in the bright air. As a result, she is always moving. Sometimes, when I see this image, I imagine my body moving toward the door, pressing the handle, the brass beneath me, opening it, calling out to her. Often this is a dream, and I call out to the open air, but she doesn't stop, only presses onward. And I stand there in that open space, waiting.

noteworthy shopping experience,

At Wal-Mart a cashier tells me, "Contractions are like menstrual cramps."
The truth is: tonight you will have a muscle spasm. It will grab your body and hold it there. It will happen while you're dreaming of water, legs and elbows floating, light as feathers. You think you could die like this. Only you awaken, your body pulling you to the floor, to your calf. All you can really do is bite your teeth and bear it.

noteworthy Freudian episode,

Once I wrote a poem about my father. How he fished early mornings, the sun a shadow on his face. Always a lovely image: the pole against his thigh, the water like black glass before him, how he'd hold the fish in his hands, watching it gasp for air, then releasing it back into the water, watching its silver body blur into murkiness. I love holding him here: his pale skin, slightly hinted with silver, his hands cracked with age.

an obsession with,

Lately, I've been dreaming of dead people. I dream everyone I know is dying. I bury them while they sleep, their hands tucked beside them, their lips pursed into rosebuds. I sit in the grass above their bodies, pulling it out, letting the wetness collect between my fingers.
I ask one of them, "What's it like?"
"It feels like smoke inside my ears."

an author's disclosure:

What you should know is that I've been collecting things: water bottles, strange conversations, faces in passing, hollow sounds. Mostly, I forget they're there. But, lately, they've been existing simultaneously, competing for space inside my head. What you should also know is that I've been trying to write about the birth of my daughter. Spontaneously, I write the images down on envelopes. These I will collect too.

a possibly related memory,

I'm maybe twelve; my sisters are fourteen & sixteen. We are crammed inside my dad's pickup truck. I'm sitting on someone's lap. We are driving

fast along country roads; all the greenery & hills are spiraling together.
We are singing along with Counting Crows, the wind blows through the
windows; we are laughing, moving, alive.

something else about Wal-Mart,

Aimlessly, I meander through the aisles. I've forgotten why I'm here. I
get overwhelmed by all the commotion—screaming kids, buzzing toys,
the man in a wife-beater reaching over me, his body odor, all these numbers, smells & sounds blurring together. I haven't told you that right
now I'm pregnant. I'm here for the baby necessities, just the necessities.
But, pretty soon, wanting & needing blur together in one continuous
line in my head. And in the baby aisle—I stop looking at brands, but
start judging by smells. I open powders, lotion, shampoo, all chamomile.
I think I could fall asleep here, all this lavender spilling over me.

what I forgot to tell you,

I haven't told you that the poem I wrote about my father was also about
my sister. Or maybe was only about my sister. I wrote it on the third
anniversary of her death. Perhaps what I wanted was for him to be fishing.
You see, there's a distance between us now.

collected fragments,

A glass of chocolate milk on the table, a silver ring on her left hand, gray
sweatshirt, a quick smile, red hair pulled into a white hair tie, distant
sirens, loose change on the counter.

collected facts from Live Science, Part II,

Long-term memories are taking up too much space, making it hard to filter
new images: the lemonade you drank yesterday, the color of your shirt,
conversations in passing. All these short-term memories are slipping
into a dark void, somewhere between then & now. Failure to filter out
long-term memories means: a constant state of motion, a meandering of
the mind, distant voices calling, singing, all of them fighting for air.

which reminds me of,

The wind drying my tongue. I am on the handlebars, one hand tightly presses into the metal, the other is dangling in the air, waving ahead. I can still taste the air, something like wet asphalt, and I remember she kept saying, "Hold on." My sister stops pedaling and we are moving faster and faster down the hill, our blood rapid inside us, our mouths open.

About the fall: pebbles and dirt inside my teeth.

the cyclical nature of,

Always, it ends up about her. I carry a photograph of my sister & me. In particular, I like the backdrop of photos: how the light meets the shadows, the mysterious people caught looking at the flash, the awkward expressions, their mouths opened in silent ovals. There is so much smoke inside these spaces, so much grayness, so many sounds to enter. The background of the one I carry is tarnished, smudged. Our faces are white, out of focus. In scribbled cursive on the back of the picture, it reads, "Ages three & one." She holds me in her lap. Her lips are fresh, ripe and pink like the inside of a grapefruit. I remember the loud flash, the flimsiness of my limbs, the sunlight seeping through the blinds.

more collected facts from Live Science,

In a study of rats, emotionally arousing events triggered activity in the amygdala, an almond-shaped part of the brain involved in emotional learning and memory. The interaction then triggers production of a protein, Arc, in neurons in the hippocampus, which is a brain region involved in long-term memory. The Arc protein stores certain memories by strengthening synapses, the connections between neurons in the brain.

the facts surrounding the accident,

I decided to stay at her house with her newborn minutes before she left. She was late; he was crying. The day was bright; sunny, cold. She came back inside the house once more after leaving because she forgot something; I'm not sure what. Sometimes, I close my eyes tight to try to recall the facts, but often all I see is the door closing over & over again.

all she does is sleep:

After my daughter was born, she closed her eyes for weeks.

Occasionally, they'd twitch, a wavelike ripple. While she slept, I pressed my index
finger onto her lids, holding the movement, like soft music beneath my fingers. I thought she must be dreaming of water—the salt on her lips, the soft drizzle on her skin.

what I can't tell you,

There was a fragment of space of seconds or less between light & darkness, sweat & dirt, words & void, wind & smoke. In the accident report, it states my sister caught the driver in her peripheral: a sudden movement, a quick twitch, and slammed her foot into her brake pedal, leaving a streak of blackness across the pavement.

how this all started,

I've forgotten the words to "Mockingbird." Or maybe I never knew them at all. Often while she sleeps, I hold my hands above her mouth to feel her breath rising into the air. What could I offer my daughter besides the truth? She sleeps under a roof so open anything could touch her.

repeat,

Often this is a dream, and I call out to the open air, but she doesn't stop, only presses onward.

A FAR CRY FROM KENSINGTON, by Muriel Spark

David Leavitt

A novel I impose upon all my graduate students, as well as most of my friends, is Muriel Spark's *A Far Cry from Kensington*. Published in 1988 and set in London just after the Second World War, *A Far Cry from Kensington* tells the story of Mrs. Hawkins, a fat young war widow who lives in a boardinghouse and works in book publishing. Possessed of a single-minded integrity that often gets her into trouble, she ends up tangling—over the course of many years—with the sinister Hector Bartlett, a dreadful and pompous writer whom she cannot keep herself from calling, usually to his face, the "*pisseur de copie.*" The plot is intricate and perfectly deployed—other elements include the occult abuse of something called "The Box," poisoning, and pregnancy—and there is a twist in the last line that makes me shudder. Yet this novel merits reading not just because it is so artfully constructed; but also because included in it—"with the price of the book," as Mrs. Hawkins says—is some of the best advice to young fiction writers ever penned. ✧

Transformations

Alice Hoffman

FOLLOW

Once a year there was a knock at the door. Two times, then nothing. No one else heard, only me. Even when I was a baby in my cradle. My mother didn't hear. My father didn't hear. But the cat looked up.

When I was ten I opened the door. There she was. A lady wearing a grey coat. She had a branch from a hazel tree. Hazel was my name. She spoke, but I didn't know her language. A big wind had come up and the door slammed shut. When I opened it again, she was gone.

But I knew what she wanted.

Me.

The one word I'd understood was daughter.

I asked my mother to tell me about the day I was born. She couldn't remember. I asked my father. He had no idea. When the grey lady next came I asked the same question. I could tell from the look on her face. She knew the answer. She went down to the marsh, where the tall reeds grew, where the river began. I ran to keep up. She slipped into the water, all grey. She waited for me to follow. I didn't think twice. I took off my boots. The water was cold. I went under fast.

SWAN

My brother stayed in his room, hiding. He watched the sky and cried. You think he'd be happy to be human, but he kept talking about needing his freedom. I had lost brother after brother, was I supposed to lose him too? He stood on the ledge outside the window. He had only one arm; if he started to fall he would dash to pieces on the rocks below.

I was always the one to save everyone. I went out at midnight to gather the reeds, though there were wild dogs and men who thought of murder. I carried sharp needles and sticks. At night I wove the reeds together while my brother cried. When I was done, I threw the cape over him. He changed into a bird and flew away.

I watched until he looked like a cloud. Now he was free. Well so was I. I walked to the city and got a job. I had a talent after all. When people asked if I had a family I didn't mention that once I'd had twelve brothers. I said I took care of myself. I said I liked it that way, and after a while I meant it.

ROSE

Everything was red, the air, the sun, whatever I looked at. Except for him. I fell in love with someone who was human. I watched him walk through the hills and come back in the evening when his work was through. I saw things no woman would see: that he knew how to cry, that he was alone.

I cast myself at him, like a fool, but he didn't see me. And then one day he noticed I was beautiful and he wanted me. He broke me off and took me with him, in his hands, and I didn't care that I was dying until I actually was. ✧

Index

The following is a listing in alphabetical order by author's last name of works published in *Post Road*. An asterisk indicates subject rather than contributor.

Abrams, Eve	REDEMPTION WINDOW (nonfiction)	PR15, 143
Aguero, Kathleen	WE DIDN'T COME HERE FOR THIS: A MEMOIR IN POETRY, BY WILLIAM B. PATRICK (recommendation)	PR15, 193
Albertsen, Dawsen Wright	CHRIS STOPS THE BOYS (fiction)	PR16, 14
Albo, Mike	KILL FEE LIT—AFTER READING GEORGE GISSING'S NEW GRUB STREET (recommendation)	PR13, 207
Almond, Steve	THE EMPEROR BY RYSZARD KAPUSCINSKI (recommendation)	PR6, 141
	ESSAY: AN INQUIRY INTO THE PSYCHOLOGICAL ROOTS OF AMERICA'S DEATH FETISH, OR, WHERE'D YOU HIDE THE BODY? (etcetera)	PR11, 197
Alvarez, Julia	RECOMMENDED READING (recommendation)	PR5, 129
Ames, Jonathan	A BOY'S GUIDE TO DRINKING AND DREAMING (recommendation)	PR2, 153
	DEEP IN QUEENS (theatre)	PR7, 123
	THE STORY OF MY SON (theatre)	PR7, 125
	TWENTY QUESTIONS (etcetera)	PR11, 216
Ansay, A. Manette	MARILYNNE ROBINSON'S HOUSEKEEPING (recommendation)	PR13, 196
Anthenien, Catherine	BAZAAR (art)	PR1, 11
Antosca, Nick	YOUNG MEN AND FIRE, BY NORMAN MACLEAN (recommendation)	PR14, 191
Armstrong, Mary	PAINTINGS (art)	PR7, 66
Attenberg, Jami	A FEAST OF SNAKES, BY HARRY CREWS (recommendation)	PR15, 90
Ausherman, Stephen	CONQUEST, TOURISM, AND ETERNAL CANADIAN RAPTURE (nonfiction)	PR15, 93
Ayala, Michael	PHOTOGRAPHS (art)	PR6, 66
Baggott, Julianna	MARY MORRISSEY, OLENA KALYTIAK DAVIS, AND MARISA DE LOS SANTOS (recommendation)	PR5, 132
Baker, Aaron	NOTEBOOK (poetry)	PR6, 27
	BONES (poetry)	PR6, 30
Bakerman, Nelson	WILDWOOD (art)	PR3, 96
Bang, Mary Jo	A SELECTION (recommendation)	PR4, 98
Barnes, Rusty	O SADDAM! (fiction)	PR15, 129
Barot, Rick	SELF-PORTRAIT AS VIDEO INSTALLATION (poetry)	PR9, 128
	DECEMBER SONNET (poetry)	PR9, 130
Bauer, Douglas	THE GOODLIFE, BY KEITH SCRIBNER (recommendation)	PR1, 157
Beam, Alex	VARIOUS (recommendation)	PR6, 155

Beck, Sophie	CUT TO THE CHASE (nonfiction)	PR13, 209
Beeder, Amy	BOTANY NOTES (poetry)	PR9, 121
	NO CHILD WILL CHOOSE IT (poetry)	PR9, 122
Bell, Currer (see also Brontë, Charlotte)	NOTE: BIOGRAPHICAL NOTICE OF ELLIS AND ACTON BELL (etcetera)	PR15, 99
Beller, Thomas	KAROO, BY STEVE TESICH (recommendation)	PR3, 65
Bellows, Nathaniel	NAN (fiction)	PR14, 89
	THE BOOKSHOP, BY PENELOPE FITZGERALD (recommendation)	PR15, 11
Bergin, Josephine	THE SINGLE GIRL GOES TO TOWN BY JEAN BAER (recommendation)	PR9, 178
Bernard, April*	INTERVIEW (etcetera)	PR7, 169
Berne, Suzanne	SISTERS BY A RIVER BY BARBARA COMYNS (recommendation)	PR11, 169
Bibbins, Mark	HIATUS (poetry)	PR1, 87
	BY THE TIME (poetry)	PR1, 88
Bickford, Ian	INTRODUCTION TO ANGIE DRAKOPOULOS: PAINTINGS (art)	PR8, 41
Bierce, Ambrose	EXCERPT FROM THE DEVIL'S DICTIONARY (etcetera)	PR2, 119
Bird, Peter	IT'S LIKE BEING RAISED IN THE WILD, BUT WITH MORE STYLE (nonfiction)	PR2, 67
Birkerts, Sven	VARIOUS (recommendation)	PR1, 159
	REMINISCENCE: JOSEPH BRODSKY (etcetera)	PR8, 166
Bitetti, Kathleen	INTRODUCTION TO MICHELA GRIFFO: PAINTINGS AND DRAWINGS (art)	PR9, 66
Bjorklund, Patricia	SIMPLY NATURAL (fiction)	PR9, 30
Black, Sophie Cabot	THE STRAY (poetry)	PR6, 32
	PULLING INTO MORNING (poetry)	PR6, 33
Bland, Chloe	BARGAIN DONUTS (fiction)	PR5, 108
Bochan, Toby Leah	WHY (fiction)	PR4, 68
Bockman, Jeffrey M.	CITY STORMS (nonfiction)	PR7, 52
Bohince, Paula	THE GOSPEL ACCORDING TO LUCAS (poetry)	PR14, 177
	THE GOSPEL ACCORDING TO JOHN (poetry)	PR14, 178
Boobar, James	TOUR: THE DOSTOEVSKY WALK (etcetera)	PR11, 17
Booker, Brian	THE BOARDWALK (fiction)	PR12, 121
Borders, Lisa	WHAT'S IT ALL ABOUT? A NOVEL OF LIFE, LOVE, AND KEY LIME PIE, BY WILLIAM VAN WERT (recommendation)	PR9, 168
Boudinot, Ryan	LOSING THE VIRGINITY OF TIME: THE LITERARY COORDINATES OF BRUNO SCHULZ AND ISAAC BABEL (etcetera)	PR8, 193
Bourgeois, Louis E.	A LONG TIME AGO IT RAINED (nonfiction)	PR12, 15
Boyd, Rebecca	WHO I WAS SUPPOSED TO BE: SHORT STORIES, BY SUSAN PERABO (recommendation)	PR2, 158
Bradway, Becky	BLOOD AND LUCK (nonfiction)	PR12, 211

Braver, Adam	EXCITABLE WOMEN, DAMAGED MEN, BY	
	ROBERT BOYERS (recommendation)	PR12, 119
	CONVERSATION: AMY HEMPEL (etcetera)	PR14, 83
	CONVERSATION: PHILLIP LOPATE (etcetera)	PR15, 21
	CONVERSATION: MARION ETTLINGER (etcetera)	PR16, 27
Braverman, Melanie	JANE HAMILTON (recommendation)	PR4, 101
Breen, Susan	ROBERT CREELEY'S COLLABORATIONS	
	(recommendation)	PR1, 170
Bremser, Wayne	MATTHEW BARNEY VERSUS DONKEY KONG	
	(criticism)	PR10, 113
Brink, Elisabeth	I AM CHARLOTTE SIMMONS, BY TOM WOLFE	
	(recommendation)	PR15, 104
Brontë, Charlotte	NOTE: BIOGRAPHICAL NOTICE OF ELLIS AND	
(see also Bell, Currer)	ACTON BELL (etcetera)	PR15, 99
Brouwer, Joel	AND THE SHIP SAILS ON (poetry)	PR8, 24
	BECKETT'S ENDGAME (poetry)	PR8, 25
Brown, Jason Lee	MY OLDER BROTHER, JUNE BUG (poetry)	PR16, 165
	NAME I WILL NEVER FORGET (poetry)	PR16, 166
Brown, Jericho	TRACK 4: REFLECTIONS AS PERFORMED BY DIANA	
	ROSS (poetry)	PR15, 9
	TRACK 1: LUSH LIFE (poetry)	PR15, 10
Brown, Peter	SINCE IT'S YOU (fiction)	PR7, 89
Browne, Jenny	TWIN CITIES, NO SIGN (poetry)	PR5, 27
	BEFORE (poetry)	PR5, 29
Browne, Nickole	ONTOGENY (poetry)	PR15, 159
	STRADDLING FENCES (poetry)	PR15, 161
Brunner, Edward	EXTENDING HARRY CROSBY'S	
	"BRIEF TRANSIT" (etcetera)	PR3, 179
Burt, Stephen	CATHEDRAL PARKWAY SUBWAY GATE (poetry)	PR4, 25
	OUR SUMMER JOBS (poetry)	PR4, 26
Butler, Robert Olen	MIKHAIL BULGAKOV (recommendation)	PR16, 35
Campana, Joseph	SUITE FOR THE TWENTIETH CENTURY (FOR CAROLE	
	LOMBARD) (poetry)	PR16, 37
	SUITE FOR THE TWENTIETH CENTURY (FOR MARILYN	
	MONROE) (poetry)	PR16, 43
Canty, Kevin	ROBERT WALSER (recommendation)	PR7, 140
	LONG STORIES (etcetera)	PR15, 151
Capps, Ashley	READING AN EX-LOVER'S FIRST NOVEL (poetry)	PR12, 187
	HWY 51 (poetry)	PR12, 188
Castellani,	THE LIFE TO COME AND OTHER STORIES,	
Christopher	BY E. M. FORSTER (recommendation)	PR8, 151
Casey, Maud	SISTERS BY A RIVER, BY BARBARA COMYNS, THE GIRL	
	FROM THE COAST, BY PRAMOEDYA ANANTA TOER	
	(TRANSLATED BY WILLEM SAMUELS), AND "GUSEV"	
	BY ANTON CHEKHOV (TRANSLATED BY RICHARD	
	PEVEAR AND LARISSA VOLOKHONSKY)	
	(recommendation)	PR14, 217

Catone, Anna	WANTING A CHILD (poetry)	PR14, 207
	THE PARACHUTE (poetry)	PR14, 208
Cernuschi, Claude	INTRODUCTION TO PAINTINGS BY MARY ARMSTRONG (art)	PR7, 66
	INTRODUCTION TO PAINTINGS BY STONEY CONLEY (art)	PR7, 73
Chapman, Maile	A LOVE TRANSACTION (fiction)	PR1, 33
Cheever, John*	INDEX: CHARACTERS FROM THE STORIES OF JOHN CHEEVER (etcetera)	PR11, 149
Chinquee, Kim	BODY LANGUAGE (fiction)	PR16, 183
	BALLOONS AND CLOWNS AND POPCORN (fiction)	PR16, 184
	MASH (fiction)	PR16, 185
Choi, Susan	JOHN DOLLAR AND EVELESS EDEN, BY MARIANNE WIGGINS (recommendation)	PR12, 13
Church, Steven	APOLOGY TO HENRY AARON (nonfiction)	PR5, 111
	A LETTER TO THE BIONIC MAN (nonfiction)	PR5, 113
Chute, Hillary	"I SAID I'M NOT YR OILWELL": CONSUMPTION, FEMINISMS, AND RADICAL COMMUNITY IN BIKINI KILL AND "RIOT GIRL" (criticism)	PR1, 185
	COOL FOR YOU, BY EILEEN MYLES (recommendation)	PR4, 103
Clarke, Brock	THE PRIME OF MISS JEAN BRODIE, BY MURIEL SPARK (recommendation)	PR13, 171
Clarke, Jaime	DESPERATELY SEEKING PACINO (etcetera)	PR1, 143
	FIVE ESSENTIAL MODERN SHORT STORIES (recommendation)	PR3, 72
	MORVERN CALLAR, BY ALAN WARNER (recommendation)	PR8, 161
Clements, Marcelle	MADAME BOVARY, BY GUSTAVE FLAUBERT (recommendation)	PR10, 73
Clinch, Jon	MORE REAL THAN REALITY: THE FROZEN ART OF ALISTAIR MACLEOD (recommendation)	PR16, 219
Cockey, Tim	TIME'S WITNESS, BY MICHAEL MALONE (recommendation)	PR9, 174
Cohen, Leah Hager	A LONG AND HAPPY LIFE, BY REYNOLDS PRICE (recommendation)	PR11, 53
Colburn, John	IN SALES (poetry)	PR10, 13
	PAST THE BITTER END (poetry)	PR10, 20
Cole, Lori	ON THE AESTHETIC AGENDA OF THE ANTIWAR MOVEMENT (criticism)	PR7, 57
Collins, Michael	DROP IT (theatre)	PR9, 139
Collins, Wilkie	REPRINT: MY MISCELLANIES. A PETITION TO THE NOVEL-WRITERS (COMMUNICATED BY A ROMANTIC OLD GENTLEMAN) (etcetera)	PR14, 159
Conley, Stoney	PAINTINGS (art)	PR7, 73
Connelly, Shannon	THE KIN-DER-KIDS, LITTLE ORPHAN ANNIE, AND MASTERS OF AMERICAN COMICS (criticism)	PR15, 49
Connor, Jackson	RARA AVIS: HOW TO TELL A TRUE BIRD STORY (nonfiction)	PR16, 249

Cook, Kenneth	EASTER WEEKEND (fiction)	PR5, 95
Cooley, Martha	BLAISE CENDRARS (recommendation)	PR2, 160
Cooper, T	SEX AND [AUTO] GENOCIDE: THE SLUTS, BY DENNIS COOPER & SWIMMING TO CAMBODIA,, BY SPALDING GRAY (recommendation)	PR13, 126
Corbett, William	INTRODUCTION TO JOSH DORMAN DRAWINGS (art)	PR4, 82
	SHEEPSHEAD BAY, BY ED BARRETT (recommendation)	PR4, 124
Corcoran, Olisa	SHOUTING OBSCENITIES AT GEORGE BUSH THE YOUNGER (nonfiction)	PR3, 126
Corral, Eduardo C.	ALL THE TREES OF THE FIELD SHALL CLAP THIER HANDS (poetry)	PR13, 169
	OUR COMPLETION: OIL ON WOOD: TINO RODRIGUEZ: 1999 (poetry)	PR13, 170
Cowgill, Erin	NATIONS CUP (art)	PR12, 33
Cox, Elizabeth	STRONG OPINIONS BY VLADIMIR NABOKOV (recommendation)	PR11, 81
Crane, Hart*	GUGGENHEIM APPLICATION (etcetera)	PR14, 63
Crane, Kate	SEA MONSTERS (nonfiction)	PR7, 31
Crews, Harry*	ANTHOLOGY OF BLURBS (etcetera)	PR6, 186
Curtis, Rebecca	THE SWEATER, THE PAIR OF SHOES, AND THE JACKET (fiction)	PR3, 13
Czyzniejewski, Michael	VICTOR (fiction)	PR15, 163
D'Agata, John	A GENRE YOU HAVEN'T LOVED ENOUGH (recommendation)	PR15, 63
Dalton, Quinn	VARIOUS (recommendation)	PR15, 197
Dameron, Jim	TWO BIRDS (nonfiction)	PR8, 97
Daniel, David	A CONFEDERACY (poetry)	PR7, 11
	MR. SWEATNER'S PARADE (poetry)	PR7, 12
Darby, Ann	A POETICS OF RISK (etcetera)	PR4, 131
Davies, Tristan	RECEIPT: TACO BELL (etcetera)	PR9, 191
Davis, Alan	THE MOVIEGOER, BY WALKER PERCY (recommendation)	PR13, 111
Davis, Lisa Selin	"THE ORDINARY SON," BY RON CARLSON (recommendation)	PR12, 167
Davis, Olena Kalytiak	THE LAIS OF LOST LONG DAYS (poetry)	PR7, 20
	STRIPPED FROM THE WAIST UP, LOVE (poetry)	PR7, 21
Dawidoff, Nicholas	A RIVER RUNS THROUGH IT, BY NORMAN MACLEAN (recommendation)	PR4, 105
Day, Cathy	PIG BOY'S WICKED BIRD: A MEMOIR, BY DOUG CRANDELL (recommendation)	PR11, 107
Decker, Stacia J. N.	WAITING ROOM (nonfiction)	PR6, 127
de Gramont, Nina	NOW IT'S CLEAN (fiction)	PR10, 161
Dempster, Brian Komei	GRAFFITI (poetry)	PR5, 37
	THE CHAIN (poetry)	PR5, 39
Dickson, Rebecca	THE FAITH OF OUR FATHERS (nonfiction)	PR12, 191

Dickstein, Morris	KEROUAC'S ON THE ROAD AT FIFTY (recommendation)	PR16, 163
DiClaudio, Dennis	SCENES FROM THE LIFE AND TIMES OF LITTLE BILLY LIVER (theatre)	PR8, 113
Didyk, Laura	FAREWELL (nonfiction)	PR16, 61
Dierbeck, Lisa	LYNNE TILLMAN'S NO LEASE ON LIFE (recommendation)	PR14, 209
Dolin, Sharon	FIRST WHY (poetry)	PR10, 79
	AND HOW (poetry)	PR10, 80
Donner, Rebecca	ASK THE DUST, BY JOHN FANTE (recommendation)	PR9, 172
Dorman, Josh	DRAWINGS (art)	PR4, 82
Drain, Kim	FAMOUS CAKE (fiction)	PR13, 85
Drakopoulos, Angie	PAINTINGS (art)	PR8, 41
Dumanis, Michael	MY MAYAKOVSKY (poetry)	PR13, 61
	CRIME SPREE (poetry)	PR13, 63
Dunlap, Murray	ALABAMA (fiction)	PR13, 10
Dunn, Meghan	SOAP SIRENS (poetry)	PR15, 91
	ADVICE FOR A SOAP SIREN (poetry)	PR15, 92
Durham, David Anthony	A SCOT'S QUAIR BY LEWIS GRASSIC GIBBON (recommendation)	PR11, 141
Eberly, Paul	HOT WATERS (fiction)	PR5, 84
Eberlein, Xujun	A HUNDRED YEARS AT 15 (nonfiction)	PR13, 107
Egan, Jennifer	QUESTIONNAIRE (etcetera)	PR15, 219
Elam, Chris	INTRODUCTION TO DESTRUCTION AND CONSTRUCTION OF THE HUMAN FACE, BY TAKAHIRO KIMURA (art)	PR5, 194
Eldridge, Courtney	BECKY (fiction)	PR2, 35
Ellis, Sherry	INTERVIEW WITH ELIZABETH SEARLE (etcetera)	PR8, 199
Engel-Fuentes, Brian	GOD ON SIDE (poetry)	PR11, 49
	SO DIRTY A SMILE (poetry)	PR11, 51
Eno, Will	BOOKS FOR READERS AND OTHER DYING PEOPLE (recommendation)	PR2, 164
	TWO MONOLOGUES (theatre)	PR4, 39
	EXCERPT FROM GINT (AN ADAPTATION OF HENRIK IBSEN'S PEER GYNT) (theatre)	PR16, 169
Ettlinger, Marion*	A CONVERSATION (etcetera)	PR16, 27
Evenson, Brian	WHITE SQUARE (fiction)	PR3, 20
Faries, Chad	THIRD STREET. STAMBAUGH, MICHIGAN: LATE SPRING, 1972 (nonfiction)	PR7, 48
Feitell, Merrill	"SONNY'S BLUES," BY JAMES BALDWIN (recommendation)	PR11, 143
Ferrell, Monica	AFTER A REST: PALIMPSEST (poetry)	PR9, 133
	ECHO DIGRESSION (poetry)	PR9, 135
Field, Miranda	BIRTH MARK (poetry)	PR2, 85
	COCK ROBIN (poetry)	PR2, 86
Fitch, Janet	THE MEMORY ROOM, BY MARY RAKO (recommendation)	PR5, 133
Fitzgerald, F. Scott*	CONTRACT FOR THE GREAT GATSBY (etcetera)	PR1, 152

Flint, Austin   EEVA-LIISA MANNER (recommendation)   PR1, 161

Flook, Maria   INSIDE THE SKY: A MEDITATION ON FLIGHT,
                         BY WILLIAM LANGEWIESCHE, AND STICK AND
                         RUDDER: AN EXPLANATION ON THE ART OF FLYING,
                         BY WOLFGANG LANGEWIESCHE (recommendation)   PR8, 142
                         TWENTY QUESTIONS (etcetera)   PR12, 219

Flores-Williams, Jason   NORTH DALLAS FORTY, BY PETER GENT
                         (recommendation)   PR9, 164
                         THE DINNER PARTY (theatre)   PR12, 71

Fluger, Marty   DIRECTING GRAND GUIGNOL (theatre)   PR1, 61
                         COMPOSING FOR GRAND GUIGNOL (theatre)   PR1, 78

Flynn, Nick   AMBER (poetry)   PR1, 90
                         STATUARY (poetry)   PR1, 92

Foix, J.V.*   FOUR SHORT POEMS, trans. Susan Lantz (etcetera) PR9, 205

Foos, Laurie   DONALD ANTRIM'S THE AFTERLIFE (recommendation) PR14, 57

Ford, Katie   IT'S LATE HERE HOW LIGHT IS LATE ONCE YOU'VE
                         FALLEN (poetry)   PR5, 30
                         ELEGY TO THE LAST BREATH (poetry)   PR5, 31

Fortini, Franco   TRADUCENDO BRECHT (poetry)   PR4, 28
Fortini, Franco*   TRANSLATING BRECHT, trans. John P. Welle (poetry) PR4, 29

Fox, Sarah   SHADOW OF THE VALLEY (poetry)   PR5, 32
                         HOW TO GET THE LOVE YOU WANT (poetry)   PR5, 35

Franklin, Tom   TRUE GRIT, BY CHARLES PORTIS (recommendation) PR7, 145

Frumkin, Rebekah   MONSTER (fiction)   PR16, 201

Funkhouser, Margaret   ESTIMATED DRIFT (poetry)   PR6, 34
                         ITS OWNERS BECAME A DIM (poetry)   PR6, 35

Furr, Derek Lance   YELLOW PAJAMAS (nonfiction)   PR8, 93

Gaitskill, Mary   PETER PAN (recommendation)   PR14, 29

Garcia, J. Malcolm   RELIEF: AFGHANISTAN, 2001 (nonfiction)   PR9, 99

George, Diana   PATERNITY WITHIN THE LIMITS OF REASON (fiction) PR4, 67

Gerstler, Amy   HEADLESS, BY BENJAMIN WEISSMAN (recommendation) PR8, 144

Gibson, Dobby   VERTICAL HOLD (poetry)   PR12,201
                         THE WORLD AS SEEN THROUGH A GLASS OF
                         ICE WATER (poetry)   PR12,202

Gifford, Barry   THE CINÉ (fiction)   PR5, 79
                         THE ROSE OF TIBET, BY LIONEL DAVIDSON
                         (recommendation)   PR6, 144
                         HOLIDAY FROM WOMEN (fiction)   PR10, 75

Gilberg, Gail Hosking   PLAN OF A STORY THAT COULD HAVE BEEN WRITTEN
                         IF ONLY I HAD KNOWN IT WAS HAPPENING (nonfiction) PR1, 119

Gitterman, Debra   BAGGAGE CLAIM (poetry)   PR15, 107
                         THOSE WERE DESERT YEARS (poetry)   PR15, 108

Glick, Jeremy Martin   COLLATERAL DAMAGES: CONTEXTS FOR THINKING
                         OF THE LIBERATION OF JAMIL ABUL AL-AMIN
                         (H. RAP BROWN) (criticism)   PR4, 12

Goldberg, Kim   BIRTHDAY (nonfiction)   PR16, 49

Goldberg, Len   JOURNAL: BLACK ROCK CITY JOURNAL (etcetera)   PR16, 133

Goldberg, Myla	BRUNO SCHULTZ AND BOHUMIL HRABAL (recommendation)	PR3, 66
Goldberg, Tod	REPORT: VEGAS VALLEY BOOK FESTIVAL (etcetera)	PR12, 183
	THE LAWS OF EVENING, BY MARY YUKARI WATERS (recommendation)	PR16, 179
Goldstein, Naama	"THE BOUND MAN," FROM ILSE AICHINGER'S THE BOUND MAN (recommendation)	PR12, 181
Goldstein, Yael	SPIN, BY ROBERT CHARLES WILSON (recommendation)	PR16, 95
Grandbois, Peter	ALL OR NOTHING AT THE FABERGÉ (fiction)	PR11, 93
Graver, Elizabeth	A GOOD HOUSE, BY BONNIE BURNARD; AND BLINDNESS, BY JOSÉ SARAMAGO (recommendation)	PR5, 134
Griesemer, John	ERNEST HEBERT (recommendation)	PR5, 127
Griffith, Michael	THE DANGEROUS HUSBAND, BY JANE SHAPIRO (recommendation)	PR10, 29
Griffo, Michela	PAINTINGS AND DRAWINGS (art)	PR9, 66
Grimm, Mary	WAR AND PEACE AS HYPERTEXT (recommendation)	PR12, 81
Gritsman, Andrey	OVERHEARD: WAKE UP NEW YORK CITY, SEPTEMBER 2001 (etcetera)	PR10, 21
Gross, Gwendolen	STONES FOR IBARRA, BY HARRIET DOERR; AND OF KINKAJOUS, CAPYBARAS, HORNED BEETLES, SELEDANGS, AND THE ODDEST AND MOST WONDERFUL MAMMALS, INSECTS, BIRDS, AND PLANTS OF OUR WORLD, BY JEANNE K. HANSON AND DEANE MORRISON (recommendation)	PR8, 155
Grubin, Eve	THE NINETEENTH-CENTURY NOVEL (poetry)	PR7, 13
	THE NINETEENTH-CENTURY NOVEL II (poetry)	PR7, 14
Hagy, Alyson	A GOOD MAN IS HARD TO FIND, BY FLANNERY O'CONNOR (recommendation)	PR13, 93
Haigh, Jennifer	PIZZA MAN (fiction)	PR14, 113
Haines, Lise	WHY DID I EVER, BY MARY ROBISON (recommendation)	PR6, 157
Haley, Melissa	SHE, UNDER THE UMBRELLA, WENT (nonfiction)	PR11, 171
Halovanic, Maria	FEMMÁGE (poetry)	PR15, 137
	AFTERIMAGE FROM A TRAIN (poetry)	PR15, 138
Hamilton, Saskia	ROOM (poetry)	PR4, 27
	EXTEND (poetry)	PR4, 30
Harding, John Wesley (see also Stace, Wesley)	LISTERINE: THE LIFE AND OPINIONS OF LAURENCE STERNE (etcetera)	PR5, 174
	THE LOST STRADIVARIUS, MOONFLEET, AND THE NEBULY COAT: THE ABNORMAL RESPONSES OF JOHN MEADE FALKNER (recommendation)	PR11, 89
	JOURNAL: (UNEXPURGATED) TOUR JOURNAL (etcetera)	PR16, 221
Harnetiaux, Trish	THE DORSAL STRIATUM (theatre)	PR13, 129
Hart, JoeAnn	CROSS CREEK, BY MARJORIE KINNAN RAWLINGS (recommendation)	PR12, 189
Hartley, Heather	PARTNER MY PARTNER (poetry)	PR14, 59
	THE KHARMA CLUB (poetry)	PR14, 61

Harvey, Matthea	THE DIFFERENCE BETWEEN THE NEED FOR CONSISTENCY & THE STATE OF EXPECTATION (poetry)	PR4, 31
	DEFINITION OF WEATHER (poetry)	PR4, 32
Harwood, Seth	FISHER CAT (fiction)	PR12, 169
Hausler, Pete	FROM HELL, BY ALAN MOORE, ILLUSTRATED BY EDDIE CAMPBELL (recommendation)	PR1, 172
	WIND, SAND AND STARS, BY ANTOINE DE SAINT-EXUPÉRY (recommendation)	PR8, 137
Healy, Lorraine	WHAT WE'VE FORGOTTEN (poetry)	PR16, 25
Hearst, Michael	THREE SHORT STORIES (nonfiction)	PR15, 157
Hempel, Amy	PEARSON MARX (recommendation)	PR1, 16
Hempel, Amy*	A CONVERSATION (etcetera)	PR14, 83
Hero, Claire	MARGINALIA (poetry)	PR5, 41
	DIVINATION (poetry)	PR5, 42
Hershon, Joanna	MRS. BRIDGE, BY EVAN S. CONNELL (recommendation)	PR6, 145
Heti, Sheila	KURT VONNEGUT (recommendation)	PR14, 175
Higgs, Christopher	HOLD YOUR HORSES THE ELEPHANTS ARE COMING (nonfiction)	PR16, 155
Hill, Daniel	PAINTINGS (art)	PR8, 34
Hoagland, Edward	THE CIRCUS OF DR. LAO, BY CHARLES G. FINNEY (recommendation)	PR5, 135
Hoch, James	GLEANERS (poetry)	PR6, 36
	SCARIFICATION (poetry)	PR6, 37
Hodgman, Jan	SMALL WORLD (nonfiction)	PR4, 46
Hoffman, Alice	TRANSFORMATIONS (fiction)	PR16, 267
Hoffman, Richard	AFTER LONG SILENCE, BY HELEN FREMONT (recommendation)	PR10, 56
	NOTHING TO LOOK AT HERE (fiction)	PR13, 197
Holdsworth, Kevin	MOVING WATER (nonfiction)	PR3, 121
Holland, Noy	A SPORT AND A PASTIME, BY JAMES SALTER (recommendation)	PR16, 127
Hollander, David	WHATEVER HAPPENED TO HARLAN? A REPORT FROM THE FIELD (nonfiction)	PR16, 51
Holliday, Frank	DAVID SPIHER: A NEW YORK PAINTER (art)	PR13, 65
Holman, Virginia	AN AMERICAN MEMORY AND I AM ZOE HANDKE, BY ERIC LARSEN (recommendation)	PR8, 135
Hood, Ann	FIRST NOVELS (recommendation)	PR11, 47
	CROONING WITH DINO (fiction)	PR14, 145
Hotchner, A. E.	P. G. WODEHOUSE (recommendation)	PR6, 146
Hryniewiez-Yarbrough, Ewa (trans.)	DE SE IPSO, by Janusz Szuber (poetry)	PR9, 131
	NEW LABORS, by Janusz Szuber (poetry)	PR9, 132
Huber, K. M.	VISIT WITH A FORGOTTEN PEOPLE (nonfiction)	PR10, 107
Hughes, Mary-Beth	BEL CANTO BY ANN PATCHETT (recommendation)	PR4, 106
Hummel, Maria	NEW YORK SELVES: AN ELEGY (poetry)	PR11, 193
	GOD MACHINE ON ADVERSITY (poetry)	PR11, 196
Hunt, Jerry	FOUR VIDEO TRANSLATIONS (theatre)	PR10, 33

Iagnemma, Karl	ITALIAN DAYS, BY BARBARA GRIZZUTI HARRISON (recommendation)	PR7, 134
Ihara, Nathan	HITTING HARMONY (nonfiction)	PR8, 100
Ireland, Perrin	THE DOG OF THE MARRIAGE, BY AMY HEMPEL (recommendation)	PR16, 195
Ison, Tara	MENDEL'S DWARF BY SIMON MAWER (recommendation)	PR2, 166
Jackson, Major	INDIAN SONG (poetry)	PR2, 87
	URBAN RENEWAL ix. (poetry)	PR2, 88
James, Henry	ON TURGENEV (etcetera)	PR7, 183
Jenkinson, Len	THE MUSEUM OF SPEED (fiction)	PR3, 26
Johnson, Samuel	LAST WILL AND TESTAMENT (etcetera)	PR4, 149
Johnston, Mat	WHAT WE DO (fiction)	PR7, 100
Jones, Alden	SECRET LIFE, BY MICHAEL RYAN (recommendation)	PR4, 108
	POLITE SOCIETY, BY MELANIE SUMNER (recommendation)	PR9, 170
Jones, Allen Morris	WILLIAM FAULKNER'S "THE BEAR" (recommendation)	PR16, 101
Jones, Ben	THE ANCESTOR'S TALE, BY RICHARD DAWKINS (recommendation)	PR11, 200
Kadish, Rachel	LAWRENCE WESCHLER'S VERMEER IN BOSNIA (recommendation)	PR12, 65
Kalfus, Ken	CONFESSIONS OF ZENO, BY ITALO SVEVO (recommendation)	PR2, 168
Kalotay, Daphne	WOMEN IN THEIR BEDS: NEW AND SELECTED STORIES, BY GINA BERRIAULT, AND THE TEA CEREMONY: THE UNCOLLECTED WRITINGS OF GINA BERRIAULT (recommendation)	PR11, 31
Kaluza, Kobun	EXCERPT FROM INERT DEMENTIA (theatre)	PR14, 193
Kantar, Annie	FOR YOU, A POEM (poetry)	PR2, 89
	I SEE MY GRANDMOTHER AGAIN (poetry)	PR2, 90
Kennedy, X. J.	THE FICTION OF J. F. POWERS (recommendation)	PR10, 123
Kimball, Michael	EXCERPTS FROM THE SUICIDE LETTERS OF JONATHAN BENDER (B. 1967, D. 2000) (fiction)	PR12, 155
Kimura, Takahiro	DESTRUCTION AND CONSTRUCTION OF THE HUMAN FACE (art)	PR5, 194
Klass, Perri	BIRDS OF AMERICA, BY MARY MCCARTHY (recommendation)	PR12, 203
Klíma, Ivan	IRENA OBERMANNOVA (recommendation)	PR2, 169
Klink, Joanna	SHOOTING STAR (poetry)	PR2, 100
	RIVER IN DUSK (poetry)	PR2, 101
Knapp, Elizabeth	INDELIBLE (poetry)	PR11, 13
	UNINVITED GUEST (poetry)	PR11, 15
Kozma, Andrew	INVADER (poetry)	PR14, 103
	WHAT IS (poetry)	PR14, 104
Kreines, Amy	WARNINGS (etcetera)	PR8, 165
Kronovet, Jennifer	A HISTORY OF KANSAS (poetry)	PR3, 37
	SCENIC OVERLOOK (poetry)	PR3, 38

Kuo, Alex	THE LUNCH (fiction)	PR15, 85
Kuzmanovich, Zoran, et al.	LOLITA A–Z (etcetera)	PR7, 151
Lang, Andrew	EXCERPT: FROM ADVENTURES IN BOOKS (etcetera)	PR14, 127
Lantz, Susan (trans.)	FOUR SHORT POEMS, by J. V. Foix (etcetera)	PR9, 205
LaSalle, Peter	E.A.P. (etcetera)	PR9, 183
Lauenstein, Maria	BODY AND SOUL (nonfiction)	PR10, 173
Lavender-Smith, Evan	BENNETT'S CHEAP CATHARSIS (fiction)	PR15, 109
Laverty, Rory	MY LIFE OF CRIME (nonfiction)	PR9, 89
Leavitt, David	A FAR CRY FROM KENSINGTON, BY MURIEL SPARK (recommendation)	PR16, 265
LeCraw, H. H.	AUGUST (fiction)	PR8, 53
Lee, Don	MYSTERY RIDE, BY ROBERT BOSWELL (recommendation)	PR10, 81
Lehman, David	AARON FOGEL (recommendation)	PR2, 172
Lemon, Alex	BELOW THE NEARER SKY (poetry)	PR10, 157
	SILT (poetry)	PR10, 158
Lennon, Brian	SOME STORIES ARE PARABLES, BUT (fiction)	PR8, 51
Lerner, Ben	FROM THE LICHTENBERG FIGURES (poetry)	PR3, 39
LeRoy, J. T.	THE STORIES OF BREECE D'J PANCAKE, BY BREECE D'J PANCAKE (recommendation)	PR10, 211
Lethem, Jonathan*	INTERVIEW (etcetera)	PR5, 153
Lewis, Sinclair	LECTURE: THE AMERICAN FEAR OF LITERATURE (etcetera)	PR15, 119
Lifson, Hannah	TINY MONUMENTS: A LOOK AT SNAPSHOT PHOTOGRAPHY (criticism)	PR16, 83
Ligon, Samuel	ANIMAL HATER (fiction)	PR6, 83
Lima, José Lezama*	RHAPSODY FOR THE MULE, trans. G. J. Racz (etcetera)	PR4, 127
Lindquist, Mark	MOTHER NIGHT, BY KURT VONNEGUT (recommendation)	PR10, 171
Liu, Elliott	THE END OF HISTORY (poetry)	PR14, 109
	THE RISE OF THE MIDDLE CLASS (poetry)	PR14, 111
Livesey, Margot	BLOOD, BY PATRICIA TRAXLER (recommendation)	PR4, 110
Livingston, Reb	INTERVIEW WITH APRIL BERNARD (etcetera)	PR7, 169
Lock, Norman	BEYOND RECOGNITION: A MONOLOGUE IN 12 SECTIONS (theatre)	PR5, 49
Lombardi, Joyce	YAMBA (nonfiction)	PR1, 111
Lopate, Phillip*	A CONVERSATION (etcetera)	PR15, 21
Lopez, Robert	SCAR (fiction)	PR5, 82
Lorberer, Eric	SONNET (poetry)	PR4, 33
	OUR WILL (poetry)	PR4, 34
Lowenthal, Michael	ANTARCTICA, BY CLAIRE KEEGAN (recommendation)	PR7, 138
	MARGE (fiction)	PR14, 167
Lucenko, Kristina	JANE BOWLES (recommendation)	PR1, 176
Lutz, Gary	EMINENCE (fiction)	PR1, 25
Lutz, Kevin	DOWN IN THE VALLEY (nonfiction)	PR13, 145

Lynn, Allison   DIGRESSIONS ON SOME POEMS BY FRANK O'HARA,
                       BY JOE LESUEUR (recommendation)   PR16, 81

Maazel, Fiona   MY LIFE AND HARD TIMES, BY JAMES THURBER
                       (recommendation)   PR4, 112

Madden, Patrick   DIVERS WEIGHTS AND DIVERS MEASURES (nonfiction)   PR6, 133

Maher, Ronnie E.   PHOTOGRAPHS (art)   PR15, 65

Malech, Dora   FACE FOR RADIO (poetry)   PR13, 181
                       QUICK STUDY (poetry)   PR13, 182

Malzhan, Tim   INTRODUCTION TO MICHAEL AYALA:
                       PHOTOGRAPHS (art)   PR6, 66

Mamet, David   TWENTY QUESTIONS (etcetera)   PR13, 221

Manning, David   THE MAN WHO WASN'T THERE (nonfiction)   PR1, 123

Marchant, Fred   NON SUM DIGNUS (poetry)   PR12, 67
                       ARD NA MARA (poetry)   PR12, 68
                       ALMOST PARADISE: NEW AND SELECTED POEMS
                       AND TRANSLATIONS, BY SAM HAMILL (recommendation) PR13, 81

Markus, Peter   WHAT OUR FATHER IS HERE TO TELL US (fiction)   PR6, 89

Martin, Lee   MY WORD: MEMOIR'S NECESSARY BETRAYAL (nonfiction) PR3, 113

Martin, Manjula   ON THE DATING PROSPECTS OF FEMINIST
                       DAUGHTERS, OR DEAR MAUREEN (criticism)   PR12, 49

Marvin, Cate   WHY SLEEP (poetry)   PR3, 41
                       OCEAN IS A WORD IN THIS POEM (poetry)   PR3, 43

Mastroianni, Mark   PAINTINGS (art)   PR10, 50

Matthews, Sebastian   IN MY DREAM I'VE BECOME A GREAT
                       TRUMPETER (poetry)   PR6, 39
                       THE FISH HAWK AT SANDERLING (poetry)   PR6, 41

Mattison, Alice   OTHER PEOPLE'S HOUSES AND HER FIRST
                       AMERICAN BY LORE SEGAL (recommendation)   PR11, 37

McCallum, Shara   "ARE WE N,OT OF INTEREST TO EACH OTHER?":
                       THE SUBLIME IN ELIZABETH ALEXANDER'S
                       AMERICAN SUBLIME (recommendation)   PR13, 143

McCann, Richard   A SORROW BEYOND DREAMS, BY PETER HANDKE,
                       TRANSLATED BY RALPH MANNHEIM (recommendation)   PR6, 139

McCarty, Anne   THE BOOK OF DISQUIET, BY FERNANDO PESSOA
                       (recommendation)   PR3, 80

McCorkle, Jill   A MIRACLE OF CATFISH, BY LARRY BROWN
                       (recommendation)   PR15, 43

McDonough, Jill   JULY 19, 1692: SUSANNA MARTIN (poetry)   PR12,117
                       SEPTEMBER 18, 1755: MARK AND PHILLIS (poetry)   PR12, 119

McGinnis, Ralph   THE OMISSION OF COMICS (criticism)   PR11, 55

McGlynn, David   RERUNS NEVER LIE (fiction)   PR11, 130

McLeod, Eric Tyrone   SELLING OUT: CONSUMER CULTURE AND
                       COMMODIFICATION OF THE MALE BODY (criticism)   PR6, 11

McNair, Wesley   DELIGHTS & SHADOWS, BY TED KOOSER, SEARCH
                       PARTY, BY WILLIAM MATTHEWS; AND JACK AND OTHER
                       NEW POEMS BY MAXINE KUMIN (recommendation)   PR11, 191

McNally, John	THE PROMISE OF FAILURE, OR WHY YOU SHOULD DROP EVERYTHING YOU'RE DOING AND READ RICHARD YATES'S REVOLUTIONARY ROAD RIGHT NOW! (recommendation)	PR16, 113
Medina, Pablo	LETTER FOR MY FATHER (etcetera)	PR2, 131
Medwed, Mameve	VARIOUS (recommendation)	PR15, 81
Mellis, Miranda F.	FROM RUNE TO RUIN: AN ALPHABET (EXCERPTS) (fiction)	PR13, 113
Melnyczuk, Askold	NO WEDDING, NO CAKE: MOSELEY AND MUTIS (recommendation)	PR4, 114
Menger-Anderson, Kirsten	THE DOCTORS (fiction)	PR16, 117
Mentzer, Robert	LATE (fiction)	PR9, 61
Mercer, Jeremy	ESSAY: OBSERVING VICTOR HUGO (etcetera)	PR14, 211
Messer, Sarah	RABID DOG (poetry)	PR3, 44
	LOOKING AT SATAN (poetry)	PR3, 46
Michaels, Leonard	REPRINT: WHAT'S A STORY? (etcetera)	PR12, 59
Miller, Ben	V.F. GROCERY (fiction)	PR2, 54
Miller, Risa	PARTS AND PIECES: SVEN BIRKERTS, A. MANETTE ANSAY, STEVE STERN, CHRISTOPHER TILGHMAN, ELINOR LIPMAN. AND AMY HEMPEL (recommendation)	PR8, 140
Millet, Lydia	THE COMPLETE TALES OF MERRY GOLD, BY KATE BERNHEIMER (recommendation)	PR15, 155
Monahan, Jean	ANIMALS IN TRANSLATION, BY TEMPLE GRANDIN AND CATHERINE JOHNSON (recommendation)	PR11, 11
Monson, Ander	A HUGE, OLD RADIO (fiction)	PR4, 64
	EXCISION (poetry)	PR8, 28
	LIMB REPLANTATION, FAILED (poetry)	PR8, 30
Montemarano, Nicholas	LAST LAST LAST (fiction)	PR4, 73
Moody, Rick	ON MICHAEL DE MONTAIGNE (recommendation)	PR1, 163
	FLAP (fiction)	PR8, 66
	I LOVE DICK, BY CHRIS KRAUS (recommendation)	PR10, 9
	TOUR DIARY: THE DIVINERS, NORTH AMERICA, 2005 (etcetera)	PR12, 91
Moody, Rick (ed.)	LETTERS HOME FROM THE PACIFIC, 1944–46, FRANCIS ARTHUR FLYNN (etcetera)	PR3, 138
Moon, Michael	THE MEMOIR BANK (recommendation)	PR5, 139
Moore, Alison	OKLAHOMA ON MY MIND (recommendation)	PR4, 116
Moos, Kate	IN A CERTAIN PLACE, AT A CERTAIN TIME (poetry)	PR3, 47
	THE PRINCE (poetry)	PR3, 48
Moran, John	THE EMPIRICAL SOCIETY (theatre)	PR6, 49
Morris, Mary	LUCY GAYHEART, BY WILLA CATHER (recommendation)	PR8, 147
	POSSUM (fiction)	PR15, 13
Morrissey, Donna	MIDDLEMARCH, BY GEORGE ELIOT (recommendation)	PR7, 129
Moser, Barry	SACRED AND VULGAR: THE INFLUENCES OF FLANNERY O'CONNOR ON THE ILLUSTRATIONS FOR PENNYROYAL CAXTON BIBLE (recommendation)	PR6, 148

Moyer, Linda Lancione	WALKING BACKWARDS IN TAKAMATSU (nonfiction)	PR11, 209
Murphy, Sarah	BREATHLESS, MY VENOM SPENT, I LAY DOWN MY WEAPONS (poetry)	PR16, 215
	HOROSCOPE (poetry)	PR16, 217
Murphy, Tom	INDEX TO THE GREAT GATSBY (etcetera)	PR8, 172
Murray, Sabina	THREE AUSTRALIAN NOVELISTS (recommendation)	PR7, 146
Myles, Eileen	HELL (etcetera)	PR10, 83
Nankin, Sarah	UNTITLED AS OF YET (fiction)	PR7, 114
Nettleton, Taro	STREETSTYLE: SKATEBOARDING, SPATIAL APPROPRIATION, AND DISSENT (criticism)	PR8, 123
Nichols, Kelcey	AUSTIN (fiction)	PR1, 40
Niffenegger, Audrey	TRASH SEX MAGIC BY JENNIFER STEVENSON (recommendation)	PR10, 193
Nilsson, Kathy	THE SACRIFICE (poetry)	PR1, 96
	BLACK LEMONS (poetry)	PR1, 98
Nin, Anaïs*	MARRIAGE CERTIFICATE (etcetera)	PR14, 63
Nissen, Thisbe	SOME THINGS ABOUT KEVIN BROCKMEIER (recommendation)	PR8, 149
Nordbrandt, Henrik	CASA BLANCA (poetry)	PR10, 197
	ANKERPLADS (poetry)	PR10, 199
Nordbrandt, Henrik*	CASA BLANCA, trans. Patrick Phillips (poetry)	PR10, 196
	ANCHORAGE, trans. Patrick Phillips (poetry)	PR10, 198
Novakovich, Josip	BERLIN, July 18–August 11, 2002 (etcetera)	PR6, 172
Nutter, Jude	THE WINGS OF BUTTERFLIES (poetry)	PR8, 19
	THE EYES OF FISH (poetry)	PR8, 22
Nye, Naomi Shihab	THE ORANGE, THE FIG, THE WHISPER OF GRAPES (etcetera)	PR2, 137
Oates, Joyce Carol*	NOVELS OF JOYCE CAROL OATES(etcetera)	PR10, 127
O'Connor, Larry	THE MIDDLE-AGED MAN AND THE SEA (nonfiction)	PR7, 39
Offutt, Chris	VEGETABLE ON THE HOOF (fiction)	PR3, 14
O'Keefe, Michael	CONVERATION: MARK STRAND (etcetera)	PR13, 119
O'Nan, Stewart	THE TRUE DETECTIVE, BY THEODORE WEESNER (recommendation)	PR5, 141
Orlen, Steve	THE ALPHABET IN THE PARK: SELECTED POEMS OF ADELIA PRADO, TRANSLATED FROM THE PORTUGUESE BY ELLEN WATSON (recommendation)	PR3, 67
Orner, Peter	OPEN DOORS, BY LEONARDO SCIASCIA (recommendation)	PR7, 142
Page. Judith	PORTRAITS IN PLASMA (art)	PR16, 65
Paine, Tom	LITTLE BOYS COME FROM THE STARS, BY EMMANUEL DONGALA (recommendation)	PR2, 174
Parrish, Tim	HEAD, BY WILLIAM TESTER (recommendation)	PR5, 137
Parvin, Roy	MICHAEL BYERS AND THE COAST OF GOOD INTENTIONS (recommendation)	PR7, 143
Patrick, Oona Hyla	THE SHACK OF ART AND HEALING (nonfiction)	PR4, 52
Pearlman, Edith	DREAM CHILDREN (fiction)	PR7, 83

Pei, Lowry	EUDORA WELTY'S THE GOLDEN APPLES (recommendation)	PR13, 15
Perabo, Susan	HARRY POTTER AND THE HALF-BLOOD PRINCE, BY J. K. ROWLING (recommendation)	PR12, 31
Perkes, Logan	THE ILLUSION OF SYMMETRY (nonfiction)	PR15, 31
Perrotta, Tom	AUNT JULIA AND THE SCRIPTWRITER, BY MARIO VARGAS LLOSA (recommendation)	PR5, 143
	THE SMILE ON HAPPY CHANG'S FACE (fiction)	PR8, 75
	TWENTY QUESTIONS (etcetera)	PR10, 219
Petro, Melissa	WORKING NIGHTS IN THE ARTIFICIAL DAY, WORKING DAYS IN THE ARTIFICIAL NIGHT (nonfiction)	PR14, 133
Phillips, Patrick	THOSE GEORGIA SUNDAYS (poetry)	PR10, 25
	LITANY (poetry)	PR10, 26
Phillips, Patrick (trans.)	CASA BLANCA, by Henrik Nordbrandt (poetry)	PR10, 196
	ANCHORAGE, by Henrik Nordbrandt (poetry)	PR10, 198
Pinsky, Robert	JAMES MCMICHAEL (recommendation)	PR3, 71
Pippin, Stephanie	GOOD SCIENCE (poetry)	PR8, 16
	HEART (poetry)	PR8, 18
Pollack, Neal	HEED THE THUNDER, BY JIM THOMPSON (recommendation)	PR8, 146
Pomfret, Scott D.	WHAT GOD SEES (fiction)	PR6, 104
Pope, Dan	A SPORT AND A PASTIME, BY JAMES SALTER (recommendation)	PR10, 217
	DRIVE-IN (fiction)	PR11, 115
Powell, Elizabeth	I SPY (poetry)	PR12, 9
Prater, Tzarina T.	"OLD MAN YOUR KUNG FU IS USELESS": AFRICAN AMERICAN SPECTATORSHIP AND HONG KONG ACTION CINEMA (criticism)	PR2, 185
Presente, Henry	THE SAVAGE GIRL, BY ALEX SHAKAR (recommendation)	PR7, 131
Price, D. Gatling	STILL WRECK (fiction)	PR10, 185
Proulx, E. Annie	A POSTCARD (recommendation)	PR1, 156
Pruett, Lynn	PLANT LIFE BY PAMELA DUNCAN (recommendation)	PR7, 136
Pynchon, Thomas*	ANTHOLOGY: THE BLURBS OF THOMAS PYNCHON (etcetera)	PR14, 11
Rabb, Margo	HAPPY ALL THE TIME: LOVING LAURIE COLWIN (recommendation)	PR16, 153
Racz, G. J. (trans.)	RHAPSODY FOR THE MULE, by José Lezama Lima (etcetera)	PR4, 127
Raffel, Dawn	FURTHER ADVENTURES IN THE RESTLESS UNIVERSE (etcetera)	PR2, 143
Raines, Laurah Norton	SLOW FREEZE (nonfiction)	PR16, 197
Ramey, Emma	SERVANT (poetry)	PR8, 26
	SERVANT (poetry)	PR8, 27
Rawson, Joanna	LOGBOOK (poetry)	PR9, 123
	ELM & CANCER (poetry)	PR9, 127

Rector, Liam	DANGEROUS MUSE: THE LIFE OF LADY CAROLINE BLACKWOOD, BY NANCY SCHOENBERGER (recommendation)	PR3, 76
Redel, Victoria	WILLIAM BRONK (recommendation)	PR2, 175
Reifler, Nelly	SUGAR (fiction)	PR5, 103
	OCTOBER SNOW, BY SAMUEL REIFLER (recommendation)	PR16, 187
Reifler, Samuel	THE DAY THEY WERE SHOOTING DOGS (fiction)	PR16, 145
Reiken, Frederick	WINTON, MUNRO, BERGER (recommendation)	PR3, 77
Reyn, Irina	EAT, MEMORY (criticism)	PR14. 47
Rice, Jeremy	LITTLE ORANGE BOTTLES (nonfiction)	PR16. 103
Richard, Frances	ADJACENT (poetry)	PR2, 92
	GLANCING AT (poetry)	PR2, 94
Richmond, Andrew	ACTIVIST (fiction)	PR7, 116
	PHOTOGRAPHS (art)	PR11, 65
Roberts, Matt	THE DOGCATCHER HATES POLITICS (nonfiction)	PR10, 49
Robinson, Lewis	TRUMAN CAPOTE, RICHARD FORD, AND JOHN IRVING (recommendation)	PR8, 153
Rock, Peter	GOLD FIREBIRD (fiction)	PR12, 19
	ON HARUKI MURAKAMI'S A WILD SHEEP CHASE, OR HOW I GOT "SHEEPED" (recommendation)	PR13, 219
Roleke, Margaret	CURRENT ABSTRACTION (art)	PR14, 65
Rosenfeld, Natania	A YEAR ON THE PRAIRIE (nonfiction)	PR11, 33
Rosovsky, Michael	POACHERS, BY TOM FRANKLIN (recommendation)	PR1, 178
	ON BOXING, BY JOYCE CAROL OATES (recommendation)	PR9, 176
Roth, David	THE OTHER WOMAN (fiction)	PR10, 201
Ruff, John	WHAT THEY TALKED ABOUT AND WHAT THEY SAID (poetry)	PR4, 35
	DE CHIRICO SHAVING (poetry)	PR4, 36
	DREAMING OF ROME (poetry)	PR16, 129
	WHILE READING PICO DELLA MIRANDOLA'S ORATION ON HUMAN DIGNITY (poetry)	PR16, 132
Ryan, David	MY LAST SIGH: THE AUTOBIOGRAPHY OF LUIS BUÑUEL (recommendation)	PR1, 180
	STORIES IN THE WORST WAY, BY GARY LUTZ (recommendation)	PR8, 159
	JERRY HUNT: FOUR VIDEO TRANSLATIONS (theatre)	PR10, 33
Salinger, J. D.*	SALINGER V. RANDOM HOUSE, INC., 811 F.2D 90 (2nd Cir. 1987) (etcetera)	PR9, 193
Salopek, Paul	MISSIVES: FOUR WAYS OF TRYING TO HOLD ONTO IT (etcetera)	PR11, 83
Salvatore, Joe	UNHEMLECH (fiction)	PR10, 99
Sandler, Lauren	HIP HOP HIGH: MAINSTREAM BLACK CULTURE IN THE WHITE SUBURBS (criticism)	PR5, 13
Saunders, George	QUESTIONNAIRE (etcetera)	PR14, 219
Scalise, Mike	WRITING HIM OFF (nonfiction)	PR15, 201
Scanlon, Elizabeth	CLOSING TIME (poetry)	PR5, 43
	QUARRY (poetry)	PR5, 44

Schappell, Elissa	THE SELECTED LETTERS OF DAWN POWELL, 1913–1965, AS EDITED BY TIM PAGE (recommendation)	PR12, 160
Scheid, Liz	WHAT THEY DON'T TELL YOU ABOUT BREAST-FEEDING (poetry)	PR16, 259
	WHAT I'M NOT TELLING YOU (poetry)	PR16, 260
Schilpp, Margot	THE BONE PEOPLE, BY KERI HULME (recommendation)	PR4, 118
Schmidt, Heidi Jon	FUTILITY, BY WILLIAM GERHARDIE (recommendation)	PR9, 161
Schmoll, Ken Rus	RESPONSIBILITY, JUSTICE, AND HONESTY: REHEARSING EDWARD BOND'S SAVED (theatre)	PR3, 51
Schrank, Ben	ALL SOULS DAY, BY CEES NOOTEBOOM (AND OTHER BOOKS THAT YEARN) (recommendation)	PR6, 151
Schuller, Kyla	THE AMERICANS WHO MATTER: MICHAEL MOORE'S WHITE LIBERAL RACISM IN BOWLING FOR COLUMBINE (criticism)	PR9, 11
Schutt, Christine	THE ARTIST AND HIS SISTER GERTI (fiction)	PR6, 91
Schutz, Lacy	INTRODUCTION TO DANIEL HILL: PAINTINGS (art)	PR8, 34
Schutzman, Steven	THE BANK (theatre)	PR11, 119
Schwabe, Liesl	BLUE WINDOW (nonfiction)	PR8, 108
Searle, Elizabeth	BLACK TICKETS, THEN AND NOW (recommendation)	PR4, 120
	LIBRETTO: TONYA AND NANCY: THE OPERA (etcetera)	PR12, 139
Searle, Elizabeth*	INTERVIEW (etcetera)	PR8, 199
Seigel, Andrea	BEHIND THE ATTIC WALL, BY SYLVIA CASSEDY (recommendation)	PR12, 217
Semanki, David	CINÉMA VÉRITÉ (poetry)	PR11, 145
	DOUBLE FEATURE (poetry)	PR11, 147
Seward, Scott	WHY BALTIMORE HOUSE MUSIC IS THE NEW DYLAN (criticism)	PR3, 85
Shattuck, Jessica	THE STORIES OF JOHN CHEEVER (recommendation)	PR11, 139
Shelby, Ashley	A RIVER IN CHARLESTON (nonfiction)	PR5, 115
Shepard, Jim	THE INVENTION OF TRUTH, BY MARTA MORAZZONI (recommendation)	PR2, 177
Sherman, Rachel	HOMESTAY (fiction)	PR2, 57
Shields, David	LIFE AND ART (etcetera)	PR2, 147
Shippy, Peter Jay	CELLIST (poetry)	PR7, 24
	DOGS RESEMBLING THEIR OWNER (poetry)	PR7, 25
Shonk, Katherine	"THE RETURN," BY ANDREI PLATONOV, FROM THE RETURN AND OTHER STORIES (recommendation)	PR9, 165
Siegel, Gail	FALLING OBJECTS: CHICAGO (etcetera)	PR10, 191
Siegel, Robert Anthony	THE MAGIC BOX (fiction)	PR11, 178
	BLOOD MERIDIAN, OR THE EVENING REDNESS IN THE WEST, BY CORMAC MCCARTHY (recommendation)	PR15, 139
Siegel, Zoë	IMAGES OF SCULPTURES AND DRAWINGS (art)	PR2, 19
Simon, Jeremy	HOW TO REACH ME: A MANUAL (nonfiction)	PR2, 70
Sinor, Shara	GHOST OF TEN (nonfiction)	PR13, 56
Slater, Tracy	JOURNAL: ERASING GENDER: A WOMAN'S JOURNEY THROUGH MEN'S LOCKUP (etcetera)	PR13, 23

Slavin, Julia	MAILE CHAPMAN (recommendation)	PR1, 167
	DREAM TRAILERS (fiction)	PR13, 173
Smith, Charles	DAN SHEA (recommendation)	PR1, 168
Smith, Tracy K.	A HUNGER SO HONED (poetry)	PR7, 15
	SELF-PORTRAIT AS THE LETTER Y (poetry)	PR7, 17
Smithee, Alan	THE STRANGE, ENTERTAINING, AND SOMETIMES BEHIND-THE-SCENES STORY OF CLEO BIRDWELL AND DON DELILLO (etcetera)	PR2, 105
Snediker, Michael	O. HENRY (recommendation)	PR3, 70
Snyder, Laurel	THE SIMPLE MACHINES (poetry)	PR6, 43
	HAPPILY EVER AFTER (poetry)	PR6, 44
Solar-Tuttle, Rachel	WORDS—LEAN, LYRICAL, AUTHENTIC—BRING CHILDREN FROM SHADOWS (recommendation)	PR8, 157
Sorrentino, Christopher	LIGHT WHILE THERE IS LIGHT, BY KEITH WALDROP (recommendation)	PR14, 105
Spalding, Lavinia	TEACHING KOREA (etcetera)	PR4, 134
Spark, Debra	SIZE MATTERS (recommendation)	PR15, 213
Spiher, David	PAINTINGS (art)	PR13, 65
Spiotta, Dana	TRANCE, BY CHRISTOPHER SORRENTINO (recommendation)	PR14, 43
Stace, Wesley see also Harding John Wesley	LISTERINE: THE LIFE AND OPINIONS OF LAURENCE STERNE (etcetera)	PR5, 174
	THE LOST STRADIVARIUS, MOONFLEET, AND THE NEBULY COAT: THE ABNORMAL RESPONSES OF JOHN MEADE FALKNER (recommendation)	PR11, 89
	JOURNAL: (UNEXPURGATED) TOUR JOURNAL (etcetera)	PR16, 221
Standley, Vincent	TRAVELOGUE (fiction)	PR8, 71
Stattmann, Jon	TRIAL BY TRASH (nonfiction)	PR11, 39
Steward, D. E.	DESEMBRE (fiction)	PR6, 118
Stine, Alison	THREE MONTHS, NO KIDDING (poetry)	PR7, 26
	SALT (poetry)	PR7, 27
Strand, Mark*	A CONVERSATION (etcetera)	PR6, 118
Strempek Shea, Suzanne	READING THE FUTURE: TWELVE WRITERS FROM IRELAND IN CONVERSATION WITH MIKE MURPHY, EDITED BY CLIODHNA NI ANLUAIN (recommendation)	PR13, 37
Stumpf, Jason	PROOF (poetry)	PR11, 105
	THE LESSON OF THE BIRDS (poetry)	PR11, 106
Sukrungruang, Ira	SPOTLIGHTING (nonfiction)	PR12, 83
Sullivan, Felicia C.	THE BUSINESS OF LEAVING (fiction)	PR6, 94
Sullivan, Mary	THE HOLY BIBLE: KING JAMES VERSION (recommendation)	PR5, 145
Swofford, Anthony	GERHARD RICHTER'S MOTOR BOAT (FIRST VERSION) [MOTORBOOT (ERSTE ASSUNG)] (poetry)	PR13, 17
	NINE RHYTHMS IN NINE DAYS: A-FRAME NEAR SISTERS, OREGON (poetry)	PR13, 18
Szporluk, Larissa	BARCAROLE (poetry)	PR1, 100
	SENSILLA (poetry)	PR1, 102

Szuber, Janusz*	DE SE IPSO, trans. Ewa Hryniewicz-Yarbrough (poetry)	PR9, 131
	NEW LABORS, trans. Ewa Hryniewicz-Yarbrough (poetry)	PR9, 132
Tarkington, Ed	SOUTHERN CULTURE ON THE SKIDS (nonfiction)	PR9, 108
Taylor, Al	PORTRAIT, DRAWING, SCULPTURE (art)	PR2, 29
Taylor, Mark C.	L'ENTRETIEN INFINI (THE INFINITE CONVERSATION), BY MAURICE BLANCHOT (recommendation)	PR2, 178
Teicher, Craig Morgan	THE GROANING COWS (poetry)	PR15, 45
	THE STORY OF THE STONE (poetry)	PR15, 47
Thayer, Cynthia	EVA MOVES THE FURNITURE, BY MARGOT LIVESEY (recommendation)	PR14, 157
Tinkler, Alan	A COUPLE OF POLAROIDS (fiction)	PR9, 23
Topol, Jachym*	ANGEL STATION, trans. Alex Zucker (etcetera)	PR1, 131
Treadway, Jessica	RICHARD YATES'S THE EASTER PARADE (recommendation)	PR13, 205
Triant, Randi	HORRIBLE ENDINGS: MY BROTHER AND THE COMPLETE WORKS OF SAKI (etcetera)	PR10, 213
Trivett, Vincent	ONE HUNDRED DEMONS AND SELF-REPRESENTATION (criticism)	PR13, 41
Twain, Mark	FENIMORE COOPER'S LITERARY OFFENSES (etcetera)	PR6, 161
Vandenberg, Katrina	CRETACEOUS MOTH TRAPPED IN AMBER (LAMENT IN TWO VOICES) (poetry)	PR16, 97
	PALINODE FOR BEING THIRTY-FOUR (poetry)	PR16, 99
van Loenen, Rocco	TECHNICAL DRAWING I (theatre)	PR1, 59
	TECHNICAL DRAWING II (theatre)	PR1, 77
Vasicek, René Georg	CONFESSIONS OF A PILSNER DRINKER (nonfiction)	PR14, 179
Venugopal, Shubha	LALITA AND THE BANYAN TREE (fiction)	PR14, 19
Veslany, Kathleen	THE APERTURE BETWEEN TWO POINTS (nonfiction)	PR2, 76
Vida, Vendela	OLT, BY KENNETH GANGEMI (recommendation)	PR10, 189
Volkman, Karen	UNTITLED (poetry)	PR1, 104
	UNTITLED (poetry)	PR1, 105
Volpe, Eugenio	THEATER OF THE CRUEL (fiction)	PR9, 44
Waldman, Ayelet	AN ICE CREAM WAR, BY WILLIAM BOYD (recommendation)	PR14, 17
Waldrep, G. C.	LULLABYE FOR MY SISTER (poetry)	PR12, 163
	FEAST OF ALL WOUNDS (poetry)	PR12, 164
	DIE FLEDERMAUS (poetry)	PR16, 191
	SISYPHUS IN PARADISE (poetry)	PR16, 192
Warloe, Constance	INTRODUCTION TO FROM DAUGHTERS & SONS TO FATHERS: WHAT I'VE NEVER SAID (etcetera)	PR2, 129
Washington, Thomas	HAVE YOU READ MY MANUSCRIPT? (nonfiction)	PR9, 83
Watson, Brad	WILLARD AND HIS BOWLING TROPHIES, A PERVERSE MYSTERY, BY RICHARD BRAUTIGAN (recommendation)	PR10, 159
Weinberger, Eliot	AT THE SIGN OF THE HAND (etcetera)	PR9, 188
Welle, John P. (trans.)	TRANSLATING BRECHT, BY FRANCO FORTINI (poetry)	PR4, 30
Weller, Anthony	THE WORKS OF ROBERT DEAN FRISBIE (recommendation)	PR12, 151

Weller, Sam	THE ILLUSTRATED MAN, BY RAY BRADBURY (recommendation)	PR15, 147
Whitcomb, Katharine	EARLY MEDIEVAL (poetry)	PR11, 202
	DREAM ON HIS BIRTHDAY (poetry)	PR11, 206
White, Derek	COATI MUNDI (fiction)	PR11, 207
Williams, Dawn	DIRECTING GRAND GUIGNOL (theatre)	PR1, 61
Williams, Diane	WELL-TO-DO PERSON (fiction)	PR6, 103
	MY FIRST REAL HOME (fiction)	PR16, 247
Williams, Greg	BLUE ANGEL, BY FRANCINE PROSE (recommendation)	PR12, 199
Wilson, Jason	WHAT IS THE COLOR OF HOPE IN HAITI? (etcetera)	PR3, 168
Winthrop, Elizabeth Hartley	DIRT MUSIC, BY TIM WINTON (recommendation)	PR14, 81
Wisniewski, Mark	CALCULUS (poetry)	PR14, 37
	LAND (poetry)	PR14, 40
Wolff, Rebecca	MAMMA DIDN'T RAISE NO FOOLS (poetry)	PR2, 96
	A GOOD IDEA, BUT NOT WELL-EXECUTED (poetry)	PR2, 98
Wood, Ann	THE ROAD TO LOS ANGELES, BY JOHN FANTE (recommendation)	PR14, 215
Wood, Monica	WE NEED TO TALK ABOUT KEVIN, BY LIONEL SHRIVER AND GEORGE ELIOT'S LATER NOVELS (recommendation)	PR13, 179
Wormser, Baron	FICTIONAL ESSAY: JOHN BERRYMAN, B. 1914 (etcetera)	PR13, 95
Wright, Charles	W. G. SEBALD (recommendation)	PR2, 179
Wunderlich, Mark	DEVICE FOR BURNING BEES AND SUGAR (poetry)	PR8, 13
	IT'S YOUR TURN TO DO THE MILKING, FATHER SAID (poetry)	PR8, 15
Xi, Xu	THE LONG MARCH (recommendation)	PR13, 53
Yang, Jeffrey	GOOGLE (poetry)	PR15, 195
	KELP (poetry)	PR15, 196
Yang, June Unjoo	GENTILITY (fiction)	PR4, 63
Yarbrough, Steve	LARRY MCMURTRY'S THE LAST PICTURE SHOW (recommendation)	PR10, 155
Yoder, Charles	AL TAYLOR (recommendation)	PR2, 180
Yoon, Paul	ON THE HISTORY OF A BACKGAMMON BOARD (fiction)	PR12, 206
Yoshikawa, Mako	REVISITING OLD FLAMES OF LITERATURE (recommendation)	PR6, 153
Young, C. Dale	THE EFFECTS OF SUNSET (poetry)	PR1, 106
	REQUIEM (poetry)	PR1, 107
Zaiman, Elana	PSALM FOR RAFI (nonfiction)	PR11, 111
Zucker, Alex (trans.)	ANGEL STATION, by Jachym Topol (etcetera)	PR1, 131